OXFORD STUDIES IN AFRICAN POLITICS AND INTERNATIONAL RELATIONS

General Editors
NIC CHEESEMAN, PEACE MEDIE, AND
RICARDO SOARES DE OLIVEIRA

Oxford Studies in African Politics and International Relations is a series for scholars and students working on African politics and International Relations and related disciplines. Volumes concentrate on contemporary developments in African political science, political economy, and International Relations, such as electoral politics, democratization, decentralization, gender and political representation, the political impact of natural resources, the dynamics and consequences of conflict, comparative political thought, and the nature of the continent's engagement with the East and West. Comparative and mixed methods work is particularly encouraged. Case studies are welcomed but should demonstrate the broader theoretical and empirical implications of the study and its wider relevance to contemporary debates. The focus of the series is on sub-Saharan Africa, although proposals that explain how the region engages with North Africa and other parts of the world are of interest.

Multiethnic Democracy

*The Logic of Elections and Policymaking
in Kenya*

JEREMY HOROWITZ

OXFORD

UNIVERSITY PRESS

Great Clarendon Street, Oxford, OX2 6DP,
United Kingdom

Oxford University Press is a department of the University of Oxford.
It furthers the University's objective of excellence in research, scholarship,
and education by publishing worldwide. Oxford is a registered trade mark of
Oxford University Press in the UK and in certain other countries

First Edition published in 2022

Impression: 1

Published in the United States of America by Oxford University Press
198 Madison Avenue, New York, NY 10016, United States of America

British Library Cataloguing in Publication Data
Data available

Library of Congress Control Number: 2021951374

ISBN 978–0–19–885273–5

DOI: 10.1093/oso/9780198852735.001.0001

Printed and bound by
CPI Group (UK) Ltd, Croydon, CR0 4YY

Contents

Acknowledgments

This book began as an effort to study how politicians exploit ethnic differences for political gain in Africa's emerging democracies. I was inspired by a desire to make sense of how appeals to ethnic identity contribute to the polarization and violence that has accompanied multiparty elections in Kenya and other parts of Africa. Over time, however, I came to see that parties in Kenya pursue broad-based strategies on the campaign trail, rather than concentrating their efforts merely on shoring up support in their core ethnic bases. This simple observation led to a series of questions about electoral competition in diverse societies: How do campaign strategists conceptualize the electoral landscape in settings where ethnicity structures voter alignments? Why might parties opt to cast a wide net on the campaign trail rather than focusing more narrowly on their core ethnic coalitions? How do campaign goals influence policy choices after the election? This book represents my effort to answer these questions based on field work and data collection in Kenya. The answers I offer are surely not the last word. Yet, in drawing attention to the importance of the competition for swing voters, I hope this work will encourage scholars to reconsider the widely-held view that elections in Africa's diverse societies amount to little more than competitive efforts to mobilize rival ethnic factions.

I owe an enormous debt of gratitude to a great many people whose encouragement and support made this book possible. First and foremost, I wish to acknowledge Karen Ferree, my graduate advisor at UCSD, who patiently read and commented on every draft I produced from my initial dissertation prospectus to the final book manuscript. Karen's guidance over many years shaped this book—and my education as a scholar—in more ways than I can count. I also acknowledge contributions from several other faculty members at UCSD who offered advice and feedback on this project, particularly Clark Gibson, Craig McIntosh, Gary Cox, and Scott Desposato.

I wish to thank a great number of people in Kenya, starting with the many political candidates and party strategists I interviewed in 2007, for explaining to me how campaigns and elections work in Kenya. At Steadman (now part of Ipsos), I thank Tom Wolf and George Waititu, who gave me access to invaluable polling data. Thanks also to Tom for many conversations about Kenyan politics over the years. I am grateful to Kamanda Mucheke at the Kenya National Commission on Human Rights who allowed me to collaborate with their campaign monitoring team in 2007 and gave me access to an extraordinary collection of recordings from campaign rallies. The analysis in Chapter 5 would not have been possible without this collaboration. I thank also Moses Radoli for helping me collect additional campaign recordings from media correspondents scattered throughout Kenya in 2007. I am grateful to Melissa Baker and the staff at TNS-RMS for their help in implementing a national panel study in 2012–13 and a survey experiment in 2015. Several research assistants, especially Paul Kipwendui Kipchumba, John Gitau Kariuki, and Juma Ondeng, provided critical support in tracking down newspaper coverage of prior elections, coding campaign speeches, and identifying the locations of campaign rallies. I thank Adams Oloo at the University of Nairobi for helping me get my bearings when I first arrived in Kenya. Many thanks also to David Mwambari and Karen Austrian who hosted me in Nairobi in 2007 and 2008.

For comments and suggestions on various pieces of the manuscript, I thank many friends and colleagues: Leo Arriola, Jeff Conroy-Krutz, Elena Gadjanova, Dan Posner, Kris Inman, Sarah Brierely, Ryan Jablonski, Kristin Michelitch, Adam Harris, Ken Opalo, John McCauley, Eric Kramon, Nelson Kasfir, Carolyn Logan, Rebecca Simson, Brendan Nyhan, and Yusaku Horiuchi—as well as participants at several conferences and departments where I presented portions of this work. I express my gratitude also to Nic Cheeseman and Ricardo Soares de Oliveira, series editors at Oxford, and the two anonymous reviewers who pushed me to articulate key ideas more clearly and to address various concerns. Portions of Chapters 3 and 4 were published in the *British Journal of Political Science* and *Comparative Political Studies* respectively, and are reprinted with permission.

Many others provided support along the way. At Dartmouth, I benefited from the help of several undergraduate research assistants who combed through microfilm of old newspapers to find coverage of campaigns events. Miriam and Precious Kilimo translated survey questionnaires and compiled information on party switching in Kenya's 2013 election. Several colleagues gave me access to data. Mai Hassan provided data on the ethnic composition of parliamentary constituencies. James Long provided data from several public opinion surveys conducted in Kenya and Ghana. Danny Choi and Leo Arriola kindly shared data on CDF expenditures in Kenya. Jonathan Chipman provided assistance with geospatial data processing. Financial support came from the National Science Foundation, the Institute on Global Conflict and Cooperation, and Dartmouth College.

Finally, I thank my wife Amanda. Her faith in my ability to complete this book sustained me when my own faltered, which was often. Without her support in ways big and small, this book would never have seen the light of day. It is dedicated to her, and to Sophia and Joshua, our two shining stars. I thank also my parents, Paulette and Jay, for their tireless enthusiasm and support.

List of Tables

List of Figures

1

Introduction

In September 2007 Kenya's incumbent president, Mwai Kibaki, took his campaign for re-election to Western Province. At a series of campaign rallies, he made numerous promises to the area's voters: an increase in the producer price for sugar cane grown in the region, the creation of a new district, title deeds for squatters, cheap fertilizer, and a new road from Kamukuywa to Chwele.[1] Not to be outdone, Raila Odinga, the main opposition leader, offered his own list of pledges during a tour of the region a week later. In Kakamega, Odinga promised to extend electricity to all marketplaces, to increase support for small-scale farmers, and to provide free secondary education to the area's students.[2] Over the next three months leading up to the election, both candidates returned to the region multiple times.

What made Western Province an appealing area for campaigning? The answer, as any student of Kenyan politics knows, is that the region is home to the Luhya ethnic group, a community that was seen as up-for-grabs in the 2007 election.[3] Both of the major presidential candidates rightly estimated that there were few potential swing voters to be won over in their own or their rival's ethnic strong-holds. Groups like the Luhya that were less tightly linked to either of the major parties offered a more inviting target.

The competition for swing voters in Kenya's Western Province raises a number of questions about electoral politics in multiethnic societies. What makes some voters more up-for-grabs than others? How much effort do parties invest in courting swing voters relative to mobilizing core supporters? And how does this balance affect the policies leaders propose—and implement—if elected?

I examine these questions in the context of Kenya's emerging multiparty democracy.[4] Because ethnic groups are too small to serve as the basis for national electoral bids, candidates must build diverse coalitions if they are to be viable. As

[1] Nation Team. "Kibaki Woos Western Voters." *Daily Nation*, September 18, 2007, p. 4.
[2] Cyrus Kinyungu and Allan Kisia. "Raila Says He Would Ask Corrupt Leaders to Account for Their Deeds." *The Standard*, September 23, 2007, pp. 1 and 4.
[3] Ohito, David and Martin Mutua. "What Next? Battle for 14M Votes." *The Standard*, September 3, 2007, pp. 1–2. Obonyo, Oscar. "Rush for Western Votes Intensifies." *The Standard*, September 23, 2007, p. 9. See also MacArthur (2008, p. 227) and Throup and Hornsby (1998) chapter 9.
[4] Throughout this book, I refer to Kenya as an emerging democracy, reflecting the country's transition to a more open political system since the early 1990s. Kenya, like many other African countries, should be understood as a hybrid regime in which elements of democracy exist alongside aspects of autocratic regimes (e.g., Diamond 2002; Schedler 2002). I therefore use the term democracy in a minimal sense to denote countries in which multiparty electoral competition is allowed.

Multiethnic Democracy: The Logic of Elections and Policymaking in Kenya. Jeremy Horowitz, Oxford University Press.
© Jeremy Horowitz 2022. DOI: 10.1093/oso/9780198852735.003.0001

Hillary Ng'Weno, a longtime media observer, noted shortly after Kenya's return to multiparty competition, "the successful politician is the one who can build on the foundations of his or her ethnic affiliations whilst managing to build viable bridges across ethnic lines."[5] Yet, because the major candidates can often rely on strong support from coethnic voters, it is the task of "building bridges" that frequently poses the greater challenge for presidential contenders.

What tools do candidates have at their disposal for attracting out-group support in Africa's diverse democracies? The conventional answer points to elite coalition building. Candidates enter into alliances with prominent leaders from other communities who are rewarded with positions in the future government in exchange for delivering their respective ethnic groups (e.g., Arriola 2013; Mozaffar and Scarritt 2005; Elischer 2013; Oyugi 2006). The focus on elite coalition building has particular relevance to Kenya, where shifting alliances largely account for the waxing and waning of candidates' electoral fortunes over time, both during the brief multiparty period after independence in the 1960s and since the return to multiparty politics in 1992 (e.g., Gertzel 1970; Throup and Hornsby 1998; Oloo 2010; Berman, Cottrell, and Ghai 2009; Elischer 2013; Cheeseman et al. 2019).

Yet, electoral politics is about more than just coopting a sufficient number of prominent allies. Once the coalitions are set, candidates turn to campaigning.[6] To date, however, campaigns have received less attention in studies of African politics.[7] This may stem from the view that in settings where ethnicity is politically salient, as it is in many parts of Africa, campaigns do not have much effect on election outcomes. In Kenya's 2007 election, for example, it was well understood that voter preferences were driven primarily by coalition alignments, not campaign tactics.[8] Moreover, data in Chapter 4 confirms that campaigns typically have little influence on the overall distribution of support in Kenyan elections. This does not mean, however, that campaigns are inconsequential. What candidates do and say on the campaign trail matters because their actions and words may exacerbate ethnic tensions (e.g., Horowitz 1985; Reilly 2001). Campaigns also matter because of their implications for policymaking after the election—the focus of this book.

The existing literature typically presumes that in diverse societies the purpose of campaigning will be to galvanize the party's ethnic base, since voters—as ethnic

---

[5] Hilary Ng'Weno, *Weekly Review*, May 8, 1992, p. 1. Quoted in Throup and Hornsby (1998, p. 124).

[6] As described in Chapter 3, elite coalition building and campaigning are inter-connected activities. Presidential candidates in Kenya rely on their allies to play important roles during the campaigns, shoring up support and ensuring high levels of turnout in their respective ethnic areas. Allies stump on behalf of the party leaders, organize and fund local-level electoral machinery, and appear with the presidential aspirants at rallies, helping to make credible appeals that transcend ethnic divides (Oloo 2010).

[7] For relevant scholarship on campaigns, see Bleck and van de Walle (2011, 2013, 2019), Taylor (2017), Gadjanova (2017, 2021), Cussac (2008), Lynch (2008), MacArthur (2008), and Paget (2019).

[8] See Barkan (2008b) and Chege (2008).

blocs—will often be "sewn up" well in advance of election day, making efforts to appeal across ethno-partisan lines an exercise in futility (e.g., Horowitz 1985; Reilly and Reynolds 1999; Snyder 2000). A closer look at what transpires on the campaign trail in Kenya, however, shows that campaigns follow a different logic. It is the competition for swing voters—not efforts to mobilize rival ethnic factions— that takes center stage in the run-up to election day. The task of this book is to explain this pattern and to explore its implications. Using data on voters, campaigns, and policy outcomes, it shows that the pursuit of the swing encourages presidential candidates to offer broad, inclusive promises and for election winners to opt for universal policies.

This is not the first work to note the importance of swing voters in Kenya or in Africa more broadly.[9] Nor is it the first to propose that when parties seek support from multiple ethnic communities they adopt inclusive electoral strategies and policies (e.g., Horowitz 1991; Reilly and Reynolds 1999; Reilly 2001, 2006).[10] Prior work, however, has yet to answer basic questions about how party leaders balance the competing goals of securing their ethnic strongholds while also courting out-group voters, and the conditions under which they prioritize the latter over the former on the campaign trail. Likewise, the literature has yet to examine whether parties in highly-diverse countries like Kenya are better off courting out-group voters widely or focusing their campaign efforts more narrowly. And, few studies have traced through how the pursuit of swing voters affects policy choices in Africa's emerging, multiethnic democracies.[11]

In addressing these questions, this book extends prior scholarship in three specific ways. First, it develops a framework for conceptualizing core and swing groups in settings where ethnic identities play a central role in structuring voter alignments. The book's approach departs from standard literature that emphasizes cognitive factors like political interest and engagement (e.g., Kaufmann, Petrocik, and Shaw 2008) or political orientations related to policy views and ideology (e.g., Hillygus and Shields 2008). It departs also from work in Africa that draws attention to performance assessments (Lindberg and Morrison 2005; Weghorst and Lindberg 2013) or urban/rural divides (Wahman and Boone 2018; Harding 2020).

Second, it offers a novel explanation for why parties prioritize the pursuit of swing voters during campaigns. In doing so, this work differs from accounts that point to the small size of ethnic communities in African countries (e.g., Tonah

---

[9]   Throup and Hornsby's (1998) comprehensive account of Kenya's 1992 election notes that all of the major presidential candidates in that race "focused on the marginal areas" (p. 384) where groups like the Luhya are concentrated. MacArthur (2008) offers a similar characterization of the Luhya in Kenya's 2007 election. Scarritt (2006) and Casey (2015) develop related arguments in Zambia and Sierra Leone, respectively.

[10]   See also van de Walle (2007, p. 66), which notes that as political competition in Africa increases leaders may adopt more expansive distributive strategies.

[11]   Notable exceptions include Casey (2015), Carbone (2011), and Carbone and Pellegata (2017).

2007; Hoffman and Long 2013); the institutional engineering literature which expects that ethnic mobilization will be the default in the absence of moderation-inducing constitutional provisions (Horowitz 1985, 1991; Lijphart 1977); or research that highlights cross-cutting cleavages that bridge ethnic divisions (Dunning and Harrison 2010; Koter 2013). This book shows that broad-based electoral strategies may emerge in unexpected contexts because the factors described below—uncertainty, strategic imperatives, and delegation—are fairly commonplace across Africa's emerging democracies, unlike moderation-inducing institutions and cross-cutting cleavages, which are not.

Third, the book develops the logic by which campaign strategies affect policy choices. It highlights the value of universal policies that establish a concrete record of widely-shared benefits and aid in the pursuit of out-group voters on the campaign trail. This approach deviates from literature that finds that the transition to multiparty politics in Africa does little to attenuate patterns of ethnic favoritism (e.g., Kramon and Posner 2016; Franck and Rainer 2012) or may in some cases exacerbate them (e.g., Crook 1997; van de Walle 2007).

Competing Models of Electoral Politics in Diverse Societies

At its heart, this book offers a theory of campaign strategy. The standard view, which I refer to as the *core mobilization model,* proposes that in diverse societies parties have little incentive to court voters outside their core bases or to share resources beyond them. This view, articulated most fully in *Ethnic Groups in Conflict* (1985) by Donald Horowitz, suggests that in settings where ethnic identities structure electoral alignments, competing parties serve as representatives of the one or more groups from which they draw their strongest support, concentrating electoral efforts on mobilizing voters in their core coalitions, and channeling resources to them if elected (see also Rabushka and Shepsle 1973; Rothschild 1981; Reilly and Reynolds 1999; Reilly 2001, 2006; Fearon 1999; Wimmer 2002). This approach echoes the logic of a broader class of core voter models developed in other contexts (e.g., Cox and McCubbins 1986; Diaz-Cayeros, Estévez, and Magaloni 2016).

Political dynamics in Kenya are often described in precisely these terms. Ajulu (2002, p. 251), for example, notes that "political parties have been organised along ethnic identities and state-power aggressively contested on the basis of mobilised ethnicity." Writing about the 2013 elections, Barkan (2013, p. 1) observes that "as in prior elections, the leading presidential candidates are mobilizing voters along ethnic lines." And a 2011 report on election violence sums up the prevailing wisdom as follows: "Kenyan political factions have always been ethnically based and those in power tend to favour their own groups" (Sentinel Project 2011, p. 13).

This book advances an alternative approach—the *swing-targeting model*—that contends that in highly-diverse societies, parties will have incentives to concentrate their campaign efforts on courting potential swing voters outside their ethnic strongholds and to opt for universal policies in place of those that favor core ethnic clientele. While swing-targeting models are well established in the literature on electoral competition and distributive politics in the world's long-standing democracies (e.g., Lindbeck and Weibull 1987; Dixit and Londregan 1996; Stromberg 2008), there is less agreement about their applicability to settings where ethnicity—rather than ideology or policy preferences—structures the partisan landscape.[12] A central goal of this book is to demonstrate the value of the swing-targeting approach to Africa's emerging democracies. In doing so, it highlights three factors neglected in existing accounts: (1) uncertainty regarding the return on investment from alternative campaign tactics; (2) the strategic imperative of countering rivals' campaign efforts; and (3) intra-party delegation on the campaign trail.

Overview of the Argument

Kenya may seem like an unlikely place for the argument that electoral competition induces broad-based appeals and universal policies. Accounts routinely describe Kenya as a country where bare-knuckle tactics of ethnic mobilization prevail; where elites cynically play on ethnic antipathies for electoral gain; where electoral competition heightens tensions that periodically erupt into communal violence; and where incumbents favor ethno-partisan constituents in patronage allocations.[13] To be sure, these accounts capture one side of political contestation in Kenya, and they make Kenya a hard case for the arguments advanced in this book. But they cannot explain central features of electoral competition or policymaking since the return to multiparty politics in 1992.

This section provides a brief overview of the book's main arguments, connecting voters, campaign strategies, and policy choices. My focus is the period starting with the 2002 election when a "two-coalition model" became the norm in Kenyan politics (Arriola 2012; Elischer 2013). Typically, two main candidates from different ethnic communities compete for the presidency. Each heads a diverse coalition that brings together leaders from smaller parties under a single umbrella. Candidates generally enter the campaigns with strong support from their own

---

[12] Casey (2015) develops a complementary swing-targeting approach.
[13] Contributions to the literature on ethnic politics in Kenya include Berman and Londsdale (1992), Berman (1998), Throup and Hornsby (1998), Haugerud (1993), Bratton and Kimenyi (2008), Oyugi (1997), Steeves (2006b), Omolo (2002), and Ajulu (1998). On resource targeting, see Franck and Rainer (2012), Kramon and Posner (2016), Barkan and Chege (1989), Burgess et al. (2015), Jablonski (2014), and Harris and Posner (2019).

ethnic communities and their respective coalition groups—"allied" communities whose support is assured by the presence of prominent representatives in the party's leadership structure. While the elite alliances at the center of Kenya's major parties have shifted over time, the basic configuration—two main presidential candidates each heading coalition parties that draw their strongest support from distinct ethnic bases—has remained constant. Later chapters take up the question of whether the arguments developed here have relevance to earlier races when Kenya's party system was more fragmented.

Swing Voters

The book begins with voters. The central question is: if presidential hopefuls seek to attract additional supporters through campaigning, whom should they target? Who, in other words, are the swing voters? Some will doubt whether there are *any* swing voters in countries like as Kenya, where elite alliances so strongly influence voter preferences. Yet, Chapter 3 shows that a surprisingly large share of Kenyan voters—more than 20 percent in the 2013 and 2017 elections—changed their stated voting intentions in the run-up to election day. What distinguishes these floating voters from the standpatters whose intentions are more fixed?

I propose that a key distinction is between voters from groups that have a coethnic among the major contenders and those from groups that do not. While other factors influence the fluidity of electoral preferences, this simple dichotomy serves as a central dividing line and provides a ready foundation for party leaders seeking to allocate campaign resources efficiently across a highly-diverse and complex partisan map.

The starting point for this claim is the observation that in the personalized party systems that prevail across many parts of Africa, including Kenya, parties often draw their most steadfast support from voters who share the ethnic identity of their presidential candidates. Thus, in Kenya, Cussac (2008, p. 2) observes that "political parties are very often anchored in the region of their main leader." In Zambia, Posner (2005, p. 110) notes that "the home regions of party presidents have been, historically, the parts of the country where Zambian politicians have had their greatest electoral success." In Malawi, Kaspin (1995, p. 613) observes that in the 1994 election ethnic identities account "for much of the support of [Hastings] Banda in the central region, for [Chakufwa] Chihana in two of the northern districts...for [Bakili] Muluzi in three contiguous districts in the central and southern regions." Though successful aspirants in all of these cases must attract support from other groups to be electorally viable, often it is among coethnics that one finds the most ardent and reliable backing.

To document this pattern in Kenya, the next chapter assembles data from presidential elections held between 1992 and 2017. It shows that while the strength of coethnic support for presidential candidates is a variable not a constant, a clear pattern is observed: the leading contenders are routinely able count on high levels of support from coethnic voters, equal to or greater than the support they receive from other communities. Groups that do not have a coethnic among the major-party contenders are more variable in their alignments. Candidates in some cases can rely on equally strong support from coalition groups. Yet, communities that do not have a coethnic in the race tend, as a whole, to be less politically unified than those that do.

These observations provide a useful foundation for understanding how party strategists target campaign effort across Kenya's major ethnic areas, and specific-ally why it is that the leading contenders pursue voters in all areas save for those where voters from groups with a coethnic in the race predominate. The reason, I propose, is that strategists view the parties' respective ethnic strongholds as qualitatively different from other parts of the country. It is generally assumed that there is little to gain—in terms of picking up new supporters—from campaigning in areas where the candidates' coethnic voters reside, since the major-party aspirants often enter the race with near-universal support among such voters. Likewise, there is little to gain from courting opponents' coethnics, who are unlikely to forego the opportunity to support their own leader on election day. Voters from other groups—including the parties' main coalition groups—provide a more attractive target for persuasive appeals.

Chapter 3 provides micro-level evidence for these propositions. Drawing on panel surveys conducted prior to Kenya's 2013 and 2017 elections, it shows that less than 10 percent of voters from groups with a coethnic in the race changed their stated voting intentions during the campaign period in each election year, relative to about 25 percent of those from groups without a coethnic in the race. These data show, moreover, that voters in coalition groups, which are often treated as akin to the candidate's own coethnic communities in terms of the intensity of partisan attachments, tend to hold weaker initial preferences and are more likely to update their electoral preferences during the campaigns, relative to voters from groups with a coethnic in the race. To account for these differences, the chapter argues that voters from groups that do not have a coethnic in the presidential race often hold more fluid preferences both because prominent coethnic politicians tend to be more divided across the major parties, and because these leaders exert less influence on policymaking after the election than the presidential aspirants.

Several caveats are warranted. First, readers may object that this approach overlooks other factors that make some voters more or less up-for-grabs in elections. Scholars have shown that a range of cognitive, demographic, and attitudinal variables help to distinguish core and swing voters.[14] I do not discount the importance of these factors; rather, I assert that after accounting for such variables, ethnicity remains an important influence. Moreover, because the goal of this book is to provide a foundation for theorizing campaign strategies, I emphasize group-level factors that are easily observed by candidates and their advisors. While strategists would surely like to tailor campaigns to reach individual voters who, for example, are less cognitively engaged with politics, identifying such individuals is difficult simply because there are no visible markers that allow parties to distinguish them from others (Hersh 2015).[15] By contrast, ethnicity is a readily-observable feature that conveys information about the broad categories of voters that will be more or less receptive to candidates' electoral appeals.

Second, while the book builds on the observation that the major-party contenders in Kenya are generally able to rely on their strongest support from their own ethnic communities, it is important to bear in mind that candidates do not always succeed in garnering the full support of coethnics. Minor-party candidates, in particular, often struggle to unify their ethnic communities. As shown in the next chapter, competitors including Charity Ngilu (1997), Michael Wamalwa (1997), Simeon Nyachae (2002), Kalonzo Musyoka (2007), and Musalia Mudavadi (2013) have been less successful at monopolizing coethnic support than the top competitors in each race. Likewise, the strength of coethnic support tends to be lower for candidates who face viable opponents from within their own ethnic communities, as in the 1992 election when Mwai Kibaki and Kenneth Matiba (both Kikuyu) stood for election or in 2002 when Kibaki and Uhuru Kenyatta (both Kikuyu) headed the two major parties. Yet, these instances are relatively rare; more often the leading competitors do not face serious challengers from within their own groups.

Third, in highlighting the distinction between groups that do and do not have a coethnic in the election, the book does not imply that there will be an equally large number of potential swing voters in all groups that do not have a candidate from their community in the race. The strength of coalition alignments means that presidential aspirants may in some cases draw equally strong support from allied groups as from their own communities. However, the strength of support from major coalition groups is highly variable, and candidates frequently do not garner universal backing from them. Thus, for example, in 2007 Odinga's support among

---

[14] As noted in Chapter 3, several studies from similar contexts suggest the relevance of performance assessments (Lindberg and Morrison 2005; Weghorst and Lindberg 2014) and urban/rural divisions (Wahman and Boone 2018; Harding 2020). Literature from the U.S. suggests also that cognitive engagement with politics may affect the likelihood of individuals updating their voting intentions during campaigns (e.g., Converse 1964; Zaller 2004; Kaufmann, Petrocik, and Shaw 2008).

[15] Similar arguments have been made regarding campaigns in the U.S. For example, Hillygus and Shields (2008, p. 108) note that "candidates in the 1960s and 1970s largely had to infer the policy preferences of voters based on region, race, or other broad characteristics, so that strategic policy decisions were made on this rather imprecise information."

Kalenjin and Luhya voters, groups routinely described as part of the Orange Democratic Movement (ODM) coalition, was roughly 76 percent and 68 percent respectively at the start of the race, well below his support among coethnic Luos (94%).[16] Moreover, data on campaign strategies assembled in subsequent chapters indicates that on the campaign trail party leaders do not make fine-grained distinctions between the many groups that do not have a candidate in the race according to the strength of their coalition ties. The more important divide is simply between those groups that have a coethnic in the race and those that do not. Strategists, I argue, know that the former have typically supported coethnic leaders at very high rates while the latter have historically been more variable in their alignments.

Fourth, this book devotes little attention to sub-tribe and clan divisions within the country's major ethnic groups. Sub-group identities are particularly relevant to the Luhya, Kenya's second largest ethnic community, which generally does not act as a unified political force. Prior research demonstrates that party leaders are attuned to sub-group differences and calibrate their electoral appeals to them (Throup and Hornsby 1998; MacArthur 2008). Yet, because the data assembled in this book is not sufficiently detailed to examine how sub-group differences affect voter preferences or campaigns, I do not focus on them. Despite this omission, the analysis in this book provides a starting point for understanding how party leaders in highly diverse societies conceptualize the electoral landscape and tailor campaign strategies to it.

Fifth, it is important to note that while this book refers to some ethnic communities as "swing groups," it does not imply that entire blocs of voters move collectively as the result of campaign persuasion. Rather, swing groups are defined as ethnic communities in which there is a larger share of potential fence-sitters—those who might be persuaded to shift their voting intentions due to campaign influences—relative to core groups. The margin may be small, but for campaign strategists seeking to determine how best to allocate the available campaign resources, even small differences are important.

Finally, it is important to note that the approach to core and swing offered here is most relevant to countries like Kenya with weakly-institutionalized party systems, where electoral alignments are shaped more by elite alliances than by enduring party structures. Personalized party systems like Kenya's are common-place in Africa's emerging democracies (Randall and Svåsand 2002b). Thus, van de Walle and Butler (1999, p. 15) observe that "African parties are plagued by weak organizations, low levels of institutionalisation, and weak links to the society

---

[16] Maupeu (2008, p. 207), for example, notes that ODM was "commonly viewed in Kenya as an agreement to join majority forces between the Luos, the Luhyas, and the Kalenjins." Data on electoral preferences is from a national survey (n=2,020) conducted by Steadman (now Ipsos) on September 21–25, shortly after the major parties announced their presidential nominees.

they are supposed to represent." However, in countries with more institutional-ized party systems like Ghana (the focus of Chapter 7), core and swing are not structured as fully by whether ethnic communities have coethnic leaders in the race. The major parties in Ghana maintain durable ties to particular ethnic constituencies that persist even as the ethnic identities of the parties' presidential candidates changes across election years. Yet, as in Kenya, the electoral landscape in Ghana is one in which each party can count on its strongest support from a distinct ethnic base while voters in other groups are more up-for-grabs. As a result, the core/swing approach outlined in this book provides a useful framework for making sense of campaign strategies and policy choices, despite differences in how the party system is structured.

Campaigns

Chapter 4 uses data on the location of campaign rallies to show that the major presidential aspirants in Kenya consistently opt for broad campaign strategies rather than narrow efforts to mobilize voters in their respective coalitions. These findings corroborate what I heard from campaign strategists interviewed prior to the 2007 election. One senior official from the Party of National Unity (PNU) explained that the party was appealing to voters throughout the country, including in areas that favored the opposition.[17] Though party leaders understood that they were not going to win over many voters in these zones, they hoped nonetheless to pick up "a few votes." Likewise, several opposition strategists in the Orange Democratic Movement relayed that the party had not given up on areas that leaned toward Kibaki and PNU.[18]

Why, though, do parties campaign extensively, including in areas where oppon-ents hold an advantage? The answer proposed in this book builds on two key ideas. First, party leaders face considerable uncertainty about the potential return on investment from targeting campaign resources toward voters in different ethnic areas. The conventional tools available to party strategists—opinion polls and past election results—provide only limited information about which types of voters will be most responsive. And, given that ethnic bloc voting is always partial and incomplete, it is not unreasonable to think that there may be some benefit—however small—from appealing to voters in rivals' strongholds. Second, campaigns are designed to blunt opponents' advances.[19] Failure to compete in parts of the country where rivals hold an advantage would allow opponents to press their

---

[17] Interviews with PNU secretariat personnel in Nairobi, October 11, 2007.

[18] Interviews with ODM secretariat personnel in Nairobi, October 8–11, 2007.

[19] On the strategic nature of campaigning, see Box-Steffensmeier, Darmofal, and Farrell (2009), Carsey, Jackson, Stewart, and Nelson (2011), and Banda and Carsey (2015).

case freely. The strategic imperative of countering opponents therefore reinforces the incentive for each party to campaign widely. There is, however, one exception to the rule: the candidates' own coethnic strongholds. Data in Chapter 4 shows that the major-party candidates generally devote very little effort to these areas, recognizing that there is little to be gained from campaigning in areas where few potential converts can be found.

One might object that campaigns are designed not only to court potential fence-sitters but also to increase turnout among existing supporters. Campaigns, of course, serve not only to persuade but also to mobilize (e.g., Holbrook and McClurg 2005). Thus, it might seem that the leading candidates would allocate considerable effort to whipping up their staunchest supporters in their coethnic strongholds to turn out on election day. Subsequent chapters show, however, that the ability to rely on lower-level actors to mobilize supporters in their coethnic strongholds allows the presidential candidates to focus their efforts elsewhere.

Chapter 4 develops the logic of these arguments and tests them using data on the location of rallies held by the leading candidates in Kenya's multiparty elections. It demonstrates that the swing-targeting approach holds most fully when the leading candidates come from different ethnic groups and when they enjoy strong coethnic support at the start of the race. Candidates who face viable competitors from within their own group tend to allocate greater effort to coethnic areas. Likewise, when candidates enter the race with less universal support from coethnic voters, they spend more time appealing to voters in their own groups. Yet, despite these variations, the data show that broad-based campaigning is universally chosen over narrow efforts to mobilize voters in the one or more ethnic groups from which the candidates draw their strongest support.

Chapter 4 also examines alternative explanations for this pattern, particularly the role of Kenya's electoral institutions. The chapter shows that electoral rules, which require presidential winners to obtain a minimum of support across geographic areas, cannot on their own account for the choice to campaign widely because these requirements typically have little bite for the major-party contenders. While institutions may encourage aspirants to broaden their elite alliances (see Cheeseman, Lynch, and Willis 2019), they offer little help in explaining campaign strategies after the coalitions are set.

In emphasizing the importance of the competition for swing voters, readers may worry that this book gives insufficient attention to the strategies parties use to shore up support and increase turnout among voters in their coalitions. In the Kenyan context, where ethnic mobilization during elections is thought to sharpen communal tensions and increase the risk of inter-group violence, this may seem like a critical oversight. However, the argument that electoral competition encourages parties to adopt broad-based campaign strategies does not imply that they allocate no effort toward mobilizing their ethnic bases, or that the pursuit of the swing leads parties to eschew divisive ethnic rhetoric. Parties in Kenya simultaneously work to court a diverse set of potential swing voters with broad, inclusive appeals while also exploiting communal fears, resentments, and antagonisms to galvanize support in their respective coalitions (KNCHR 2008; HRW 2008; CIPEV 2008; Barkan 2008b; Chege 2008; Kagwanja 2009; Klopp and Kamungi 2008; Klaus 2020). This book shows, however, that electoral politics is about more than whipping up the base.

Policymaking

Finally, I link campaign strategies to policymaking. Because voters in multiethnic settings like Kenya may view promises to share resources across group lines as cheap talk (Posner 2005), incumbents must work to overcome a credibility deficit with out-group voters. Coopting leaders from target communities is useful in this regard, providing a costly signal of a candidate's intentions to share resources (Chandra 2004; Ferree 2011; Keefer 2007). So too are universal policies that establish clear, unambiguous methods for allocating benefits, typically by adopting formula-based rules or by creating new entitlements. For incumbents, tying one's hands in this way reduces the discretionary power to favor supporters, a power that leaders in Africa have carefully guarded since independence, but signals inclusion to prized out-group voters.

To illustrate the connection between campaign strategies and the adoption of universal policies, I examine reforms in Kenya's education sector. Recent empirical work has documented a history of ethnic favoritism in the education sector in Kenya and elsewhere in Africa (Kramon and Posner 2016; Franck and Rainer 2012), making education an especially useful case for this analysis.

I draw on data on primary school enrollment and school construction to show that ethnic favoritism in Kenya is observed only during the single-party era (1979–1992) but not after the return to multiparty competition in 1992. This change is explained both by the re-introduction of free primary education in 2003 and decisions related to the allocation of resources for school construction. Notably, major reforms adopted during the multiparty era have concentrated benefits *outside* presidents' coethnic areas—a finding at odds with the view that electoral competition encourages leaders to channel benefits to ethno-partisan clientele.

Though electoral considerations are likely not the sole driver of policy reforms in the education sector, there is a clear connection between campaign strategies and education policies: incumbents and challengers routinely make promises of universal education reform central to their election platforms and tout accomplishments in this sector when they seek re-election, highlighting the inclusive nature of their policies. Once in office, incumbents work to make good on their pledges, establishing a record that will aid their re-election bids.

The effects documented in the education sector are part of a general movement away from particularistic policymaking in Kenya's multiparty era. Since 1992 leaders have introduced a number of formula-based programs and constitutional reforms that have restricted their ability to engage in discretionary targeting. For example, the Local Areas Transfer Fund (LATF), launched in 1998, allocates 5 percent of national tax revenue to local governments using a formula based on population size and urban population density. The Constituency Development Fund (CDF), introduced in 2003, allocates a minimum of 2.5 percent of ordinary revenue to parliamentary constituencies according to a set formula in which three-quarters of all funding is divided equally across constituencies and one-quarter is targeted toward poorer areas. Most important, a new constitution adopted in 2010 stipulates that a minimum of 15 percent of national revenue must be transferred to county governments. Finally, though findings from other sectors are mixed, research on road construction and the allocation of title deeds (Burgess et al. 2015; Hassan and Klaus 2020) documents a pattern of ethnic favoritism during the single-party era but not under democracy, consistent with the arguments in this book.[20]

The most striking feature of changing patterns of distributive politics in Kenya is that incumbent leaders have embraced reforms that limit their discretionary powers—often initiating major changes—rather than fighting tooth and nail to retain the ability to target resources for political purposes. To be sure, the reforms initiated since the early 1990s have not eliminated all forms of ethnic and partisan particularism (e.g., Harris and Posner 2019). Yet, the movement toward non-targeted policies is undeniable and consequential. This defies the commonplace expectation that African leaders will resist changes that undercut their ability to use patronage to build and maintain political support (e.g., Berman 1998). While a variety of factors—including international donor pressure and moments of polit-ical crisis—explain the reform agenda in Kenya, a central contribution of this book is to show that multiparty electoral competition increases the value of universal policies and encourages elites to opt for inclusive reforms rather than opposing them at every turn.

These arguments are consistent with other research showing that democracy incentivizes leaders to improve social services, both globally and in Africa's emerging democracies (Lake and Baum 2001; Baum and Lake 2003; Ansell 2008; Stasavage 2005a; Stasavage 2005b; Harding and Stasavage 2013; Harding 2020; Carbone 2011, 2012; Carbone and Pellegata 2017; Kjær and Therkildsen 2013; Travaglianti 2017). The difference here is the emphasis on the *ethnic logic* of universal policies in settings where the need to cultivate support across ethnic lines is a central electoral imperative. In such contexts, the value of universal

---

[20] For work showing that ethnic favoritism persists across the single-party and multiparty eras in Kenya see Franck and Rainer (2012), Kramon and Posner (2016), and Jablonski (2014).

policies is not only that they provide benefits to many voters (see Harding 2020), but also that they allow incumbents to demonstrate, in concrete and visible terms, the delivery of benefits across ethnic lines—aiding their efforts to appeal to swing voters outside their core ethnic bases.

Kenya in Context

In the early 1990s many African countries took steps toward democracy, legalizing opposition parties, reducing restrictions on the media, and holding multiparty elections. While the pace of reform varied across the continent and progress has been halting in many cases, the movement toward more open political systems represents a significant break from the past in a region where military dictatorships and single-party systems had been the norm (Bleck and van de Walle 2019). This book seeks to understand the logic of politics in Africa's emerging multiparty democracies by examining electoral competition in one country: Kenya. To situate the case in the broader regional context, this section briefly describes several factors that define presidential elections in Kenya and throughout the region. It shows that despite some unique features, electoral competition in Kenya mirrors trends in Africa's multiparty systems. Chapter 7 takes up the question of whether the swing-targeting approach advanced in this book has broader relevance by examining a second case—Ghana—that differs from Kenya in several key respects.

Ethnic Diversity

Kenya's major ethnic groups (those that comprise 2 percent or more of the national population) are shown in Table 1.1. Like most African countries, Kenya is a country of ethnic minorities. The largest group, the Kikuyu, make up only about 17 percent of the population according to the 2009 census. While the Kikuyu are typically allied in politics with two closely-related communities, the Meru (5%) and Embu (1%), these groups together comprise less than a quarter of the population. Given the small size of ethnic communities, national politics revolves around coalition building, and multiethnic coalition parties predominate in Kenya (Elischer 2013). Demographically, Kenya is similar to most other African countries. Data from Fearon (2003) shows that within Africa only 12 of 43 countries (28%) with a population greater than a million contain an ethnic group that on its own makes up a majority.

Throughout this book, I focus on the "higher-level" ethnic divisions shown in Table 1.1—the major ethnic fault lines in national politics. It is important to bear in mind, though, that ethnic groups in Kenya, as in other parts of Africa, do not

Table 1.1 Major ethnic groups in Kenya (percentages)

	Population Share	Geographic concentration
Kikuyu	17	63
Luhya	14	61
Kalenjin	13	61
Luo	10	64
Kamba	10	78
Kisii	6	68
Somali	6	83
Mijikenda	5	63
Meru	4	78
Other (each < 2%)	13	—

Notes: Population shares are based on the 2009 census. Geographic concentration is defined as the percent of each group living in constituencies where it makes up 75 percent or more of the population, measured using survey data from multiple polls conducted between 2007 and 2009 (total sample 39,062).

constitute unified social or political entities.[21] The rich literature on the historical construction of ethnicity in Kenya highlights the evolving nature of ethnic boundaries and their salience to politics (Lonsdale 1994; Berman 1998; Ogot 2000; Muigai 1995; Lynch 2010). These works emphasize in particular the continued relevance of sub-group identities including clan and sub-tribe divisions. As noted, the focus on higher-order ethnic identities is not intended to discount the importance of these attachments. Rather, it stems from practical limitations related to the available data, as well as the conceptual goal of tracing through how one factor—whether groups have a coethnic among the major presidential contenders—affects electoral alignments, and the implications of this factor for campaign strategies and policy choices.

Ethnic communities in Kenya remain geographically concentrated to a considerable extent despite decades of urbanization and internal migration. Table 1.1 shows the percentage of each group that lives in the group's "ethnic homeland," which I define as parliamentary constituencies in which the group makes up 75 percent or more of the population.[22] Spatial segregation in Kenya is similar to other countries in Africa. Alesina and Zhuravskaya (2011) generate national-level estimates of ethnic segregation, using a measure that ranges from 0 for countries where regional-level ethnic composition matches the national-level distribution exactly to 1 for countries in which each ethnic group occupies a separate region.

---

[21] The fluid and multidimensional nature of ethnicity has been examined extensively in the broader literature on ethnic politics. See Chandra (2001) and Laitin and Posner (2001) for overviews.

[22] Geographic concentration estimates were created by aggregating 12 nationally representative surveys (with a total sample size of 39,065) conducted between November 2006 and January 2009. Details are provided in the appendix.

Their sample includes 23 African countries, in which segregation ranges from 0.002 for Lesotho to 0.49 for Uganda. The measure for Kenya (0.27) is above the median but is not an extreme value. The literature has long noted the importance of spatial segregation for patterns of distributive politics (e.g., Bates 1983; Ejdemyr, Kramon, and Robinson 2018). In the context of this study, it matters for a more mundane reason: it allows me to make inferences about campaign targeting by observing where the major-party candidates hold campaign rallies, a strategy that forms the basis of Chapter 4.

Ethnic bloc voting is widely understood to be a central feature of Kenyan elections. The next chapter details bloc voting patterns in Kenya since 1992 and finds that while common impressions are not without foundation, treating ethnic groups as unified electoral blocs conceals the partial and varying nature of electoral coordination. In this regard, Kenya is similar to many other African countries. Data from Afrobarometer (round 6) surveys conducted in 29 countries in 2014 and 2015 shows that across Africa, bloc voting ranges from 0.33 for Lesotho to 0.76 for Namibia.[23] Kenya's value (0.66) is above the median, but in the same range as several other countries, including Ghana (0.61), Nigeria (0.66), and South Africa (0.67).[24]

Parties, Candidates, and Multiethnic Coalitions

The trend since the return to multiparty competition in the early 1990s has been toward a more consolidated party system in Kenya. In the first two elections after the reintroduction of competitive elections, opposition leaders failed to coalesce around a single candidate in their efforts to unseat the incumbent president, Daniel arap Moi, leading to a highly fragmented partisan landscape. Starting with the 2002 election, however, the party system consolidated into what is essentially a two-party configuration in which two main parties—usually coalitions of several smaller parties—compete for the presidency. This can be seen in Figure 1.1, which plots the effective number of parties (ENP) and the vote share of the leading candidate in presidential races from 1992 to 2017.[25] ENP declined from an average of 3.7 in 1992 and 1997 to an average of 2.2 in the four subsequent races. The share of the vote won by the leading candidate has trended upward. In 1992 and 1997 Moi won re-election with relatively small pluralities, 37 percent

---

[23] This measure is defined as the mean bloc voting rate for groups that make up ≥2 percent of each country sample, weighted by group size.

[24] Other measures of party system ethnicization developed in Huber (2012) similarly show that Kenya is at the higher end of the spectrum.

[25] These figures are based on official election results. The 2017 data is based on the first election, held on August 8, not the re-run held on October 26, which was boycotted by the leading opposition candidate, Odinga.

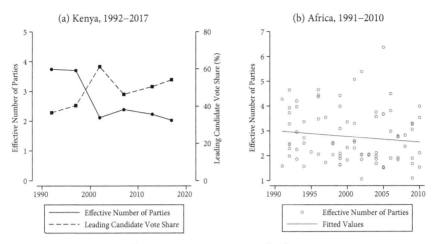

Figure 1.1 Party-system fragmentation in Kenya and Africa

Notes: Data on election outcomes is based on official results, compiled by the African Elections Database (https://africanelections.tripod.com/). Data in (b) is for all multiparty elections between 1991 and 2010 listed in the NELDA data set (Hyde and Marinov 2012). Elections were excluded if opposition parties were not allowed to form, there was only one legal party, there was only one candidate on the ballot, opposition leaders were prevented from running, or some opposition leaders boycotted the election.

and 40 percent of the official vote, respectively. In the four subsequent races, the winner gained an average of 53 percent of the vote, as reported by official sources. The trend toward a more consolidated party system in Kenya matches the broader pattern for Africa, as shown in the right panel of Figure 1.1, which indicates a downward trend in the effective number of parties for African elections as a whole between 1991 and 2010.[26]

In one respect, however, Kenya differs from most of Africa's other multiparty systems: presidential elections are highly competitive. The average margin of victory, according to official sources, in the six presidential races from 1992 to 2017 was 11.2 percentage points, relative to a median of 24.8 points for elections in other countries included in Figure 1.1(b). The competitiveness of Kenya's elections generates an especially strong incentive for parties to invest in campaigning and other related strategies to maximize their appeal to voters.

As noted above, the leading presidential candidates in Kenya usually come from different ethnic groups. Table 1.2 displays the ethnicity of all candidates receiving at least 1 percent of the popular vote since 1992. Two exceptions are noteworthy: the 1992 election in which Kenneth Matiba and Mwai Kibaki (both Kikuyu) challenged the incumbent, Daniel arap Moi, and the 2002 race when Kibaki and

---

[26] The universe of cases is defined by the NELDA version 3 dataset (Hyde and Marinov 2012). Election results were obtained from a variety of online sources, mainly africanelections.tripod.com.

Table 1.2 Ethnicity of major-party candidates (>1%) and official vote shares

Year	Candidate	Ethnic group	Vote share
1992	Daniel arap Moi	Kalenjin	37%
	Kenneth Matiba	Kikuyu	26%
	Mwai Kibaki	Kikuyu	20%
	Oginga Odinga	Luo	17%
1997	Daniel arap Moi	Kalenjin	40%
	Mwai Kibaki	Kikuyu	31%
	Raila Odinga	Luo	11%
	Michael Wamalwa	Luhya	8%
	Charity Ngilu	Kamba	8%
2002	Mwai Kibaki	Kikuyu	61%
	Uhuru Kenyatta	Kikuyu	30%
	Simeon Nyachae	Kisii	6%
2007	Mwai Kibaki	Kikuyu	46%
	Raila Odinga	Luo	44%
	Kalonzo Musyoka	Kamba	9%
2013	Uhuru Kenyatta	Kikuyu	51%
	Raila Odinga	Luo	44%
	Musalia Mudavadi	Luhya	4%
2017	Uhuru Kenyatta	Kikuyu	54%
	Raila Odinga	Luo	45%

Notes: Data compiled by author. Vote shares are based on official sources.

Uhuru Kenyatta (both Kikuyu) competed for the presidency following Moi's retirement. In every other instance, the major-party candidates have been from different communities.[27] As shown in later chapters, this means that the leading candidates are typically not forced to compete for coethnic voters and can instead concentrate their efforts elsewhere.

This pattern tracks with elections across Africa's emerging multiparty systems. Data collected from presidential elections in 38 countries between 1990 and 2010 shows that the top two contenders came from different ethnic communities in 83 percent of elections, and that candidates only faced a significant coethnic competitor (defined as one or more candidates who received 5 percent or more of the vote) in 24 percent of all races.[28] Thus, the electoral landscape in presidential

[27] Presidential elections in Kenya, as in other parts of Africa, typically feature a handful of also-rans who have little chance of victory and fail to garner more than a tiny share of the vote. Given their limited influence on electoral politics, I do not focus on these competitors.

[28] This data is based on elections in the 38 African countries for which it was possible to determine the ethnic identity of the main candidates (those who received 5 percent or more of the vote), and for which it was possible to estimate the population share of the candidates' ethnic groups using the classifications in Fearon (2003).

elections across Africa is typically defined by a small number of candidates from different ethnic groups, as in Kenya.

A central feature of presidential elections in Kenya is that elite coalitions, not parties, structure electoral politics. Thus, competitive efforts to construct diverse coalitions of senior politicians from the country's major ethnic communities take center stage in the run-up to presidential contests (Throup and Hornsby 1998; Cussac 2008; Cheeseman 2008; Oloo 2010). Despite some notable exceptions, these alliances have generally been short-lived. In Kenya there are no permanent allies or enemies, only coalitions of convenience, to use Horowitz's (1985) apt phrase. These unstable alliances give Kenya's weak party system its personalized and volatile character.

The shifting tides of elite alliances make voter alignments more fluid than in other parts of the continent. Weghorst and Bernhard (2014) provide a measure of the change in vote share across parties from one election to the next (at the legislative level) that can be attributed to parties entering and exiting the system— referred to as Type A volatility. Where elite coalitions are more fluid, Type A volatility will be higher. Between 1992 and 2007, Type A volatility in Kenya averaged nearly 20 percent, meaning that on average 20 percent of voters in each election supported parties that did not exist in the previous race. In this regard, Kenya ranks among the most volatile party systems in Africa, in league with countries like Malawi, Benin, and Mali, where party systems also revolve to a considerable extent around personalities rather than institutionalized parties. As discussed in later chapters, the personalized nature of Kenya's party system means that conceptions of core and swing differ from other parts of the continent where more established parties structure electoral alignments.

Plan of the Book

Chapter 2 provides an overview of presidential elections in Kenya's multiparty era and describes the connection between ethnicity and voter behavior. Chapter 3 then demonstrates that having a coethnic among the major presidential contenders shapes the intensity of partisan orientations and the fluidity of electoral preferences during campaigns. The chapter draws on survey data from three national elections, including two panel studies of voter preferences conducted prior to the 2013 and 2017 elections.

The book then turns from voters to campaigns. Chapter 4 demonstrates that the pursuit of swing voters is at the heart of electoral competition in Kenya. It examines the ethnic logic of campaigns by studying where presidential candidates hold public rallies, showing that they converge on the country's main swing groups, as defined in this book, and largely avoid their own—and their rivals'— coethnic strongholds. Data on household canvassing prior to the 2007 election confirms that the important task of mobilizing core supporters in the parties' coethnic areas is delegated to lower-level actors.

Chapter 5 charts how the pursuit of swing voters affects campaign appeals. Drawing on a large sample of campaign speeches from rallies in the 2007 election, the chapter shows that incumbents and challengers opt for broad-based, universal appeals over narrow, particularistic promises. And while parties do make targeted promises to specific localities and ethnic communities, they do so in a universal fashion, offering pledges of localized benefits to many groups—not just those in their core coalitions. The chapter also demonstrates that a focus on courting swing voters helps to explain the negative appeals employed on the campaign trail. While the content of negative messages varies across incumbent and challenger, both use negative messages to limit their opponent's appeal in swing areas.

Chapter 6 explores the implications for policymaking. Focusing on the education sector, it documents that since the transition to multiparty politics, Kenyan politicians have made universal reforms central to their electoral strategies. Using data on primary school enrollment and school construction, the chapter shows that the reforms implemented by incumbents since 1992 have upended patterns of ethnic favoritism observed in prior years. These reforms, particularly the removal of school fees, have dramatically increased enrollment and have gone a long way toward equalizing access at the primary-school level across ethnic groups, attenuating group inequalities that have existed since before independence.

Chapter 7 investigates whether the arguments in this book apply to other African cases, focusing on Ghana. It shows that despite differences in the nature of the party system and the salience of ethnicity to electoral politics, the swing-targeting model helps to explain key aspects of electoral competition and policy-making in Ghana. Chapter 8 concludes by exploring the implications of the book's arguments. Additional details on data sources and quantitative tests from empirical chapters are available in an Online Appendix on Dataverse (dataverse.org).

2

The Ethnic Foundations of Electoral Politics in Kenya

This chapter sets the stage for the arguments developed in subsequent chapters by accomplishing four tasks. First, it provides a brief overview of presidential elections in Kenya since the reintroduction of multiparty competition in 1992. Second, it describes the ethnic foundations of voter behavior. Consistent with instrumental theories of ethnic voting that predominate in the literature, it marshals new and original data on voter behavior at the individual and group level in Kenya to show that ethnicity is important for the information it conveys about patronage allocations and communal representation. Third, the chapter examines the connection between voters' preferences for coethnic leaders and the coalition-building strategies that presidential aspirants employ. To illustrate, it focuses on the rise to power of one of the central political figures in the multiparty era, Mwai Kibaki, Kenya's third post-independence president. Consistent with standard accounts, the data shows that voters routinely line up *en masse* in support of coethnic candidates or the coalition that best incorporates prominent coethnic leaders, and switch partisan allegiances as elite alliances shift. Yet, the data also reveals that the impression that ethnic groups move as unified electoral blocs is only partially correct. Thus, the fourth task of this chapter is to examine bloc voting rates across ethnic groups over time. The analysis shows that ethnic bloc voting is never uniform and that it tends to be lower on average for ethnic groups that do not have a coethnic leader in the race.

Multiparty Presidential Elections in Kenya

Kenya's political trajectory mirrors trends across Africa.[1] Like most African countries, Kenya, which gained independence in 1963, inherited a multiparty political system based on that of its departing colonizer, in this case Britain. In the terminal phase of the colonial era, the British oversaw the creation of a local legislative body, the Legislative Council, and presided over elections in 1961 and

---

[1] For comprehensive accounts of Kenya's modern political history, see Branch (2011) and Hornsby (2013).

Multiethnic Democracy: The Logic of Elections and Policymaking in Kenya. Jeremy Horowitz, Oxford University Press.
© Jeremy Horowitz 2022. DOI: 10.1093/oso/9780198852735.003.0002

1963 to select members of the legislature and the Prime Minister who would serve as the chief executive when power was transferred to Kenyan authorities.

The basic contours of an ethnically-oriented party system were evident in Kenya's two pre-independence elections. The Kenya African National Union (KANU) emerged as the main political party in the 1950s, led by prominent independence-era figures like Tom Mboya, a trade union leader, and Jomo Kenyatta, a British-trained anthropologist who would become Kenya's first Prime Minister (later President). Fears that KANU served the interests of the country's larger ethnic groups—especially the Kikuyu and Luo—led to the formation of a competing party, the Kenya African Democratic Union (KADU), which brought together leaders from smaller communities, including the Kamba, Kalenjin, and Mijikenda. Election outcomes closely followed coalition dynamics, with ethnic groups lining up in large numbers on different sides of the ethno-partisan divide according to which party best included prominent leaders from their ethnic communities (Bennett and Rosberg 1961; Sanger and Nottingham 1964).

As in other parts of Africa, Kenya's early experiment with democracy was not to last (Collier 1982). Kenyatta and other KANU leaders saw little value in preserving the constitutional structures left behind by the British. In short order, KANU leaders altered basic constitutional provisions, switching from a parliamentary to a presidential system, dissolving the Senate by merging it with the lower house, and scrapping provisions for a federal structure (Anyang' Nyong'o 1989; Okoth-Ogendo 1972; Kyle 1999). Party leaders induced KADU's top officials to cross the aisle and merge with KANU. In exchange, Kenyatta rewarded KADU's Chairman, Daniel arap Moi, with the vice presidency. The lone remaining opposition party, The Kenya People's Union, which would not yield to KANU's entreaties, was simply harassed into submission and then banned in 1969, creating a *de facto* single-party state (Mueller 1984). The government later passed legislation officially banning opposition parties, making Kenya a *de jure* single-party system in 1982.

Throughout the 1970s and 1980s, Kenya continued to hold parliamentary elections at regular intervals within a single-party framework (Throup 1993). Though all candidates stood on the KANU ticket, competition at the constituency level was often intense, and turnover rates for members of parliament were high. Presidential elections, however, were not competitive: incumbent presidents ran unopposed in every race from 1969 to 1988. The only transition in power during this era occurred in 1978 when Kenyatta died in office and was succeeded by Moi.

After solidifying his hold on power, Moi showed few signs of vulnerability even as the economy went into decline, the nation's infrastructure began to crumble, and public services eroded during the 1980s—Africa's "lost decade." Moi presided over an increasingly repressive regime in which harassment, detention, and the alleged assassination of regime opponents were regular occurrences (Throup

1993; Widner 1993). However, with the end of the Cold War, new pressures for reform appeared. Demands for political liberalization came both from a resurgent domestic opposition and the international donor community (Ogot 1995; Throup and Hornsby 1998; Muranga and Nasong'o 2007). As one of Africa's top recipients of Western aid, Kenya was especially vulnerable to donor demands (Brown 2007). Sensing that the tides had shifted, Moi took the initiative. To the surprise of many within the ruling party, Moi announced at a 1991 convention of KANU delegates that the constitutional provision prohibiting opposition parties was to be removed, freeing the opposition to compete in the parliamentary and presidential elections scheduled for the following year.

The transition to multiparty competition in 1992 initially appeared to be a hollow victory (Barkan 1993). Moi and his allies in KANU deployed an extensive bag of tricks to tilt the playing field in their favor: harassing opposition leaders, monopolizing state-run media, fomenting violence against opposition supporters, exploiting state resources for campaigns, manipulating election tallies, and so forth (Throup and Hornsby 1998; Southall 1998; Klopp 2001; HRW 1993; KHRC 1997, 1998). For its part, the opposition fragmented along ethnic lines, failing to coalesce around a single candidate in the 1992 and 1997 presidential elections. Kenya's permissive electoral system (only a plurality was required in presidential elections at the time) allowed Moi to win both contests with relatively meager shares of the vote: 37 percent and 41 percent respectively, according to official statistics—figures that were likely inflated on Moi's behalf by electoral fraud (Barkan 1993; Barkan and Ng'ethe 1998).

Yet, as in several other African cases, political liberalization eventually paved the way for alternation. Barred from seeking a third term under Kenya's multiparty constitution, Moi stepped down in advance of the 2002 election, choosing Uhuru Kenyatta, the son of Kenya's first president, to stand as KANU's presidential nominee. Having learned the painful lessons of the past decade, the opposition finally unified behind a single candidate in 2002, bringing Mwai Kibaki, a longtime government insider turned opposition leader, to power as the head of the National Rainbow Coalition (NARC), a broad multiethnic alliance (Anderson 2003; Barkan 2004). Many greeted Kibaki's victory as a triumph for democracy after decades of corruption and misrule—a "second liberation" (Ndegwa 2003).

Hopes for a new dawn were quickly dashed under Kibaki, whose years in office proved polarizing and divisive. Though the pragmatic leader presided over a sustained period of economic growth and the rehabilitation of the country's ailing infrastructure and social services, infighting in the senior ranks of the NARC coalition led in 2004 to the departure of several top allies from outside Kibaki's core ethnic support base among the "GEMA" communities, those that made up the Kikuyu (also Gikuyu), Embu, and Meru Association formed in the early 1970s to advance the shared interests of these closely-related groups (Barkan 2008b). Key coalition partners whose support had been instrumental to Kibaki's 2002 victory—including Raila Odinga (Luo), Musalia Mudavadi (Luhya), and Kalonzo Musyoka (Kamba)—abandoned NARC when it became clear that Kibaki did not intend to make good on a package of constitutional reforms promised before the 2002 election. These leaders joined forces with prominent opposition figures, especially William Ruto, who by this time had emerged as the most influential Kalenjin leader, to oppose a 2005 constitutional referendum pushed through by Kibaki's administration. The referendum, which failed by a wide margin, was a bitter public contest that pit opposition-aligned ethnic communities against Kibaki and the GEMA communities (Lynch 2006; Kagwanja 2009).

Kibaki entered the 2007 elections with a narrowed coalition facing a broad-based opposition movement, dubbed the Orange Democratic Movement (ODM)—an appropriation of the symbol (an orange) used to represent a "No" vote in the 2005 referendum (Kagwanja and Southall 2009). Headed by Raila Odinga, the son of long-time Luo opposition leader Oginga Odinga, ODM looked poised to defeat Kibaki. Pre-election polls uniformly showed Odinga to be in the lead prior to election day (Horowitz and Long 2016). The Electoral Commission's announcement of Kibaki as the 2007 winner amid allegations of electoral fraud sparked an intense period of ethnic violence, leading to over 1,300 deaths and the displacement of hundreds of thousands more (Anderson and Lochery 2008; ICG 2008; KNCHR 2008; Mueller 2008; Kagwanja 2009). A peace deal brokered by former UN Secretary General Kofi Annan and several other foreign dignitaries resulted in a power-sharing arrangement in which Kibaki retained the presidency and Odinga was appointed to a temporary position as Prime Minister (Kanyinga and Walker 2013).

Following Kibaki's retirement at the end of two terms, Uhuru Kenyatta won both the 2013 and 2017 elections as the head of the Jubilee coalition (later Jubilee Alliance Party), built around an unlikely pairing with William Ruto as his vice-presidential running mate. Observers speculated that the logic of the Kenyatta–Ruto alliance stemmed from the leaders' shared interest in resisting cases brought against the two by the International Criminal Court for their alleged roles in the 2008 post-election violence (Lynch 2014; Malik 2016). Whatever the rationale, the alliance proved to be a winning formula, edging out coalition parties headed by Odinga in both races—the Coalition for Reform and Democracy (CORD) in 2013 and the National Super Alliance (NASA) in 2017—though allegations of election fraud again marred these contests (Cheeseman, Lynch, and Willis 2014; Cheeseman, Kanyinga, Lynch, Ruteere, and Willis 2019). The 2017 election was especially noteworthy in this regard: for the first time in Kenya (or anywhere else in Africa) the Supreme Court annulled the election results based on procedural irregularities and called for a new election. Nevertheless, Kenyatta was re-elected in the repeat election after Odinga boycotted the contest on the grounds that administrative reforms did not adequately safeguard against fraud in the second election (Chege 2018).

Ethnicity and Voter Behavior

While ethnicity's importance to Kenyan politics has been widely documented, much of the literature on voter behavior in Kenya relies on anecdotal sources or aggregate election returns. The increasing availability of high-quality survey data makes it possible to explore the micro-foundations of ethnic voting with greater precision. This section turns to data from several opinion polls conducted between 2007 and 2017 to examine the connections between ethnic identities and individual preferences.

The comparative ethnic politics literature has greatly advanced understanding of how ethnicity influences electoral decisions in diverse societies. The predominant approach takes an *instrumental* view that emphasizes the material motivations underlying electoral choices and shows that ethnicity matters to voters because it conveys useful information about how candidates will behave in office. In contexts where voters have come to expect that political leaders will "favor their own" once in office, there is a strong incentive to elect members of one's own community to positions of power. As van de Walle (2007, p. 65) observes, "citizens may feel that only a member of their own ethnic group may end up defending the interests of the group as a whole, and that voting for a member of another ethnic group will certainly not do." Thus, candidate ethnicity provides a useful cue—or shortcut—for voters: by observing the ethnic identities of alternative leaders, voters can make rough inferences about which leader will better represent their communal interests.[2]

Instrumental theories of ethnic voting have particular relevance to Kenya, where expectations of ethnic favoritism are widespread. In a 2012 national survey I asked respondents, "How much of the time do government leaders favor their own ethnic groups?"[3] An overwhelming majority (84%) reported that leaders routinely engage in favoritism, with 53 percent saying "almost always" and another 31 percent saying "some of the time" (13% chose "rarely" and 3% "never"). Another survey I conducted in 2016 in Kenya's capital city, Nairobi, asked, "In your view, do members of parliament usually favor their own tribe when it comes to distributing jobs, bursaries, and funds for development, or do they usually make sure that people from all ethnic groups receive benefits?"[4] Nearly 70 percent of respondents reported that parliamentary leaders usually favor their own tribes, the common term for ethnic groups in Kenya. And in a

---

[2] This approach builds on a rich literature on the informational value of ethnic identities, especially Chandra (2004), Posner (2005), Ferree (2006, 2011), Carlson (2015), Adida (2015), Chauchard (2016), and Conroy-Krutz (2013).

[3] Data come from the first round of a national panel survey (n=1,246) conducted between December 6, 2012 and January 6, 2013.

[4] Data come from a survey conducted in Nairobi county (n=2,203) between June 8 and July 9, 2016.

2014 national Afrobarometer survey a large majority (76%) of Kenyans reported that ethnic considerations "often" or "always" play a role in government appointments.[5]

A growing body of scholarship on distributive politics in Kenya indicates that these beliefs are not without foundation. Quantitative work has documented ethnic favoritism across multiple sectors, including road construction, health and education, foreign aid allocations, and local development funds (Burgess et al. 2015; Franck and Rainer 2012; Kramon and Posner 2016; Jablonski 2014; Harris and Posner 2019; Barkan and Chege 1989). While other sectors have yet to receive such detailed examination, scholarship suggests a history of favoritism also in land (Harbeson 1973; Leys 1975; Boone 2011), government recruitment and promotions (Nellis 1974; Leonard 1991; Throup 1987), and commercial lending (Marris and Somerset 1971; Meisler 1970).

Kenyans, it should be noted, tend to view the historical record through an ethno-partisan lens. In the 2012 national survey referenced above, I asked about perceptions of government favoritism by successive Kenyan administrations since independence. A large portion of respondents—at least 40 percent—believed that current and former administrations *favored certain groups* rather than serving the interests of all ethnic communities (Table 2.1). In each case, though, the president's coethnics were less likely to view the leader as having engaged in favoritism, in some instances by a large margin. Thus, for example, only 36.7 percent of Kalenjin respondents believed that Moi favored some groups over others, relative to 63.1 percent among respondents from other groups. Voters, it appears, take a charitable view of coethnic leaders.

Beliefs about favoritism in the past naturally influence expectations about how future leaders will behave. I have asked Kenyans about favoritism expectations using a variety of questions—some narrow, others more general—in surveys conducted

Table 2.1 Did the government of [LEADER] serve the interests of all ethnic groups or favor certain groups? (% saying favored certain groups)

	All	Coethnics	Non-coethnics	Difference
Jomo Kenyatta (Kikuyu)	45.8	41.8	44.1	−2.3
Daniel arap Moi (Kalenjin)	63.1	36.7	63.1	−26.5***
Mwai Kibaki (Kikuyu)—first term	46.2	26.9	47.9	−21.0***
Mwai Kibaki (Kikuyu)—second term	42.5	32.1	42.4	−10.3***

Notes: Data come from the first round of a national panel survey (n=1,246) conducted between December 6, 2012 and January 6, 2013. ***$p<0.01$, **$p<0.05$, *$p<0.1$.

[5] Afrobarometer round 6 survey, conducted in Kenya from November 12 to December 5, 2014 (n=2,397).

over a decade from 2007 to 2017. The results are unambiguous: Kenyans, in large measure, believe that they and their ethnic communities will be treated better by coethnic leaders and the coalitions that best incorporate prominent coethnics in their senior ranks than by non-coethnic candidates and parties that include few coethnics in top positions. The 2012 survey, for example, asked about favoritism expectations in advance of the 2013 election using three different questions:

o If the coalition led by [Uhuru, Ruto, and Mudavadi / Raila, Musyoka, Ngilu, and Wetangula] wins the election, do you think it will serve the interests of all ethnic groups or favor certain groups over others?
o How well do you think each of the following candidates would represent the interests of your ethnic group if elected: very well, somewhat well, not well, or not at all? [Uhuru Kenyatta / Raila Odinga]
o If [Uhuru Kenyatta / Raila Odinga] is elected president, how much government funds will this area receive for development: a lot, some, a little, or none?

It makes little difference how these questions are phrased. Figure 2.1 shows that in the 2013 election Kikuyus generally expected their coethnic leader, Kenyatta, and his party (Jubilee) to serve the interests of all ethnic groups, to represent their group somewhat or very well, and to deliver funds for development to their areas, as was true for voters in the broader coalition of groups aligned with Jubilee. Kikuyus and Jubilee voters held the opposite expectations for Odinga and the party he headed (CORD). The reverse was true for Luos and CORD-aligned groups.

Given the belief that party leaders favor their own supporters, it is unsurprising that voters routinely express a preference for coethnic candidates. To document this, I conducted a simple survey experiment in 2015 with 819 respondents in Nairobi in which participants were asked to choose between two hypothetical candidates for a fictitious parliamentary by-election as part of a larger household survey (details are provided in the appendix). Each pairing included one coethnic candidate and one non-coethnic (signaled by surname). Other details (first name, age, education, and campaign pledges) were randomized, as was the order in which enumerators described the candidates. As shown in Figure 2.2(a), coethnicity increased the likelihood of respondents selecting a candidate by 38 percentage points, from a base of 31 percent for non-coethnic candidates. The size of the coethnicity bump was similar across respondents from the five ethnic groups included in the survey. The survey experiment then asked respondents how much they would trust each candidate to represent "people like you," with responses measured on a seven-point scale. Figure 2.2(b) shows a coethnic differential for the full sample and by ethnic group, suggesting that—in line with instrumental theories of ethnic voting—the preference for coethnic leaders stems in large part

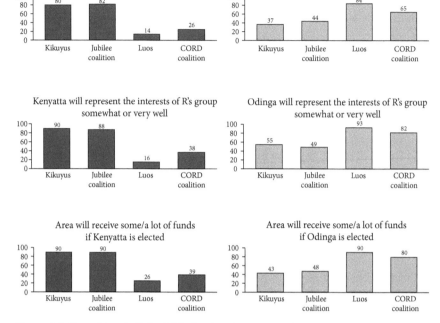

Figure 2.1 Favoritism beliefs, 2013 election (percentages)

Notes: Data come from the first round of a national panel survey (n=1,246) conducted between December 6, 2012 and January 6, 2013. Jubilee and CORD coalitions are defined as groups in which 60 percent or more of respondents in the survey registered an intention to vote for each party's leader in the 2013 presidential election. Jubilee-aligned groups are the Kikuyu, Meru, and Kalenjin. CORD-aligned groups are the Kamba, Kisii, Luo, Luhya, and Mijikenda. Only groups with a sufficient sample size are included.

from the perception that coethnics will more faithfully represent voters' communal interests.

Given these expectations, many Kenyan voters form preferences across competing presidential candidates by looking to the candidates' ethnic identities and those of their top coalition allies (see also Oyugi 1997; Haugerud 1993)—much like voters in other similar settings (Posner 2005; Chandra 2004; Ferree 2006, 2011). Voters assume that having a coethnic leader positioned in the upper ranks of a party will ensure that their group's interests will be well represented if the party wins the election, an assumption borne out by past research on distributive politics. Kramon and Posner (2016), for example, show that in education, groups in Kenya benefit not only when they have a coethnic president in power but also when the Minister of Education is from their community. Leonard (1991) shows that civil servants were more likely to receive pay raises in the late-1960s when the ministry in which they worked was headed by a coethnic permanent secretary (the most senior civil servant position).

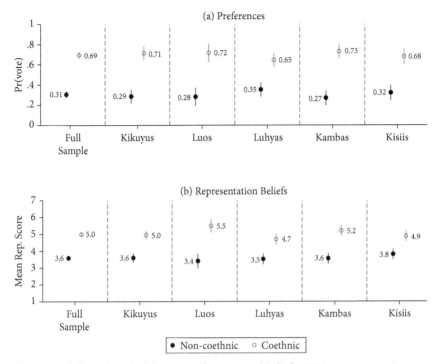

Figure 2.2 Effect of coethnicity on preferences and beliefs, 2015 survey experiment

Notes: Data come from a survey (n=819) conducted in Nairobi, Kenya from January 22 to February 16, 2015. Details are provided in the appendix. Figures show point estimates and 95 percent confidence intervals.

It is important to emphasize that the preference for coethnic leaders persists in Kenya even though many voters disdain the centrality of ethnicity in public affairs. Afrobarometer surveys show that Kenyans are substantially more likely to identify in national rather than ethnic terms.[6] Inter-group hostilities also appear to be less intense than one might expect given the polarized nature of electoral politics and the history of ethnic violence in Kenya. For example, Kenyans express little opposition to living next to neighbors from other ethnic communities and report that ethnicity has little or no influence on their choice of friends.[7] Behavioral measures less prone to potential self-censoring also produce similar

---

[6] Afrobarometer surveys conducted from 2005 to 2016 (rounds 3–6) show that between 83 percent and 91 percent of respondents in each survey round report that their national identities are equal to or stronger than their ethnic identities.

[7] In the 2014 and 2016 Afrobarometer surveys, less than 10 percent of respondents reported that they would strongly or somewhat dislike having neighbors from other ethnic communities. In a 2007 study conducted by the Afrobarometer and Oxford University (n=1,206) only 6 percent of respondents said they choose friends with the same ethnic background, while 77 percent said that ethnicity plays no role in these choices (see Dercon and Gutiérrez-Romero (2012) for survey details).

results. Berge et al. (2020), for example, find no evidence of ethnic bias in a range of behavioral games and an implicit association test commonly used to gauge inter-group sentiments for a large sample of urban respondents. Inter-marriage rates, a standard indicator of inter-group accord, show that while frequencies in Kenya are low by African standards, more than 10 percent of all couples cross ethnic lines, with rates considerably higher in urban areas (Dulani et al. 2021; Bandyopadhyay and Green 2021; Crespin-Boucaud 2018).[8]

Moreover, there is evidence that many Kenyan voters disapprove of ethnic favoritism and ethnic political mobilization. A 2003 Afrobarometer survey found that an overwhelming majority (86%) of Kenyans agreed with the statement that "since everyone is equal under the law, leaders should not favour their own family or group" and only 11 percent agreed that "once in office, leaders are obliged to help their own family or group." In a separate national poll in 2007, a majority of respondents (57%) agreed that political parties should not be allowed to form on an ethnic or religious basis.[9] Of course, these data may reflect a degree of self-censorship, as respondents likely hesitate to publicly pronounce their enthusiasm for favoritism or ethnic political parties. Nonetheless, they suggest that opposition to the politicization of ethnicity is widespread.

The persistence of ethnic voting in a context in which ethnic political behavior is largely disfavored supports the proposition that voters may find themselves locked in a prisoner's dilemma of sorts: despite the widespread disapproval of ethnic politics, voters are compelled to support coethnic candidates and parties that best include coethnics in positions of power for fear that failure to do so will mean that they and their community will not receive a fair share of government resources (Posner 2005; Bratton and Kimenyi 2008). Consistent with this notion of defensive ethnic voting, Kenyans routinely report that ethnicity plays little or no role in *their own* electoral calculations but that it does influence *others'* choices. In a 2007 survey, for example, 49 percent of respondents said they thought that the ethnic origins of presidential candidates were important to voters overall. In contrast, less than 1 percent of respondents listed a candidate's ethnicity as the most important criterion upon which *they* made electoral decisions, insisting instead that service to the community (27%), honesty in handling public funds (24%), concern about the community (22%), and experience (19%) matter more.[10]

---

[8] For example, the 2014 Demographic and Health Survey (DHS) in Kenya shows that nationally 12.6 percent of couples married or living together are ethnically mixed, and the inter-marriage rate is 18.5 percent in urban areas.

[9] Data come from a national survey conducted in the two weeks prior to the 2007 elections (n=1,207). See Dercon and Gutiérrez-Romero (2012) for details.

[10] See prior footnote for data source.

Elite Coalitions and Ethnic Bloc Voting

Because the preference for coethnic politicians leads many voters to support the party or coalition that best includes prominent figures from their community, building elite alliances that incorporate out-group leaders is a central task for presidential aspirants. Cussac (2008, p. 3), for example, describes the 2007 election as follows:

> Politicians have no choice but to mobilise voters outside of their ethnic block. Presidential aspirants were therefore heavily involved in mobilising their allies across the country quite early on, in an attempt to play the multi-ethnic card. For example, M. Kibaki relied on Daniel Moi and Kipruto Kirwa (both Kalenjin) in the Rift Valley, on Chirau Ali Makwere (Mijikenda) in the Coast, on Musikari Kombo (Luhya) in the West, and on Simeon Nyachae (Gusii) in the Kisii region. R. Odinga, on his part, benefited from Musalia Mudavadi's (Luhya) popularity in the West, from Najib Balala (Arab) at the Coast, from Joseph Nyaga (Mbeere) in central Eastern, and from Fred Gumo (Luhya) and Reuben Ndolo (Luo) in Nairobi.

To illustrate how these elite alliances influence voter alignments, I examine the electoral fortunes of one candidate, Mwai Kibaki, in election contests from 1992 to 2007, presenting group-level estimates of bloc voting for Kenya's eight largest ethnic communities that collectively make up about 86 percent of the national population.[11] Bloc voting estimates are generated using ecological inference techniques based on electoral returns for early contests in which public opinion survey data is not available (1992, 1997, and 2002) and survey data for 2007. Both types of data suffer from various limitations (the appendix describes the data sources, estimation methods, and potential sources of error). Nonetheless, the estimates provide a valuable illustration of how elite alliances shape group alignments in Kenyan elections.

Kibaki's entry into presidential politics came in 1992, the first election after the return to a multiparty system. By this time, Kibaki was a consummate regime insider. Trained as an economist, he was first elected to parliament in 1963 and then held various cabinet positions during both the Kenyatta and Moi presidencies, including serving as vice president under Moi from 1978 to 1988.

Despite his extensive experience, Kibaki fared poorly in 1992, capturing only 19.6 percent of the vote and coming in third behind Moi (36.6%) and Kenneth Matiba (25.7%).[12] As shown in Figure 2.3, Kibaki failed to garner substantial

---

[11] Estimates for smaller ethnic communities cannot be generated given the limitations of the available data.

[12] I rely upon election results from official government sources. It is important to note that domestic and international observers have routinely raised concerns about election fraud in Kenya both in the balloting process and during the vote tabulation.

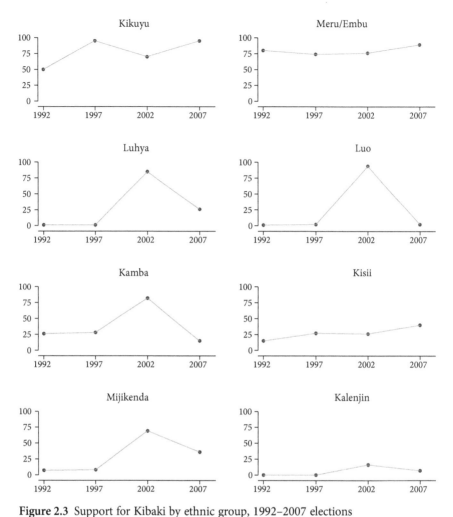

Figure 2.3 Support for Kibaki by ethnic group, 1992–2007 elections

Notes: Estimates are based on ecological inference data for 1992, 1997, and 2002, and survey results for 2007. Details on the data sources and estimation approach are presented in the appendix.

support beyond his Kikuyu base and the related Meru and Embu communities—often referred to as the GEMA bloc.[13] Among coethnic Kikuyus, Kibaki split the vote with Matiba, also Kikuyu. Kibaki garnered stronger support in northern sections of Central province around Nyeri, his birthplace, while Matiba fared better in southern districts close to his birthplace in Murang'a (Throup and Hornsby 1998, pp. 471–3). Outside of the Kikuyu, Kibaki's strongest showing was in Meru and Embu areas, where his Democratic Party (DP) succeeded in

---

[13] For detailed accounts of this race, see Throup and Hornsby (1998), Oyugi (1997), and Fox (1996).

attracting prominent local figures to stand on the DP ticket (Throup and Hornsby 1998, p. 483). Kibaki's failure in 1992 had much to do with the DP's narrow leadership structure. While the party contained leaders from a diverse set of ethnic backgrounds, it included few prominent politicians from outside the GEMA communities. Thus, Throup and Hornsby (1998, p. 99) note, that "despite the party's attempts to publicise the roles of John Keen and Eliud Mwamunga, a Maasai and a Taita, the DP appeared to be a party of the Kikuyu elite." Moi, by contrast, enjoyed near universal support among coethnic Kalenjins but also managed to garner substantial support from voters in several out-groups, especially the Luhya, Kamba, Kisii, and Mijikenda (see Table A2.2 in the appendix). Moi's success was due in large part to his greater ability to build and maintain alliances with prominent leaders both within his own ethnic stronghold and in other communities, where, as the incumbent, he held the advantage (Throup and Hornsby 1998, p. 463).

Kibaki fared better in 1997, garnering 30.9 percent of the vote, but again lost to Moi, who claimed 40.4 percent in an election in which the opposition was even more fragmented than in 1992. Kibaki was again plagued by the narrowness of his support base. Figure 2.3 indicates that his gains in 1997 were largely confined to Kikuyu voters. With Matiba boycotting the 1997 election, Kibaki stood as the sole Kikuyu candidate and attracted nearly all Kikuyu voters (see Southall 1998; Cowen and Kanyinga 2002). As in 1992, he drew relatively little support from other major ethnic groups, save again for the Meru and Embu. Other candidates— Raila Odinga (Luo), Michael Wamalwa (Luhya), and Charity Ngilu (Kamba)—all did well within their respective ethnic strongholds but failed to gain substantial support elsewhere (see Table A2.3 in the appendix). Moi, as the incumbent, again proved adept at maintaining a broad coalition that extended beyond his coethnic base. Thus, one observer attributed Moi's victory to his ability to compete for out-group support more effectively than his competitors: "Luoland voted overwhelmingly for Mr. Raila Odinga, Kalenjinland for President Moi, Luhyaland for Kijana Wamalwa, and Kikuyuland for Kibaki. It was among the communities that did not have their own presidential candidate that President Moi broke away from his rivals" (*Weekly Review*, January 9, 1998, cited in Southall 1998).

The 2002 election was a watershed both for Kibaki, who finally succeeded in garnering substantial support outside his traditional ethnic strongholds, and for Kenya, which witnessed the first political transition via the ballot box since independence. As noted, Moi chose Kenyatta as KANU's nominee, likely estimating that Kenyatta would divide the Kikuyu vote and undercut Kibaki's electoral base.[14] In the event, Kibaki's support among the Kikuyu did decline relative to 1997, with geographic divisions again coming into play. As in 1992, Kibaki fared

---

[14] *Africa Confidential* volume 43, no. 21.

better among voters in northern areas of Central province, closer to his home base in Nyeri, while Kenyatta did better in southern areas near his family's home in Kiambu (Throup 2003). Kibaki's success, however, lay in his increased support among out-groups—especially the Luhya, Luo, Kamba, and Mijikenda—which propelled him to a landslide victory with 61.3 percent of the vote, relative to 30.2 percent for Kenyatta.

What changed in 2002? Certainly, it was not campaign strategies. As in previous elections, Kibaki's appeal centered around an indictment of KANU's economic mismanagement and corruption, combined with a promise to revitalize the economy and root out corruption (Steeves 2006a). Moreover, Kibaki's campaign efforts in 2002 were severely curtailed by a road accident that forced him from the campaign trail midway through the race. Rather, as many have noted, Kibaki's success was the result of the emergence of a broad elite coalition that included top leaders from several of the country's larger ethnic communities under the NARC umbrella, which chose Kibaki as its nominee (Ndegwa 2003; Barkan 2004). It was clear to all that Kibaki's ability to reach voters outside his traditional ethnic base had everything to do with these alliances. Thus, for example, Barkan (2004, p. 90) notes that "the most important factor behind Kibaki's victory was the opposition's decision to unite around a single slate of candidates."

As clearly as the 2002 election illustrates the importance of elite coalitions, so too does the race that followed in 2007. As president, Kibaki proved remarkably inattentive to coalition politics, perhaps reasoning that his reform agenda would be sufficient to maintain popular support across ethnic lines. If so, he was wrong. As Figure 2.3 shows, support among several ethnic communities—including the Luo, Luhya, Kamba, and Mijikenda—plummeted after allies from these communities broke from the NARC coalition in 2004 (Kagwanja and Southall 2009). Though Kibaki was officially re-elected for a second term in 2007, the circumstances of the elections raised serious concerns that the final tally had been altered to boost Kibaki's flagging public support (Throup 2008; Gibson and Long 2009).

This brief discussion illustrates the importance of elite alliances in explaining Kibaki's varying electoral fortunes. The same is equally true for other candidates. Thus, as noted, Moi's ability to hold onto power in 1992 and 1997 had much to do with his success in maintaining alliances with leaders from several of Kenya's larger ethnic communities including the Luhya, Kisii, and Kamba (Throup and Hornsby 1998). Likewise, the failed electoral bids of leaders including Raila Odinga, Michael Wamalwa, and Charity Ngilu in 1997, Simeon Nyachae in 2002, or Kalonzo Musyoka in 2007 stem in each case from an inability to build electoral pacts with influential politicians from other groups. And more recently, Uhuru Kenyatta's successful electoral bids in 2013 and 2017 depended critically on alliances with top leaders from other communities, above all William Ruto (Lynch 2014).

How Extensive Is Ethnic Bloc Voting?

The strength of ethnic bloc voting in Kenya sometimes leads observers to treat ethnic groups—rather than individual voters—as the building blocks of electoral politics. Thus, for example, Southall (1999, p. 98) describes the 1997 election as follows:

> The result of the 1997 election had confirmed the ethnic pattern of voting: the Kalenjin voted for KANU and Moi (107 seats and 40% of the vote in the presidential election), the Kikuyu for the Democratic Party (DP) (39 and 31%) and Mwai Kibaki, the Luo for the National Development Party of Kenya (NDPK) and Raila Odinga (21 and 11%), the Luhya for the Forum for the Restoration of Democracy (Kenya) (FORD-K) and Michael Wamalwa (17 and 8%) and so on, with the smaller ethnic communities which did not have their own presidential candidate throwing their lot in with Moi.

Yet, despite the undeniable importance of group bloc voting, it is a mistake to assume that ethnic communities in Kenya are fully united in their electoral preferences. Figure 2.4 plots bloc voting rates for Kenya's eight largest ethnic groups across six elections from 1992 to 2017.[15] The mean bloc voting rate is 76.1 percent, meaning that on average about a quarter of all voters in each group do not support their group's most-preferred candidate. This observation is important for electoral politics in one basic way: it signals to presidential candidates and their strategists that voter preferences may not be wholly determined by elite alignments, suggesting the possibility that other influences—and campaigns in particular—may offer effective strategies for increasing vote share. This creates an incentive for investing in campaigning after the elite alliances are set.

Equally important, bloc voting tends to be higher for groups that have a coethnic in the race than for those that do not: 85.6 percent vs. 71.4 percent across all election years. The extent of bloc voting varies across groups that do not have a coethnic in the race. The Luo and Kalenjin have generally voted as solid blocs even in contests when these groups did not have a coethnic in the presidential election. The Meru and Embu have been steadfast in their support for Kikuyu candidates in every race since 1992. Other groups, especially the Kisii, Luhya, Kamba, and Mijikenda, have typically been more divided, owing to sub-tribe and clan divisions that make coordinated political action more difficult. Yet, despite these differences, the general rule is clear: ethnic groups that do not have a coethnic in the race are on average less likely to unite behind a single candidate to the same extent as voters in groups that do. This finding has important

---

[15] Bloc voting rates are defined as the share of voters in each ethnic group that supports the most-preferred candidate in that group.

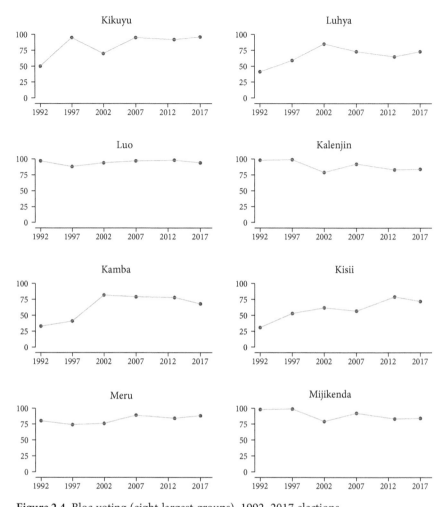

Figure 2.4 Bloc voting (eight largest groups), 1992–2017 elections

Notes: Figure shows the estimated share of each ethnic group that supported the leading presidential candidate in each group. Estimates are based on data in Tables A2.2–A2.5 in the appendix.

implications for campaign strategies: if presidential aspirants seek to increase their vote share on the campaign trail, they will be well advised to concentrate their efforts on voters in groups that do not have a coethnic in the race.

Conclusion

This chapter lays the foundation for the examination of campaign strategies in subsequent chapters by describing the electoral landscape in Kenya's multiparty contests. After providing a brief overview of presidential elections since independence, the chapter describes the connection between ethnic identities and voter behavior at the individual and group levels. Consistent with instrumental theories of ethnic voting, the chapter shows that ethnicity matters to voters in Kenya for the information it conveys about how alternative leaders are likely to behave—which groups they will favor and which they will neglect—if elected to office. While these arguments are well established in the literature on ethnic voting and in studies of Kenyan politics, the chapter assembles a range of new survey and experimental data to buttress the micro-level architecture on which future chapters build.

Turning from individual-level to group-level outcomes, the chapter explores how the preference for coethnic leaders affects elite alignments in Kenya's weak-party system. To illustrate, it traces the electoral fortunes of Mwai Kibaki, Kenya's third president, whose victory in 2002 owed to the emergence of a broad coalition of prominent allies who supported his presidential bid. This chapter provides new data on group alignments using ecological inference techniques to study the shifting tides of Kibaki's support across Kenya's major ethnic communities.

Finally, the chapter examines bloc voting rates across six multiparty elections from 1992 to 2017. The results show that accounts that view elections in Kenya as an "ethnic census" (Horowitz 1985) capture an essential kernel of truth. At the same time, the results in this chapter demonstrate the importance of not over-stating the extent of bloc voting in Kenya, which is never fully realized. Equally important, the chapter discerns a clear pattern across elections: bloc voting rates are generally lower for groups that do not have a coethnic among the main contenders in presidential elections than for those that do. This finding represents a general trend, not a universal rule, and many exceptions are observed. Yet, it provides a cornerstone for the theory of campaign strategies proposed in this book.

3

Ethnicity and the Swing Vote

While considerable effort has been devoted to conceptualizing swing voters in the world's long-standing democracies, core and swing have received less attention in emerging democracies, particularly in Africa. The lack of scholarship may stem from the view that in contexts where ethnicity is politically salient, as it is in much of Africa, few voters will be available for persuasion and conversion during elections. The lack of attention may also stem from methodological limitations. Much of the contemporary research on political behavior in Africa's emerging democracies relies on data from cross-sectional studies, aggregate election returns, or single-shot experiments—data that is poorly suited for examining preference change during campaigns. As a result, scholars know little about the factors that make some voters "up-for-grabs" during elections.

This chapter examines how one factor—whether groups have a coethnic in the race—affects the stability of electoral preferences. Drawing on survey data from Kenya's presidential elections in 2007, 2013, and 2017, the analysis shows that voters without a coethnic in the race have weaker initial preferences at the start of campaigns and are more likely to change their voting intentions during the campaign period than those with a coethnic in the race. Additional tests suggest that changes in voting intentions occur when individuals update their beliefs about how well the alternative candidates will serve the interests of their ethnic communities. These results provide a behavioral foundation for the analysis of campaign strategies in Chapter 4.

Ethnicity and Swing Voters

The approach developed here emphasizes variation in the *informational value of ethnic cues*. As described in the prior chapter, many Kenyan voters seek to elect coethnic leaders to positions of power and influence at all levels in government. Voters form electoral preferences in presidential elections by identifying the coalition or party that best incorporates prominent coethnic representatives in its ranks, relying on ethnic cues—the identities of the presidential aspirants and their main allies—to decide between alternative options. This chapter proposes that the informational value of ethnic cues varies in systematic ways across communities, leading to stronger and more durable ties at the start of the campaign period among voters from groups that have a coethnic leader among

Multiethnic Democracy: The Logic of Elections and Policymaking in Kenya. Jeremy Horowitz, Oxford University Press.
© Jeremy Horowitz 2022. DOI: 10.1093/oso/9780198852735.003.0003

the major contenders. This is because political institutions in Africa concentrate extensive powers in the hands of chief executives and because lower-level politicians that share the ethnic background of the main presidential contenders tend to be more unified in their party affiliations than office-seekers from other groups.

First, chief executives in Africa have historically enjoyed high levels of discretion over distributive allocations (Jackson and Rosberg 1984; van de Walle 2003). Despite three decades of political liberalization since the early 1990s, chief executives remain relatively unconstrained in their ability to control policymaking and implementation. Thus, van de Walle (2003, p. 310) observes that "throughout the region, power is highly centralised around the president. He is literally above the law, controls in many cases a large proportion of state finance with little accountability, and delegates remarkably little of his authority." In Kenya, the powers of the presidency are so extensive that the office is sometimes referred to as the "imperial presidency" (Prempeh 2008), despite reforms that have strengthened other branches of government and loosened restrictions on the media and civil society since the early 1990s (Barkan 2008a; Opalo 2014; Hassan 2015). The strength of presidential power means that the president exerts considerable influence over how myriad benefits are distributed across ethnic communities (Branch and Cheeseman 2006; Mueller 2008).

Given the concentration of power in the hands of chief executives in Africa, voters look above all to the ethnic identities of the presidential candidates to form expectations about which group(s) each leader will favor if elected, particularly in weak party systems where individual politicians, not parties, structure electoral competition. The identities of lower-level actors within parties are less informative simply because such actors have less control over patronage allocations. Thus, Posner (2005, p. 109) observes that in Zambia, "the overwhelming tendency is for voters to ignore the vice presidents, secretaries general, and party chairpersons . . . and to draw their inferences about the party's patronage orientations from the ethnic background of its top leader." Likewise, in Kenya voters look above all to the ethnic identities of the presidential aspirants for information about future patronage dynamics. Haugerud (1993, p. 42) reports that "Kenyans I talked with in both town and countryside in mid-1993 discussed the nation's political future in explicit ethnic and regional terms, and assumed that the ethnic identity of a new president would define patterns of favoritism." Voters from groups that do not have a coethnic in the race may form preferences in presidential elections by examining which coalition better incorporates coethnic leaders in senior positions.[1] Yet because lower-level actors within parties have less direct control over distributive decisions, the ethnic identity of these leaders will often be less informative, relative to the identities of the top candidates.

---

[1] This account draws on an extensive literature that examines ethnic and partisan cues in multi-ethnic settings (e.g., Chandra 2004, Posner 2005, and Ferree 2011).

Second, ethnic cues may be less informative for voters from groups that do not have a coethnic among the major contenders because prominent politicians—including those who seek election as governors, members of parliament, and local councilors—from such groups tend to be less unified in their party affiliations than elites from groups that do have a candidate in the race. Presidential aspirants compete intensely to recruit leaders from across the country, an imperative given greater urgency by institutional requirements that presidential winners gain a minimum of support across geographic areas in Kenya.[2] The most senior regional leaders in Kenya—figures like William Ruto, Musalia Mudavadi, or Kalonzo Musyoka—have considerable latitude in deciding which coalition to join, stemming from their ability to influence the electoral choices of coethnic voters. However, most office-seekers must affiliate with whichever party is dominant in their locality due to the strength of coattail effects in down-ballot races.[3] This is particularly true for candidates seeking election in the presidential candidates' ethnic strongholds, where running for office on an opposition ticket is usually a non-starter.

In Kenya, the power of presidential coattails means that the real contest in the candidates' ethnic strongholds is at the nominations stage; whoever gains the nomination on the locally dominant party ticket is assured to prevail in the general election.[4] Thus, Oloo (2001, p. 447) notes that in the Rift Valley in 1992, "most aspirants...viewed the real battle to be at the primaries stage rather than during the general election. This was based on the belief that once an aspirant won the KANU nomination ticket, the general election would be a mere formality" (see also Kimathi 1993 and Throup and Hornsby 1998). Coattail effects tend to be strongest in each presidential contender's ethnic stronghold, where support for the presidential candidate—and distrust of rival aspirants—is often most uniform and intense. Lower-level candidates in these areas have little choice but to seek the dominant party's nomination, to affiliate with allied parties, or to sit out the race. In other areas, local candidates may have more latitude to seek alternative party affiliations, meaning that local elites will often be more divided across party platforms.

[2] From 1992 to 2007 Kenya's constitution required that the presidential winner gain at least 25 percent of the vote in five of eight provinces. A new constitution adopted in 2010 changed this requirement to at least 25 percent of the vote in half of the 47 counties that replaced districts as administrative divisions. The constitution was also amended to require that the presidential winner gain a majority rather than a mere plurality of the national vote. For a discussion of these institutional changes, see Cheeseman, Lynch, and Willis (2019).

[3] Candidates for lower-level offices are elected from single-member districts and typically seek election in areas where their own ethnic group makes up a large share of the local electorate. As a result, most Kikuyu candidates, for example, seek election in Kikuyu-majority areas, as is true of candidates from other ethnic communities (Horowitz 2012).

[4] On coattail effects in weakly-institutionalized party systems, see Conroy-Krutz, Moehler, and Aguilar (2016) and Carlson (2016). Candidates may also face social pressures not to affiliate with rival parties that are seen as a threat to communal interests (Posner 2005).

Data from Kenya's 2007 parliamentary elections illustrate this point. Table 3.1 shows the party affiliations for 725 candidates who sought parliamentary seats.[5] Most candidates from the ethnic groups of the two leading contenders—Kibaki (Kikuyu) and Odinga (Luo)—sought to affiliate with those candidates' parties (or allied parties) and avoided running on rival party tickets. Thus, 79 percent of Kikuyu candidates ran on the PNU ticket headed by Kibaki or on the ticket of allied parties that were part of PNU's broader coalition.[6] Those not affiliated with PNU or its coalition partners ran on minor parties not linked to the opposition or as independents. Few ran on the ODM ticket headed by Odinga or on ODM-K, which was led by the minor-party candidate Kalonzo Musyoka (Kamba). Likewise, nearly all Luo candidates sought election as part of ODM or allied parties, and very few affiliated with the parties headed by Odinga's major rivals.[7] Candidates from other groups that did not have a coethnic among the leading

Table 3.1 Party affiliations for parliamentary candidates, 2007 election (percentages)

Candidate ethnicity	PNU coalition	ODM & allied parties	ODM-K	Other
Kikuyu (136)	79	4	0	17
Luo (41)	2	83	0	15
Kamba (69)	30	7	28	35
Luhya (90)	32	38	6	24
Kalenjin (77)	30	48	10	12
Mijikenda (46)	37	24	13	26
Kisii (49)	47	24	8	20
Meru (43)	84	0	0	16
Somali (46)	50	26	7	17

Notes: Table includes candidates who received 5 percent or more of the vote. Candidates' ethnic groups were coded by research assistants from the University of Nairobi. The number of candidates from each ethnic group is shown in parentheses.

[5] The analysis excludes also-rans, defined as candidates who gained less than 5 percent of the vote. Results are similar if I use a higher threshold to distinguish also-rans or if I include all candidates who competed in the election.

[6] PNU's coalition partners include DP, FORD-KENYA, FORD-PEOPLE, KANU, NARC-KENYA, New Ford-Kenya, Shirikisho, Agano, Community Development Party, Ford-Asili, Forepa, KENDA, Kenya Republican Reformation Party, Kenya Union of National Alliance, Mazingira Green Party, National Alliance Party of Kenya, National Renewal People's Party, New Aspirations Party of Kenya, New Generation Party, Republican Liberty Party, Saba Saba Asili, SAFINA, Sheda Party, Sisi Kwa Sisi, United People's Congress, Vijana Progressive Alliance, and Workers Congress. ODM's allied parties include NARC and UDM. Sources: PNU Manifesto and Cheeseman (2008, p. 183).

[7] These patterns do not obtain because office seekers were inhibited from joining rival parties. To the contrary, the parties in 2007 actively sought candidates from outside their core strongholds in order to convey their national reach. Thus, for example, PNU made great fanfare of the one major Luo candidate who joined the party's ranks—Raphael Tuju, the sitting incumbent from Rarieda constituency, a Luo-majority area in Nyanza Province.

presidential contenders including the Luhya, Kalenjin, and Kisii, were typically more divided across the main parties.[8]

The partisan alignments of lower-level politicians have implications for voters seeking to determine which presidential candidate will best represent their communal interests.[9] When political leaders from one's group are united in their party affiliations, ethnic cues all point toward the same conclusion. Thus, for Kikuyu and Luo voters in 2007, the partisan alignments shown in Table 3.1 reinforced the view that Kikuyu interests would be best served by Kibaki and Luo interests by Odinga. However, when coethnic leaders are more divided across parties, elite cues point in different directions, increasing uncertainty about which of the presidential candidates will better represent the interests of one's group. Because of these differences in the informational value of ethnic cues, voters from groups that do not have a coethnic in the race should, on average, be less certain at the start of the race about which of the alternative parties or candidates will best serve their group's interests. These voters should therefore hold weaker initial preferences and should be more willing to update their voting intentions during the campaign period, relative to voters from groups that have a coethnic in the race.

Coalition Groups

Emphasizing the distinction between voters from communities that do and do not have a coethnic in the race may seem contrary to intuition given the importance of multiethnic coalitions in Kenya. The major presidential candidates are routinely able to draw on equally strong support (or nearly so) from voters in coalition groups as from their own. Given this, one might expect that voters in coalition groups would be just as steadfast in their support at the start of the race and equally unwilling to update their voting intentions during the campaigns, blurring the distinction between voters from groups that do or do not have a coethnic in race. Thus, for example, ODM in 2007 is often described as a coalition of the Luo, Kalenjin, and Luhya (e.g., Maupeu 2008). Yet, as shown in Table 3.1, Kalenjin leaders seeking office in the legislature were less united in support of Odinga's presidential bid than Luo elites: only about half (48%) affiliated with ODM or allied party tickets, compared to 83 percent of Luo candidates. Nearly as many (40%) affiliated with PNU or ODM-K. And, at the most senior level, the former

---

[8] Of course, not all lower-level politicians are equally influential with voters. In Kenya, the most prominent leaders—the regional kingpins—hold more sway in their home areas than other political actors. Thus, for example, William Ruto's decision to ally with ODM in 2007 surely had more influence on Kalenjin voters than did decisions by less prominent leaders such as Kipruto Kirwa, Patrick Kiplagat, or Moses Cheboi who stood with Kibaki. While the data in Table 3.1 do not account for these differences, they nonetheless demonstrate that elites are often more divided in communities that do not have a coethnic in the race than in those that do.

[9] See also Ferree (2011, ch. 6).

president, Moi, supported Kibaki, as did numerous other prominent Kalenjin leaders, including several incumbent MPs. Likewise, among the Luhya, only 38 percent of parliamentary aspirants stood for election on the ODM ticket; an equal number sought election on the PNU or ODM-K platforms. Moreover, at the senior level, Luhya politicians were well placed in all three parties, each of which chose a Luhya as the vice-presidential running mate (Moody Awori in PNU; Musalia Mudavadi in ODM; and Julia Odhiambo in ODM-K).

Elite divisions among ethnic groups that are commonly viewed as coalition allies mean that voters in such groups may hold weaker initial orientations and be more willing to update electoral preferences during campaigns, relative to voters from the candidates' own ethnic communities. There are, however, instances in which coalition partners are more akin to the candidates' own groups. As illustrated in Table 3.1, Meru leaders were as unified in their partisan affiliations as were Kikuyu leaders: no Meru parliamentary aspirants sought election on the ODM or ODM-K tickets, and no prominent leaders from the group supported Odinga or Musyoka. Given this, one might expect that Meru voters in 2007 would hold strong and durable electoral ties to Kibaki. Yet, as a general rule, elites from coalition groups tend to be more divided than elites from the leading candidates' own communities. And, as shown below, voters from coalition groups tend to update their electoral preferences during the campaigns at higher rates than voters who have a coethnic in the race.

Caveats

Several caveats are in order. First, the emphasis on how ethnic identities influence core and swing does not imply that other, non-ethnic factors are irrelevant. Studies from Kenya and other similar contexts demonstrate that a host of influences—including performance evaluations, issue priorities, candidate assessments, ideology, urban/rural divisions, and others—may shape voter preferences (Bratton and Kimenyi 2008; Youde 2005; Gibson and Long 2009; Hoffman and Long 2013; Ferree, Gibson, and Long 2014; Carlson 2015; Harding 2015; Whitfield 2009; Wahman and Boone 2018). Research on swing voters in Ghana (Lindberg and Morrison 2005; Weghorst and Lindberg 2013) argues that performance assessments largely explain voter shifts across elections. Scholarship from long-standing democracies shows that voters who are less cognitively engaged with politics are more prone to update their electoral intentions (e.g., Converse 1964; Zaller 2004; Kaufmann, Petrocik, and Shaw 2008). My goal in the tests below is to show that ethnic identities exert a substantively meaningful effect on the fluidity of electoral preferences in Kenya after accounting for a range of other attitudinal, cognitive, and demographic factors suggested by these prior works. Moreover, as noted in the introduction, the account offered in this book highlights the role of ethnicity because it seeks to link voter preferences to campaign strategies. Unlike many of the other factors that may make some voters more up-for-grabs in elections, ethnicity is visible to party strategists. By observing the ethnic composition of localities, strategists can make rough inferences about whether it is worth allocating campaign resources toward them. Other factors that are less easily observed are less useful to party strategists (Hersh 2015).

Second, throughout this book I refer to groups that do not have a coethnic in the race as "swing groups" and those that do as "core groups." As noted in the introduction, this terminology serves as a shorthand for ethnic communities in which there will be *marginally more or less persuadable voters* who might potentially be convinced to change their vote during the campaign period. I do not imply that entire groups will be up-for-grabs or that they might be persuaded—as a bloc—to swing from one party to another. Nor does the terminology used here imply that all voters within swing groups will be persuadable or that none within core groups will be. Indeed, most voters in both core and swing groups generally will not be up-for-grabs in the months leading up to a national election. Rather, what distinguishes core and swing is the marginal difference in the share of potential swing voters. Though the margin may be small, for candidates seeking to maximize the return on campaign investments, even a small differential can be important.

Further, swing groups are defined by the greater number of *potential* swing voters, not the number of *actual* party switchers. Scholars have long understood that campaigns typically have minimal effects on the overall distribution of support (Lazarsfeld, Berelson, and Gaudet 1944; Berelson, Lazarsfeld, and McPhee 1954; Finkel 1993). Because the leading competitors often have similar resources available for campaigning, their efforts may be offsetting (Gelman and King 1993). It is a mistake, therefore, to define swing voters only as those who do in fact change their intentions, though the tests below find that voters in groups that do not have a coethnic in the race are consistently more likely to update their voting intentions, relative to voters in groups that do.

Third, endogeneity may be a concern. Groups that are more internally cohesive may be more likely to have coethnic candidates in presidential races than groups for which sub-tribal and clan differences have greater relevance. It may be that this underlying cohesiveness produces more homogenous and stable electoral preferences, not the fact of having a coethnic leader in the race. This concern is difficult to fully allay because Kenya's electoral history provides only so many opportunities to observe voter behavior and because a small group of leaders from a narrow set of ethnic groups has dominated electoral competition since 1992. As a result, it is not possible to test whether attitudes and behaviors among Kikuyus, for example, vary across elections when they do or do not have a coethnic leader in the race, as every election since 1992 has included one or more prominent Kikuyu candidate. Concerns about endogeneity are especially relevant to the Luhya, which typically does not have a coethnic among the major contenders. Aspiring Luhya presidential candidates may demure from running (or may fail to gain the nomination of the parties they join) due to the expectation that they will not be able to unify the Luhya vote in support of their candidacy. It is, however, difficult to tease apart whether the Luhya tend not to have coethnic leaders in the race because sub-group divisions inhibit voter coordination, or whether sub-group divisions remain relevant because the group often does not have a coethnic option among the major-party contenders—both are likely true.

I draw on survey data later in the chapter to demonstrate that group cohesion—as measured by the strength of ethnic identification—is not systematically higher among groups like the Kikuyu and Luo that frequently have coethnic leaders in presidential elections in Kenya. Nonetheless, the available data cannot fully resolve the question of whether groups with a coethnic in the race act as unified blocs due to the presence of coethnic representatives on the ballot rather than underlying group propensities to coordinate around a single party. At the proximate level, however, what matters is simply that the electoral landscape is one in which the major-party contenders enter the race knowing that their strongest support—and that of their rivals—will likely come from coethnic voters, while other groups will typically be more divided and hold weaker initial preferences.

Finally, this book does not test the specific mechanisms through which campaigns alter voting intentions. Rather, it treats campaigns as a bundle of activities that includes rallies, household canvasing, media coverage, public deliberation, and so forth. Scholarship from a variety of contexts provides evidence that these aspects of the campaign can influence attitudes and preferences (e.g., Arcenaux 2007; Baker, Ames, and Renno 2006; Bartels 1993; Boas and Hidalgo 2011; Greene 2011; Huckfeldt and Sprague 1995; Iyengar and Kinder 1987; Ladd and Lenz 2009; Lawson and McCann 2004; Wantchekon 2003). I propose that it is the greater *receptivity* to these various aspects of the campaign that makes voters from groups without a coethnic in the race more likely to update their preferences.

Data and Tests

To explore how ethnic identities shape core and swing, the analysis draws on data from national surveys conducted prior to Kenya's 2007, 2013, and 2017 elections. Data for 2007 are from a survey (n=2,020) conducted on September 21–25, shortly after the major parties announced their presidential nominees. This data is used to examine initial preferences at the start of the campaign. For 2013 and 2017, I draw on panel surveys that allow me to investigate initial preferences and to track changes in voting intentions across the campaign periods by re-interviewing the same individuals at the start of the campaigns and again just prior to the elections. The 2012–13 panel study interviewed 1,246 wave 1 respondents shortly after the main coalitions, Jubilee and CORD, formed in early December 2012, with 846 respondents re-interviewed prior to the March 4 election. For the 2017 panel study, wave 1 was fielded roughly three months before the election (May 11–23) as part of a larger omnibus poll that reached 2,026 respondents. The second wave was conducted by telephone prior to the August 8 election, and reached 730 wave 1 respondents. Additional details for all surveys are provided in the appendix.

Testing the argument requires first categorizing ethnic groups according to whether they had a coethnic candidate in each presidential election. While conceptually this should be a straightforward task, it is complicated by the large number of also-rans who compete in Kenya's presidential elections—minor-party candidates who have little chance of victory and are generally viewed as after-thoughts by most voters. My approach is to exclude also-rans and focus on the major contenders, those candidates who garnered 5 percent or more of the national vote (shown in Table 3.2).[10]

The Effect of Having a Coethnic in the Race on Initial Attitudes

To explore how having a coethnic leader in the presidential race affects initial preferences, I examine responses to several questions that might plausibly make some voters more willing to update their voting intentions in response to campaign persuasion. I use four measures shown in Table 3.3, which provides

Table 3.2 Major candidates in presidential elections, 2007–2017

2007	Mwai Kibaki (Kikuyu), Raila Odinga (Luo), Kalonzo Musyoka (Kamba)
2013	Uhuru Kenyatta (Kikuyu), Raila Odinga (Luo)
2017	Uhuru Kenyatta (Kikuyu), Raila Odinga (Luo)

[10] The decision to exclude also-rans who received less than 5 percent of the vote is based on the assumption that most voters do not seriously consider supporting marginal contenders. For example, in 2013 the ballot included Mohamed Dida (Somali), James Kiyiapi (Maasai), and Musalia Mudavadi (Luhya) in addition to the two major-party candidates, Uhuru Kenyatta (Kikuyu) and Raila Odinga (Luo). Yet it hardly makes sense to consider the Somali, Maasai, and Luhya as core groups, because it was well understood prior to the start of the campaigns that candidates from these groups were not viable contenders. Likewise, the 2013 ballot included three Kikuyu candidates in addition to Kenyatta (Martha Karua, Paul Muite, and Peter Kenneth). Again, however, it was well known at the start of the race that these candidates were not serious contenders. For these reasons, it is sensible to treat the 2013 election as a contest between Kenyatta and Odinga, and therefore to view their respective communities as the core groups in 2013. Support for this approach comes from a national public opinion survey (n=2,000) conducted by Ipsos Synovate in November 2012 that found that the vast majority of Kenyans supported the four candidates who went on to lead the CORD and Jubilee coalitions. When asked who respondents would vote for if the election were held now, 33% chose Odinga, 26% Kenyatta, 9% Ruto, and 8% Musyoka. Among the other candidates who went on to contest the election, Mudavadi's support was 4%, Peter Kenneth's was 3%, and Martha Karua's was 2%. None of the other eventual contenders (Paul Muite, Mohamed Dida, or James Kiyiapi) cleared 1% in the poll.

Table 3.3 Survey items used to measure initial preferences

Measure	Survey question	Coding notes
1. Partisan		
2007	Which political party do you feel closest to, if any?	1 if "close" to any; 0 otherwise
2013	Do you feel close to any particular political party? If yes: Which party is that?	Same as above
2017	Which political party or coalition do you feel closest to, if any?	Same as above
2. Strong partisan		
2007	Not available.	
2013	*If close to any:* Do you feel very close to this party, somewhat close, a little close, or not very close?	1 if "very close"; 0 otherwise
2017	*If close to any:* How close do you feel to this party/coalition? Do you feel: very close, somewhat close, or not very close?	Same as above
3. Undecided		
2007	If an election for president were held now, whom would you vote for if the person was a candidate?	1 if "undecided"; 0 otherwise
2013	If the election were between only Raila Odinga and Uhuru Kenyatta, which candidate would you vote for?	1 if "don't know"; 0 otherwise
2017	If the election was held tomorrow, who would you want to vote for president and deputy president?	Same as above
4. Representation gap		
2007	Regarding each of these leaders I am going to mention, do you expect them to treat your tribe favorably, unfavorably, or the same as other communities if they were elected president?	1 if difference between Kibaki and Odinga ≥ 1; 0 otherwise
2013	How well do you think each of the following candidates would represent the interests of your ethnic group if elected: very well, somewhat well, not well, or not at all?	1 if difference between Kenyatta and Odinga ≥ 2; 0 otherwise
2017	How well do you think each of the following candidates would represent the interests of your ethnic group if elected in the next election: very well, somewhat well, not well, or not at all?	Same as above

question wording and coding details. The first two measures relate to *partisan affinities*: one is a measure of whether respondents identify as partisans ("feel close") of any party; the second measures whether individuals identify as strong partisans of a party (available only for 2013 and 2017). The third measure captures whether respondents are *undecided* about their voting intentions in the presidential election. The fourth measure examines the perceived *representation gap* in how well each of the two leading candidates would represent the interests of each voter's ethnic group if elected. I examine the share of respondents who perceive the gap between the candidates to be large, as defined in Table 3.3. The questions used to measure these variables in the 2007, 2013, and 2017 surveys vary, making comparisons across election years inappropriate. Nevertheless, it is possible to compare attitudes and beliefs for those with and without a coethnic in the race for each election year. Data are taken from surveys conducted prior to the main period of campaigning in each election.

Table 3.4 shows that having a coethnic in the race is consistently associated with differences in initial attitudes. Regarding partisan affinity, those without a coethnic in the race were less likely to feel close to a political party in 2013 (60.1% vs. 79.6%) and 2017 (87.6% vs. 94.2%), though in 2007 no difference was observed, perhaps because of the intensely polarized nature of that election and the 2005 referendum that preceded it.[11] Large differences in partisan intensity are observed in both 2013 and 2017. Those with a coethnic in the race were substantially more

Table 3.4 Initial attitudes and beliefs (percentages)

	Coethnic in race?		
	No	Yes	Difference
2007 Election:			
Partisan	91.4	88.9	−2.5
Undecided	6.0	3.6	−2.4**
Representation gap	65.2	73.1	7.9***
2013 Election:			
Partisan	60.1	79.6	19.0***
Strong partisan	54.6	72.3	17.7***
Undecided	11.1	2.8	−8.3***
Representation gap	40.0	50.7	10.8***
2017 Election:			
Partisan	87.6	94.2	6.6***
Strong partisan	52.8	71.5	18.7***
Undecided	9.1	4.6	−4.5***
Representation gap	59.2	70.4	11.3***

Notes: Initial attitudes are measured using survey data collected prior to the start of the main period of campaigning in each election year. Data for 2007 are from a survey (n=2,020) conducted by Steadman (now Ipsos) on September 21-25, 2007. Data for 2013 are from the first wave of a panel study (n=1,246) conducted by TNS/RMS from December 6, 2012 to January 6, 2013. Data for 2017 are from the first wave of a panel study (n=2,026) conducted by Ipsos on May 11–23, 2017. Additional details are provided in the appendix. Differences based on two-sided t-tests. ***p<.01, **p<.05, *p<.1.

[11] The null finding on partisanship in the September 2007 survey may reflect the question used in the survey, which asked respondents which party they were "closest" to (rather than asking whether they feel close to any party). A separate survey conducted just prior to the election employed a two-part question that first asked whether respondents felt close to any party, and then probed which party for those who gave an affirmative response. The data show that, despite being conducted shortly before the election, a noticeable difference is observed between those who had a coethnic in the race and those who did not: 90.8% vs. 85.5% (difference = 5.3, p<0.01) in partisans and 75.6% vs. 67.2% (difference =

likely to identify as strong partisans: 72.3% vs. 54.6% in 2013 and 71.5% vs. 52.8% in 2017. In all three elections, those without a coethnic in the race were more likely to be undecided between the two leading candidates at the start of the race: 6.0% vs. 3.6% in 2007; 11.1% vs. 2.8% in 2012; and 9.1% vs. 4.6% in 2017. And those without a coethnic in the race were less likely, on average, to see a large disparity between the two leading candidates regarding group representation: 65.2% vs. 73.1% in 2007; 40.0% vs. 50.7% in 2012; and 59.2% vs. 70.4% in 2017.[12]

In sum, voters from groups that do not have a coethnic in the race are less likely to feel close to a party, less likely to register strong partisan affinities, more likely to be uncertain at the outset, and less likely to perceive a large disparity between the leading candidates with regard to how well each of the two would represent their group's interests. For all of these reasons, such voters should be more willing to update their voting intentions as a result of campaign persuasion.

Preference Change during the Campaigns

To examine preference change during campaigns, I draw on the panel data from the 2013 and 2017 elections (similar data is not available for 2007). Recall that the 2013 election was an open race in which the incumbent, Mwai Kibaki, was barred from running after having completed two terms. The race was mainly a contest between Kenyatta, who headed the Jubilee Alliance, and Odinga, who led the Coalition for Reform and Democracy (CORD). Kenyatta emerged as the official winner, though opposition leaders disputed the results (Cheeseman, Lynch, and Willis 2014). The 2017 race again featured the same candidates, and again Kenyatta came out as the official winner, though the results were subsequently overturned by the Supreme Court.[13] Kenyatta ultimately prevailed in a re-run election that was boycotted by Odinga.

Table 3.5 presents voting intentions across survey waves in 2013.[14] It shows that 19.5 percent of respondents updated their preferences during the campaign.[15]

8.4, p<0.01) in strong partisans. The survey (n=1,207) was conducted by the Afrobarometer and Oxford University (implemented by Ipsos) in December 2007.

[12] Similar differences are also found with regard to beliefs about material transfers rather than general beliefs about group representation. To probe expectations regarding material transfers, the survey asked, "If [Raila Odinga / Uhuru Kenyatta] is elected president, how much government funds will this area receive for development?" The data show that those without a coethnic in the race perceive a smaller initial disparity between the candidates (1.13 vs. 1.49, p<0.001) on a three-point scale that measures the absolute value for Kenyatta minus Odinga, in which the answer options for each candidate were none, a little, some, and a lot.

[13] Kenyatta's initial victory in 2017 was annulled by the Supreme Court on procedural grounds. In the repeat election, Kenyatta won with 98 percent of the vote after Odinga boycotted the contest (Chege 2018). I focus on the campaign period prior to the first election in August.

[14] I exclude respondents who did not indicate a preference or who stated that they would not vote in the election (n=44, 5.3 percent of the sample).

[15] The overall magnitude of preference change is similar to that found in studies of older democracies. It is difficult to directly compare these results to those from other contexts because of differences in survey methods. Nonetheless, it is useful to note that Zaller (2004) estimates that, on average, about

Table 3.5 Changes in vote intentions, 2013 election (percentages)

	(1)	(2)	(3)	(4)
	Total	Groups *without* a coethnic in the race	Groups *with* a coethnic in the race	Diff. (3−2)
From candidate to candidate				
Kenyatta => Odinga	5.6	6.4	4.0	−2.3
Odinga => Kenyatta	4.7	6.5	1.1	−5.5**
Total	10.4	12.9	5.1	−7.8**
From don't know to candidate				
Don't know => Kenyatta	2.8	3.3	1.6	−1.8
Don't know => Odinga	4.6	6.1	1.6	−4.5**
Total	7.4	9.4	3.2	−6.2**
From candidate to don't know				
Kenyatta => Don't know	0.9	1.1	0.6	−0.05
Odinga => Don't know	0.8	1.0	0.5	−0.5
Total	1.8	2.0	1.1	−0.9
TOTAL	19.5	24.4	9.5	−14.9**

Note: Difference-in-mean estimates in Column 4 are based on two-sided t-tests using weighted data to account for attrition between rounds (see Online Appendix for weighting procedures). Due to rounding, some cell entries do not sum to total. ***$p<0.01$, **$p<0.05$, *$p<0.1$.

While some of the movement (7.4%) can be attributed to respondents who were initially undecided picking a candidate, a larger portion (10.4%) is from respondents who switched candidates. An estimated 5.6% of respondents shifted from supporting Kenyatta in round 1 to Odinga in round 2, while a similar share (4.7%) shifted in the opposite direction. Most important for the present analysis, respondents from groups that did not have a coethnic candidate in the presidential race were roughly two and a half times more likely to update their preferences than respondents from groups that had a coethnic in the race (24.4% vs. 9.5%, difference = 14.9, p<0.001). Part of this difference can be attributed to higher rates of uncertainty at the start of the campaign: 9.4 percent of those who did not have a coethnic in the race switched from "don't know" to one of the leading candidates, while only 3.2 percent of those with a coethnic in the race did so. But a substantial difference is also observed with regard to movement between the two leading candidates: while 12.9 percent of those without a coethnic in the race switched between Kenyatta and Odinga, only 5.1 percent of those with a coethnic in the race did (difference = 7.8, p<0.001).[16]

---

15 percent of voters changed their intentions during U.S. campaigns between 1948 and 2000. Hillygus and Jackman (2003), by contrast, estimate that 45 percent of voters changed their preferences during the 2000 presidential race in the U.S.

[16] Additional details are provided in the Online Appendix available on Dataverse (dataverse.org).

Table 3.6 repeats the analysis with data from the 2017 panel survey and finds nearly identical results: 19.4 percent of respondents reported changing their voting intentions during the campaign period, and a large gap is again observed between those from groups with and without a coethnic in the race: 6.7% vs. 25.3%, a differential of 18.6 percentage points (p<0.001). The findings for 2017 are particularly striking since the election was essentially a repeat of 2013. Given this, one might expect that there would be few voters whose minds were not already made up heading into the 2017 campaigns.

To examine rates of preference change for Kenya's major ethnic groups, Figure 3.1 plots the share of respondents that reported changing voting intentions in each panel study for all groups with a sufficiently large sub-sample. While estimates are imprecise due to small sample sizes, they demonstrate that the difference between groups with and without a coethnic among the major contenders is consistently observed. Thus, in both election years the likelihood of a voter switching his or her voting intentions was systematically greater for voters in all major groups that did not have a coethnic in the race. One partial exception is the Meru and Embu, which I aggregate in Figure 3.1 due to the small samples from these groups. The likelihood of updating electoral preferences among these groups was akin to those that had a coethnic in the race. It is noteworthy also that among voters in coalition groups, preferences are generally more fluid than for voters in

Table 3.6 Changes in vote intentions, 2017 election (percentages)

	(1)	(2)	(3)	(4)
	Total	Groups *without* a coethnic in the race	Groups *with* a coethnic in the race	Diff. (3−2)
From candidate to candidate				
Kenyatta => Odinga	4.4	6.1	0.9	−5.1***
Odinga => Kenyatta	7.1	9.6	1.7	−7.9***
Total	11.5	15.7	2.6	−13.1***
From don't know to candidate				
Don't know => Kenyatta	2.3	2.8	1.3	−1.5
Don't know => Odinga	2.3	3.0	0.8	−2.2*
Total	4.6	5.9	2.1	−3.7**
From candidate to don't know				
Kenyatta => Don't know	1.7	1.9	1.1	−0.9
Odinga => Don't know	0.6	0.6	0.5	−0.1
Total	2.2	2.6	1.6	−1.0
TOTAL	19.4	25.3	6.7	−18.6***

Note: Difference-in-mean estimates in column 4 are based on two-sided t-tests using weighted data to account for attrition between rounds (see Online Appendix for weighting procedures). Due to rounding, some cell entries do not sum to total. ***p<0.01, **p<0.05, *p<0.1.

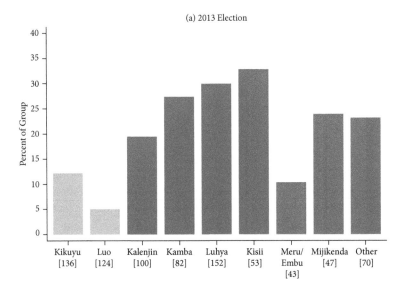

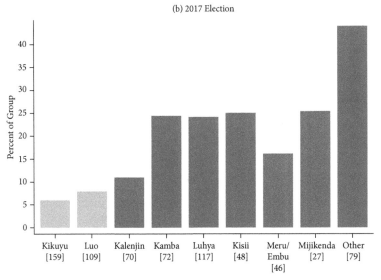

Figure 3.1 Preference change by ethnic group, 2013 and 2017 elections

Notes: Figures show the proportion of respondents that changed stated electoral preferences between survey rounds for all ethnic groups that make up 5 percent or more of the population (and a residual "other" category). Groups with a coethnic among the major contenders in the presidential race are shown in light grey, and other groups are shown in dark grey. Sample sizes are in brackets. Data are weighted to account for panel attrition.

the president's own ethnic groups. Thus, among the Kalenjin and Kamba, groups seen as allied to Jubilee and CORD/NASA respectively, voters exhibit higher rates of change than among Kikuyu and Luo voters that had co-ethnic leaders among the presidential candidates—though this difference is less pronounced for the Kalenjin in 2017.

Regression Analysis

While the data in Tables 3.5 and 3.6 suggest that having a coethnic leader in the race affects the likelihood of changing one's vote during the campaign, it is possible that members of groups that had a coethnic in recent elections differ in systematic ways from members of groups that did not, and that these underlying differences explain the results in Tables 3.5 and 3.6. To address this possibility, I estimate a series of logit models of preference change that control for a wide range of potential confounds suggested by prior literature. In all models, the dependent variable takes a value of 1 for respondents whose voting intentions changed during the campaign period, and 0 otherwise. All control variables are taken from the first rounds of the 2013 and 2017 panel surveys. A richer set of covariates is available for 2013 than for 2017. Details on the measures and descriptive statistics are provided in the appendix.

First, following studies that show that voters from mixed social backgrounds have more fluid preferences (Berelson, Lazarsfeld, and McPhee 1954; Campbell et al. 1960), I include measures of whether respondents come from mixed lineages (parents from different ethnic groups) or are married to (or live with) a non-coethnic partner. Second, in line with research showing that the diversity of social networks and localities can affect preferences (Baker, Ames, and Renno 2006; Carsey 1995; Huckfeldt and Sprague 1995; Ichino and Nathan 2013; Nathan 2016), I include measures of the ethnic diversity of respondents' social networks (2013 only) and local environments. Third, literature has shown that information access, knowledge and political interest are linked to preference stability (Converse 1964; Delli Carpini and Keeter 1996; DellaVigna and Kaplan 2007; Flores-Macias 2009; Greene 2011; Kaufmann, Petrocik, and Shaw 2010; Ladd and Lenz 2009; Lawson and McCann 2004; Zaller 2004). Following these works, I include measures of political interest, education, media consumption, and whether respondents mainly get radio news from national-language stations that broadcast in Swahili and/or English or "vernacular" stations that broadcast in the language of a particular ethnic group (2013 only). Finally, I include standard demographic controls—age, gender, and wealth—that other studies have shown to be associated with preference change (e.g., Hillygus and Jackman 2003; Kaufmann, Petrocik, and Shaw 2010), and I control for the number of days between interviews (2013 only). Models employ inverse propensity weights to

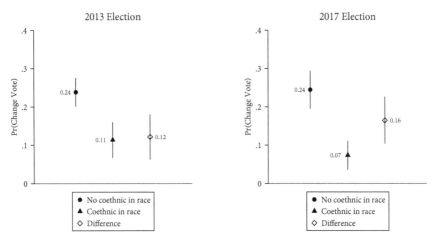

Figure 3.2 Preference change during campaign period, 2013 and 2017 elections

Notes: Figures show the predicted probability of changing voting intentions across survey waves in the 2013 and 2017 panel surveys based on logit models in the Online Appendix, with covariates held at mean values.

account for attrition on observables using methods developed by Fitzgerald, Gottschalk, and Moffitt (1998).

Results are shown graphically in Figure 3.2.[17] The estimates confirm that those with a coethnic in the race are less likely to change their voting intentions during the campaign by a substantial margin: holding all control variables at their mean values, having a coethnic in the race is associated with 12 and 16 percentage-point decreases in the predicted probability of changing one's preferences in the 2013 and 2017 campaigns respectively, relative to a rate of 24 percent for respondents from groups that did not have a coethnic in each race. These results are similar in magnitude to the uncontrolled results in Tables 3.5 and 3.6.

I briefly discuss several robustness tests, details of which can be found in an Online Appendix. First, I re-estimate the models excluding respondents who changed to or from "don't know" between survey rounds in order to test whether those who do not have a coethnic in the race have more fluid preferences *solely* because they tend to be more undecided at the start of the race. The results indicate that the findings do not stem only from higher levels of initial uncertainty. Second, I test whether the observed effects hold for both groups with a coethnic in the 2013 and 2017 races, the Kikuyu and the Luo, and show that they do. Third, given that the analysis relies on panel data, there is a risk that attrition could bias the results in ways that would favor the main hypothesis. However, additional analysis suggests that attrition likely biased the sample in the opposite

---

[17] Full logit results and details of all robustness tests described in this chapter are provided in the Online Appendix.

direction.[18] Moreover, as noted, all analysis presented above employs weights to account for attrition on observables. Fourth, I examine whether the results stem from interviewer effects. Results in the Online Appendix show no significant differences across core and swing groups with regard to the likelihood of being interviewed by a non-coethnic, and that the results presented above are robust to the inclusions of variables for interviewer ethnicity.

Connecting Initial Attitudes to Preference Stability

A key assumption in this chapter is that ethnicity make some voters more or less willing to update their electoral preferences during the campaign due to differences in initial attitudes at the start of the race. To confirm this, I estimate a series of bivariate logit models using data from the 2013 and 2017 panel surveys. The dependent variable for all tests is again a dichotomous measure of whether individual respondents changed their stated voting intentions from the first wave to the second in each election year. The independent variables are the four measures of initial attitudes and beliefs reported in Table 3.4 above. The results in Table 3.7 show that voters who identify as partisans and strong partisans or who perceive there to be a large gap between the candidates regarding how well each will represent the interests of one's community are substantially less likely to change their vote. Those who are undecided at the outset are more likely to do so. Predicted probabilities shown in Table 3.8 indicate that all four variables are highly predictive of whether individuals update their electoral preferences.

Linking Preference Change to Beliefs about the Candidates

Next, I offer evidence that instrumental theories of ethnic voting can help explain the observed changes in voting intentions in 2013 and 2017. Instrumental theories imply that if electoral choices depend on beliefs about how well each candidate will represent the interests of one's ethnic group, voters should update their preferences if their beliefs about the candidates' representational intentions change.

To test this proposition, I use logit regressions to estimate transition models that examine the *direction* of change across survey waves in 2013 and 2017. In the first model for each election year, which examines transitions to Kenyatta, the dependent variable takes a value of 1 for respondents who registered a preference for Kenyatta in the second survey round but not in the first, and 0 otherwise.

---

[18] See additional results in the Online Appendix.

Table 3.7 Logit models of preference change, 2013 and 2017 elections

	2013 Election				2017 Election			
	(1)	(2)	(3)	(4)	(5)	(6)	(7)	(8)
Partisan	−1.41*** (0.20)				−0.96** (0.38)			
Strong partisan		−1.54*** (0.20)				−0.88*** (0.25)		
Undecided			4.26*** (0.49)				2.90*** (0.47)	
Representation gap				−0.74*** (0.11)				−0.37** (0.15)
Constant	−0.58*** (0.14)	−0.60*** (0.13)	−1.88*** (0.11)	−0.59*** (0.15)	−0.56 (0.35)	−0.93*** (0.19)	−1.68*** (0.15)	−0.92*** (0.25)
Observations	763	772	775	741	648	648	649	611
Pseudo-R^2	0.07	0.09	0.23	0.08	0.01	0.03	0.10	0.02

Notes: Logit models of preference change. Partisan, Strong partisan, and Undecided are dichotomous variables. Representation gap ranges from 0 to 3, with higher values indicating a larger gap in perceptions of how well the leading candidates would represent one's ethnic group. Definitions for the independent variables are in Table 3.4.

***p<0.01, **p<0.05, *p<0.1.

Table 3.8 Predicted probability of changing one's vote (with 95 percent confidence intervals)

	Min	Max
2013		
Partisan	0.36 [0.30, 0.42]	0.12 [0.09, 0.15]
Strong partisan	0.35 [0.30, 0.41]	0.11 [0.08, 0.13]
Undecided	0.13 [0.11, 0.16]	0.92 [0.84, 0.99]
Representation gap	0.36 [0.29, 0.42]	0.06 [0.03, 0.08]
2017		
Partisan	0.36 [0.20, 0.52]	0.18 [0.14, 0.22]
Strong partisan	0.28 [0.21, 0.36]	0.14 [0.10, 0.18]
Undecided	0.16 [0.12, 0.19]	0.77 [0.62, 0.93]
Representation gap	0.28 [0.19, 0.38]	0.11 [0.06, 0.17]

Notes: Predicted valued based on models in Table 3.7. Partisan, Strong partisan, and Undecided are dichotomous variables. Representation gap ranges from 0 to 3, with higher values indicating a larger gap in perceptions of how well the leading candidates will represent one's ethnic group. 95 percent confidence intervals are shown in brackets.

The second model repeats the analysis for transitions to Odinga. The key independent variables in both models measure changes in respondents' beliefs about group representation, based on the question that asked, "How well do you think each of following candidates would represent the interests of your ethnic group if elected: very well, somewhat well, not well, or not at all?"[19] Models include the same controls used in the previous models of preference change in Figure 3.2. I add controls for respondents' initial beliefs about the candidates' ethnic representation intentions, as measured in the first survey round of each panel survey, and variables that measure changes in overall favorability ratings (like/dislike) for each candidate in order to distinguish the effects of changes in beliefs about the candidates' ethnic representation intentions from more general attitudes toward each candidate (2013 only).[20]

The association between changes in beliefs about the candidates' representational intentions and electoral preferences is presented in Table 3.9. The models show that a positive change in beliefs about how well either candidate would represent one's ethnic group is associated with an increase in the probability of

[19] Results are similar when I use a more narrow question about resource targeting instead of this general question about group representation. The narrow question asks, "If [Uhuru Kenyatta / Raila Odinga] is elected president, how much government funds will this area receive for development: a lot, some, a little, or none?"

[20] Favorability ratings are constructed from questions on both surveys that asked, "For each of the following politicians, please tell me whether you like the candidate very much, like him somewhat, neither like him nor dislike him, dislike him somewhat, or dislike him very much." Changes in beliefs about each candidate are defined as the round 2 response minus the round 1 answer.

Table 3.9 Logit models of direction of change, 2013 and 2017 elections

	2013 Election		2017 Election	
	(1) New Kenyatta supporter	(2) New Odinga supporter	(3) New Kenyatta supporter	(4) New Odinga supporter
Δ in beliefs about group representation, Kenyatta	0.81*** (0.28)	−0.70*** (0.20)	1.26*** (0.33)	−0.54* (0.30)
Δ in beliefs about group representation, Odinga	−0.58** (0.27)	0.98*** (0.25)	−0.68** (0.28)	1.84*** (0.49)
Group representation, Kenyatta (round 1)	0.58** (0.30)	−0.56** (0.28)	0.11 (0.33)	0.25 (0.52)
Group representation, Odinga (round 1)	−0.01 (0.20)	0.38 (0.27)	0.06 (0.27)	0.97** (0.48)
Δ in overall evaluation of Kenyatta	0.46*** (0.14)	−0.18 (0.15)		
Δ in overall evaluation for Odinga	−0.23* (0.13)	0.78*** (0.18)		
Observations	689	689	541	541
Pseudo R-squared	0.24	0.34	0.39	0.40

Notes: Models include controls for wealth (income in 2017), age, gender, the number of days between survey rounds (2013 only), measures of mixed parentage, spouse from different ethnic group, non-coethnics in social network (number), non-coethnics in sample area (share), political interest, education, radio, TV, and newspaper consumption, and vernacular radio source (2013 only). Data is weighed to account for attrition (see Online Appendix for details). Robust standard errors in parentheses.
***p<0.01, **p<0.05, *p<0.1.

becoming a supporter and a decrease in the likelihood of becoming a supporter of the rival candidate.

Figure 3.3 plots these associations, holding all other variables at their mean values. It shows that the probability of becoming a new Kenyatta or Odinga supporter is less than 0.05 for a respondent whose views of the candidates were unchanged during the campaign period. Negative changes in beliefs about either candidate reduce the probability of becoming a new supporter close to 0, while positive changes sharply increase the likelihood of becoming a new supporter of either candidate.

I treat these estimates as suggestive evidence because changes in beliefs about the candidates' ethnic intentions could be endogenous to changes in electoral preferences and the models cannot account for all possible confounds that might correlate with both beliefs about the candidates' ethnic intentions and electoral preferences. Nonetheless, the evidence is consistent with the proposition that campaigns work by shifting voters' perceptions of which candidate will best represent the interests of their ethnic communities.

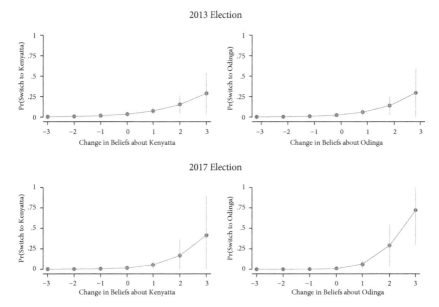

Figure 3.3 Estimated effects of changes in beliefs about the candidates on vote intentions

Notes: Figures show the estimated effect of changes in perceptions about how well each candidate will represent the respondent's group, based on results in Table 3.9. Estimated effects are calculated with other covariates held at their mean values. Error bars show 95 percent confidence intervals.

Are Preference Changes Attributable to the Campaigns?

Can the observed micro-level shifts in voting intentions be attributed to the effects of the parties' campaign efforts rather than other factors? Because of the well-known limitations associated with estimating campaign effects using observational data, this chapter infers the effects of the campaigns by observing changes in voting intentions during campaign periods rather than seeking to directly estimate the effects of campaign exposure.[21] However, because it is indirect, this approach provides only suggestive evidence that differences in receptivity to campaign persuasion explain the documented shifts in voting intentions. To bolster confidence in the proposed mechanism, this section rules out several alternative explanations, focusing on the 2013 election for which richer data is available.

---

[21] Several well-known challenges limit the ability to examine campaign effects using observational data: parties target their activities strategically, voters select into participating in rallies and other face-to-face events, and recall of campaign exposure may be biased by political orientations. As a result, research designs that do not draw on exogenous variation in campaign exposure cannot provide credible estimates of campaign effects (Iyengar and Simon 2000).

One concern is that changes in voting intentions might be attributable to events other than the campaigns. The short time frame for campaigning (roughly three months) in Kenya helps to mitigate this risk.[22] Moreover, the median time between the first and second survey waves in the 2012–13 panel was only 66 days. Despite this, it is possible that other events could affect voter intentions. Particularly relevant is elite party switching, which could prompt some voters to update their views of the candidates and their parties. To explore this possibility, I collected information on politicians who switched parties during the campaign from Kenya's two leading newspapers, *The Nation* and *The Standard*.[23] I then coded the ethnicity of each party switcher and classified each as major or minor in terms of prominence.[24] The data (presented in the Online Appendix) show that party switching was relatively rare during the 2013 campaigns, and of the 61 politicians who switched parties, only 15 where prominent leaders. More importantly, there is no clear relationship between party switching and rates of preference change across ethnic groups.[25]

While overall trends in party switching appear not to account for differences in preference change, it is worth further exploring the possible effects of one important defection in 2013, Musalia Mudavadi's departure from the Jubilee coalition to stand for the presidency as the head of his own party. One way to control for the potential effects of Mudavadi's departure is to rerun the main test in Figure 3.2 without respondents from Mudavadi's Luhya ethnic group, those who in all likelihood would have been most affected by his departure from Jubilee. The results show that the main findings are not affected by this exclusion (see Online Appendix). An alternative is to include variables that track individual support for Mudavadi, in order to account for possible differential effects caused by his exit from Jubilee. I employ two measures, one that probed sentiments toward the candidate by asking how much respondents liked or disliked Mudavadi, and a second that asked respondents how well they thought the candidate would represent the interests of their ethnic group if elected. The results, presented in the Online Appendix, show that the main findings in Figure 3.2 are robust to the inclusion of these variables.

A second concern is that differences in the stability of preferences may stem from differential *exposure* to the campaigns, rather than *receptivity* to campaign persuasion. Perhaps Kikuyus and Luos in the 2013 and 2017 races were less likely to update their preferences because they had fewer opportunities to interact with

---

[22] Surveys were designed to capture preference changes during the main period of campaigning, not the official period, which is shorter.

[23] While there undoubtedly were other party switchers not captured by news reporting in these outlets, such individuals are likely to have been relatively minor given that the country's main newspapers did not deem them sufficiently important to report.

[24] Prominence is coded as a dichotomous variable (major or minor) based on years of experience in office, past positions held, and subjective assessments of national profile.

[25] See Online Appendix.

the campaigns. Data from the second survey round of the 2012–13 panel, how-ever, show that Kikuyus and Luos were no less likely to have attended campaign rallies, to have been contacted at home by the leading parties, to have received an SMS message related to the election, or to have been offered money for their vote (see Online Appendix). And in some instances, Kikuyus and Luos were *more* likely than voters from other groups to have been exposed to these campaign activities. These data suggest that Kikuyus and Luos were less likely to change their voting intentions because the strength of their initial preferences made them less receptive to campaign influences, not because they received a smaller "dose" of the campaigns.

A third alternative explanation relates to the strength of ethnic identities. The expressive voting literature (e.g., Horowitz 1985) suggests that strong bonds of ethnic affinity may incline voters to support coethnic candidates or the party that best includes coethnic leaders. If such bonds are more widespread or intense within some ethnic communities, or if they only come into play when voters have a coethnic in the race, we might expect to find lower rates of preference change within such groups. While the panel surveys did not include questions on the strength of ethnic identification, data from a previous study conducted in 2007 is useful.[26] The survey found that among Kikuyus and Luos, 19 percent identified in terms of their language or tribal group while 20 percent of other groups did so, suggesting that communal attachments are not more pronounced for voters in groups that had a coethnic in the 2013 and 2017 elections. The relatively small share of respondents identifying in ethnic terms, moreover, suggests that even if ethnic attachments do matter only when voters have a coethnic in the race, such attachments are not sufficiently widespread to account for differences in the stability of preferences across core and swing groups in Kenya's 2013 and 2017 elections.

Finally, I explore whether the results might reflect social pressure or in-group sanctioning. Kikuyus and Luos have frequently been at the center of political contestation and conflict in Kenya. Perhaps as a result of this history of political mobilization, stronger norms against "defecting" from group behavior (and net-works to enforce such norms) have developed within these two communities. During elections, members of these groups might therefore face stronger potential sanctions that would lead to more homogenous voting intentions at the start of the race and a reduced likelihood of changing one's vote (or confessing such changes during a household survey) over the course of the campaign. To test this possibility, the second round of the 2012–13 panel survey asked about two types of

---

[26] These data come from a nationally representative survey (n=6,111) conducted in December 2007 by Steadman (now Ipsos). To probe identification, the survey asked: "We have spoken to many Kenyans and they have all described themselves in different ways. They describe themselves in terms of their language, tribe, race, religion, gender, occupation, age and class. Which specific group do you feel you belong to first and foremost?"

possible external sanctions: social marginalization and physical violence. The survey first asked respondents which candidate they believed was the leading presidential contender in their area. It then asked respondents how afraid they would be that others in the area would (1) exclude them from social gatherings or (2) attack or harm them if they voted against the leading local candidate. The data reveal that voters from groups with a coethnic in the race (Kikuyus and Luos) are slightly more fearful of reprisals on both measures, but that these differences are substantively small and not statistically significant (see Online Appendix).

Conclusion

Making sense of what presidential candidates seek to accomplish on the campaign trail requires first understanding the electoral landscape they confront: which types of voters can be relied upon for support, which voters are out of reach, and who will be available for persuasion and conversion. This chapter develops the proposition that ethnicity plays a role in differentiating such groups in Kenya, building on the widely-noted observation that presidential aspirants often find their strongest electoral support among voters from their own ethnic communities. The chapter proposes that from the perspective of the campaign strategist, core and swing can be meaningfully distinguished simply based on whether groups have a coethnic among the major-party contenders. The chapter argues that these differences can be attributed to the varying informational value of elite cues that provide greater clarity about which of the prospective leaders will best represent one's communal interests to voters who have a coethnic in the race than to those who do not.

This chapter does not offer a systematic accounting of other factors—including sub-tribe and clan identities or non-ethnic determinants of vote-choice—that may make some voters more or less up-for-grabs at election time. The goal is not to offer a comprehensive overview of all relevant factors; rather, it is to provide a foundation for explaining why presidential aspirants consistently devote little campaign effort to their own and rivals' coethnic strongholds, and instead concentrate their efforts in areas where other ethnic groups predominate.

To test the chapter's key propositions, I draw on micro-level data from surveys conducted prior to Kenya's 2007, 2013, and 2017 elections, including two panel studies that track attitudes and preferences during the campaign periods. The results show that voters from groups that do not have a coethnic among the major contenders systematically hold less consistent and intense preferences at the start of the race and more frequently update their voting intentions during the campaigns. The next chapter explores the implications of these findings for campaign strategies.

4

Campaign Strategy

Appealing to a Diverse Electorate

Reports in the Kenyan press routinely note the importance of the competition for swing voters during elections. For example, one account summarizes the 2017 campaigns as follows: "With their strongholds' votes deemed intact, the two main presidential candidates have concentrated their energies on the so-called battleground zones—counties where it was felt the votes were up for grabs."[1] This assessment captures an essential truth about campaigning in Kenya: the leading candidates typically devote little time to voters in their own or their rivals' ethnic strongholds, concentrating instead on "battleground zones." This observation, however, raises a number of questions. Why do candidates dedicate more effort to trying to convert voters who are "up-for-grabs" than to mobilizing existing supporters? How do they decide how much effort to allocate across the many potential ethnic communities that reside in "battleground areas"? Do these decisions vary according to the extent of a candidate's coethnic support at the start of the race? To answer these questions, this chapter develops a theoretical approach that highlights three factors that define the context in which party strategists make decisions about how best to allocate campaign resources: uncertainty, strategic imperatives, and intra-party delegation.

Campaigns are complex operations involving many actors working at different levels in support of the party leader and to advance their own interests. This chapter abstracts from the full complexity of campaigns by focusing on the presidential race rather than lower-level contests. It develops the logic of the swing-targeting approach in the Kenyan context and shows empirically that the pursuit of swing voters—not the mobilization of existing supporters—is the focus of presidential campaigns. The inspiration for these arguments comes from interviews with campaign strategists in 2007 who universally noted that their parties sought to implement broad-based campaign strategies, seeking to increase support even in areas where rivals held the initial advantage.[2]

---

[1] Ngirachu, John. "Jubilee, Nasa Flagbearers Confident of Winning." *Daily Nation* (online). August 7, 2017.

[2] ODM officials interviewed at the party's headquarters in Nairobi (October 8–9, 2007) noted that the party was directing campaign effort to all areas of the country and had not given up on PNU's strongholds in Central and Eastern Provinces. Likewise, officials at the PNU Secretariat in Nairobi (interviewed on October 11, 2007) conveyed that PNU was appealing to voters widely, including in

Multiethnic Democracy: The Logic of Elections and Policymaking in Kenya. Jeremy Horowitz, Oxford University Press.
© Jeremy Horowitz 2022. DOI: 10.1093/oso/9780198852735.003.0004

To study how presidential candidates allocate campaign effort across ethnic areas, I examine the location of rallies held by the main presidential contenders in the months prior to the 2007, 2013, and 2017 elections, following an approach used in studies of U.S. elections (Shaw 2007; Stromberg 2008; West 1983; Althaus, Nardulli, and Shaw 2002; Herr 2002; Jones 1998). I complement this analysis by examining household-level contact during campaigns, relying on information from a large, national public opinion poll conducted after the 2007 election. The results provide consistent evidence in favor of the proposition that the leading contenders concentrate their campaign efforts on converting potential swing voters rather than mobilizing their most steadfast core supporters.

On the Campaign Trail

A distinctive feature of electioneering in Kenya, like much of Africa, is that campaigns are conducted primarily through in-person contact with voters, rather than paid media advertising. In the months leading up to the election, presidential candidates and their allies engage in two main activities: campaign rallies and door-to-door canvasing. The presidential aspirants rely on local allies at all levels to stump on their behalf and to organize the local-level machinery that reaches voters in villages and neighborhoods across the country. Most local allies are also candidates for positions as governors, legislators, and local councilors. Elections for these seats are held simultaneously with the presidential election and are filled using single-member districts with plurality winners.

As noted in the introduction, the candidates' major coalition allies—often referred to as regional kingpins—play an especially important role in the campaigns, mobilizing support for presidential aspirants in their ethnic areas where, by virtue of shared ethnic ties, they often have greater influence with voters (Kramon 2018; Arriola et al. 2021).[3] Senior coalition partners are expected to deliver support from their respective ethnic communities simply through their

ODM strongholds where the party hoped to pick up "a few votes." One official noted that PNU was concentrating its efforts for the presidential campaign on Western, Rift Valley, and Coast Provinces—areas that overwhelmingly supported the opposition.

[3] Evidence suggests that senior allies concentrate their efforts in areas where coethnic voters reside. Data compiled from newspaper accounts of the 2013 election provides information on the location of rallies attended by the parties' vice-presidential nominees: William Ruto, Uhuru Kenyatta's running mate in PNU, and Kalonzo Musyoka, Odinga's running mate in CORD. Both leaders spent the majority of their time campaigning with the party leader outside of their home ethnic areas. Thus, Ruto appeared at 51 rallies, 31 of which were held in conjunction with Kenyatta, and only six of these were held in Kalenjin-majority areas. Musyoka appeared at 56 rallies, 31 of which were held with Odinga, and only 2 of these were held in Kamba-majority areas. However, when the vice-presidential nominees held rallies on their own, both disproportionately focused their effort on coethnic voters: Ruto held 40 percent (8 of 20) of his solo rallies in Kalenjin-majority areas, and Musyoka devoted 40 percent (10 of 25) of his solo appearances to Kamba-majority areas, suggesting that both vice presidential nominees were tasked with increasing support for their respective tickets in their home ethnic areas.

presence in the coalition and also by stumping for the party leader in their home ethnic areas. On the campaign trail, regional allies appear with the party leader, lending credibility to his or her efforts to garner support across ethnic lines. As shown in the next chapter, these allies frequently appeal to shared communal interests, attesting to the party leader's inclusive intentions. They also articulate the more bellicose attacks against rival candidates.

At the local level, there is generally little coordination between central party leaders and candidates who are competing for governor, parliamentary, and local council seats.[4] Lower-level candidates typically receive little assistance in raising the funds needed to operate an effective campaign.[5] The costs of campaigning can be substantial. In interviews conducted in 2007, parliamentary candidates estimated that the minimum required to run a full-fledge campaign was about USD $100,000, a sum that has likely increased with time.[6] Funds are used to hire vehicles and drivers, to recruit village-level representatives who canvas households and distribute small gifts, and to pay for the handouts voters expect at rallies and public events (Kramon 2018).

Available data suggest that at the presidential level campaigning has become more extensive since the return to multiparty elections in 1992. Newspaper coverage in Kenya's two leading dailies—*The Nation* and *The Standard*—provides a rough indication of the number of rallies held by the leading presidential candidates (those who received 5% or more of the vote). In the first three multiparty elections (1992, 1997, and 2002) the newspapers recorded an average of 30 rallies attended by each of the major presidential aspirants in the three months prior to each election. In the next three races (2007, 2013, 2017), the same papers recorded an average of 83 rallies held by each leading candidate. While this increase likely reflects the papers' growing capacity to cover the campaigns, it also suggests that the major candidates are ratcheting up their efforts to reach voters through public events.[7]

---

[4] This point was made in interviews with party leaders from both major parties in 2007. One senior ODM official noted that while the party expected parliamentary candidates to project ODM's message, it was not possible to control what they did and said (interviewed in Nairobi on October 8, 2007). Another official from the ODM Communications Office noted that the party sought to avoid becoming overly hierarchical and instead encouraged local candidates to adapt the party platform to local conditions so that it would have greater relevance in different localities (interviewed on October 9, 2017). The lack of coordination between lower-level actors and party leaders was also noted by several parliamentary candidates interviewed in December 2007.

[5] This point was made in several interviews conducted with parliamentary candidates between December 9 and 21, 2007.

[6] Parliamentary candidates interviewed in 2007 bemoaned the cost of running an effective campaign, particularly the "listening fees" that attendees expected at rallies. One candidate noted that because these handouts had become commonplace during the Moi era, it was difficult to avoid offering gifts when speaking to crowds. Several candidates noted that the total cost of their campaigns ranged from USD $50,000 to $100,000, with funds mostly coming from their own resources and friends and family.

[7] These numbers likely provide an undercount of the extent of campaigning since the papers do not mention all rallies held by the candidates. For example, in 2017 the Kenyatta campaign claimed that it held 504 rallies in the months before the election, suggesting that—if correct—the papers covered only a small portion of the actual number. See Ngirachu, John. "Jubilee, Nasa Flagbearers Confident of Winning." *Daily Nation* (online). August 7, 2017.

Survey data demonstrates the considerable reach of the campaigns. Afrobarometer surveys from 2011 and 2014 find that nearly half of all respondents in Kenya attended one or more campaign rally in the 2007 and 2013 elections.[8] Other opinion polls find that large portions of the electorate report having been contacted in their homes by party agents during the campaigns: 49.8 percent in the 2007 election and 27.0 percent in the 2017 election.[9]

The Ethnic Logic of Campaign Strategies

Presidential candidates and their strategists must decide how to divide campaign effort between persuasion (seeking to convert potential swing voters) and mobilization (attempting to increase turnout among existing supporters), and if they invest in persuasion, which voters to target. In Kenya, this entails deciding how to allocate campaign effort across ethnic communities and the geographic areas where they are concentrated. The theory developed here relies on three key principles—uncertainty, strategic dynamics, and delegation—that guide my understanding of the competitive environment. First, decisions about campaign targeting are made under high levels of uncertainty. While uncertainty is a universal challenge for campaign strategists in all electoral contests, it is particularly acute in emerging democracies where information about voters is more scarce. Second, campaign decisions are strategic, in the sense that what candidates do on the campaign trail depends on what their rivals do. Third, party leaders are able to delegate campaign duties to lower-level actors, allowing for a division of labor on the campaign trail. Appreciating the benefits of delegation helps to make sense of why national party leaders focus on persuasion among out-groups rather than mobilization within their own ethnic communities.

Persuasion versus Mobilization

The arguments offered here build on existing literature on distributive politics (Cox and McCubbins 1986; Dixit and Londregan 1996; Lindbeck and Weibull 1987; Casey 2015) as well as research on the allocation of campaign resources in

---

[8] Data are from the Afrobarometer Round 5 survey (n=2,399) conducted in November 2011, which asked about the 2007 election, and the Round 6 survey (n=2,397) conducted in November–December 2014, which asked about the 2013 election. The surveys show that 47.9 percent and 50.4 percent report having attended one or more rally in 2007 and 2013 respectively.

[9] Data on household contact in 2007 come from a survey (n=3,600) that was conducted about a year after the election as part of an evaluation of Kenya's national civic education program (see Finkel, Horowitz, and Mendoza (2012)). Data for 2017 come from a survey (n=2,468) conducted as part of a study on popular support for Kenya's Supreme Court conducted in the month following the August 8 election that was annulled by the court (see Bartels, Horowitz, and Kramon (2021)).

long-standing democracies (Shaw 2007; Stromberg 2008; Bartels 1998, 1985; Brams and Davis 1974; Colantoni, Levesque, and Ordeshook 1975; Snyder 1989). The central insight from these works is that if the goal of campaigning is persuasion, parties ought to focus their efforts on areas where potential swing voters are concentrated. If the goal is mobilization, parties ought to target areas where existing supporters predominate.

The previous chapter showed that in Kenya presidential candidates can typically rely on the steadfast support of voters in their respective ethnic communities. Voters in other groups are often less committed, and as a result it is within these groups that a larger number of potential swing voters will be found. This understanding of core and swing implies that there will be few potential swing voters available for conversion in parties' ethnic strongholds or in opponents' core coethnic areas. This point is well understood by Kenyan media observers. Writing in advance of the 2007 election, for example, *The Standard* observed that "When the starter's gun is fired and the General Election gets under way, it is expected that Raila will have Nyanza Province under lock and key. President Kibaki will have Central Province sewn up and Kalonzo will have Eastern Province, especially Ukambani, in his column."[10] These areas, of course, are the regions where each of the candidates' ethnic groups were concentrated. Thus, if the goal of campaigning is to attract new supporters, parties should target areas primarily inhabited by groups that do not have a candidate in the race. If, on the other hand, the goal is mobilization, parties should target areas where there is a high density of existing supporters, particularly their own coethnic strongholds and perhaps also areas where major coalition groups reside.[11]

How, then, do parties allocate campaign effort across ethnic areas? Much of the existing literature on electoral strategies, especially work on distributive politics, presumes that parties will invest *only* in persuasion or mobilization (Cox and McCubbins 1986; Dixit and Londregan 1996; Lindbeck and Weibull 1987; Casey 2015). These conclusions are driven by the implicit assumption that party leaders have perfect information about the potential returns from alternative strategies.

---

[10] Ohito, David, and Martin Mutua. "What Next?" *The Standard*, September 3, 2007, p. 1.

[11] Parties, of course, may micro-target their campaign effort within ethnic areas based on sub-tribe or clan divisions, geographic factors, or the presence of strong local allies in particular areas. Thus, for example, in the 1992 race Kibaki may have focused his efforts in Central Province in and around his home base in Nyeri while Matiba may have concentrated on the southern Kikuyu arears around his base in Murang'a, though Throup and Horsnby (1998, pp. 387–8) suggest that both candidates competed throughout the Central Province. Likewise, in Luhya areas, presidential aspirants may train their sights on voters from particular sub-groups that are viewed as potentially better targets due to the presence of elite allies from such groups. Thus, for example, Odinga in 2007 may have prioritized the Maragoli due to the presence of Musalia Mudavadi as part of ODM's senior leadership team. However, equally plausible is that Odinga would focus on other sub-groups, given the candidate's strength in areas where key allies secure the vote. Due to data limitations, the analysis presented in this chapter does not explore how sub-group divisions or other more idiosyncratic factors affect campaign targeting.

I propose, by contrast, that uncertainty about the likely return from each activity makes diversification a more appealing strategy.

There are likely to be potential gains both from persuasion and mobilization in African elections. As shown in the previous chapter, a surprisingly large share of the electorate may be up-for-grabs during campaigns, even in cases like Kenya where ethnic identities exert a strong influence on electoral preferences. At the same time, turnout in Africa's multiparty elections is sufficiently low that mobilization may also yield positive returns.[12] Under such conditions, it is reasonable to think that there may be benefits from investing both in converting potential fence-sitters and from using campaign resources to increase turnout among existing supporters.

Parties everywhere face uncertainty regarding the relative return on mobilization and persuasion. Within the scholarly literature on campaigns, there are important on-going debates about the effectiveness of each strategy (Arcenaux, 2007; Bailey, Hopkins, and Rogers 2013; Gerber and Green 2000; Gerber and Green 2005; Imai 2005). These debates attest to the fact that even in long-standing democracies significant uncertainty exists regarding the benefits of persuasion and mobilization. In emerging democracies information constraints are greater. Voter files that provide information about whether voters have participated in past elections, which now form a crucial resource for parties in the U.S. (Hersh 2015), do not exist in African countries. Prior election results provide only a rough guide to how voters will behave in the current election due to high rates of volatility in African elections (Kuenzi and Lambright 2005; Ferree 2010; Weghorst and Bernhard 2014). And while opinion polling is now commonplace across Africa, parties may lack the resources for analyzing results and developing strategies tailored to them.

Diversification is a standard solution for managing risk in the face of uncertainty (Little et al. 2001; Tufano 1996; Valdivia et al. 1996; Di Falco and Perrings 2005). If parties knew with certainty that persuasion, for example, would yield the greater return, they might invest solely in the pursuit of swing voters. Absent this knowledge, party leaders, if they are risk-averse, should invest in both persuasion and mobilization. While it is impossible to assess the risk profile of presidential candidates, there is good reason to expect that they and their advisors will typically be risk-averse. A large body of scholarship shows that risk-aversion increases as the stakes go up (Markowitz 1952; Binswanger 1980; Holt and Laury 2002). Given the winner-take-all nature of elections, presidential contests represent high-stakes affairs. Accordingly, office-seeking aspirants should generally opt for strategies that reduce risk.[13] Thus, with regard to the choice

---

[12] Kuenzi and Lambright (2007) show that the average turnout rate in Africa's multiparty elections between 1990 and 2004 was 64 percent of registered voters.

[13] While risk acceptance varies across individuals, most people become more risk averse as stakes increase (Fehr-Duda et al. 2010).

between persuasion and mobilization, if party leaders are uncertain about the potential return on investment from each activity and are risk averse, they will devote resources to both.[14]

This does not imply, however, that presidential candidates will allocate equal effort to persuasion and mobilization. Delegation allows for a division of labor within parties: by delegating the job of mobilizing existing supporters to turn out on election day to lower-level actors—including coalition allies, candidates for lower-level offices, local party operatives, and civil society groups—within their strongholds, party leaders free themselves to focus their efforts on courting potential swing voters in other parts of the country.[15] This division of labor stems from the parties' need to garner support from multiple ethnic communities to be competitive in national elections. To do so, presidential aspirants must project an inclusive image.[16] If a candidate is viewed as the champion of one group or a narrow subset of groups, he or she will have little appeal to members of other communities. Moreover, when candidates hold rallies in their home ethnic areas, these events tend to be well attended by the most loyal and ardent supporters. The massive outpouring of support at these homecoming rallies conveys the wrong message to voters from other communities, reinforcing the connection between the candidate and his own ethnic group—a liability when one is trying to court out-group voters. The need to project an inclusive image therefore discourages presidential candidates from campaigning extensively in their home ethnic areas. At the same time, presidential candidates have less need to campaign in their ethnic strongholds relative to other parts of the country. As noted in the previous chapter, parties hold an advantage in recruiting candidates for lower-level races within their home ethnic areas. As a result, the presidential candidates are assured that they will have a capable team working on their behalf

[14] In highlighting uncertainty and risk aversion, the approach developed here differs from much of the literature on distributive politics. Gans-Morse, Mazzuca, and Nichter (2014) provide a notable exception. Yet, in their theoretical framework diversification is driven by cost/benefit calculations that indicate that benefits can be obtained both from using resources to convert opposition supporters and from targeting resources to existing supporters who would otherwise stay home on election day. These returns are known with certainty. Here, the proposition is that diversification emerges where uncertainty about the relative return on investment is high, as long as strategists believe that there may be potential gains from both persuasion and mobilization.

[15] The role of lower-level actors and particularly parliamentary candidates was noted in several interviews I conducted in 2007. Thus, a campaign consultant for ODM (interviewed on September 27, 2007) reported that the role of lower-level candidates is to ensure turnout and spread ODM's message in their areas, noting that "they become campaign agents" along with candidates for councilor seats. This point was made also in interviews with PNU's Regional Coordinator for Coast Province (December 21, 2007) and ODM's Branch Secretary for Central Rift Valley (December 9, 2007).

[16] This point was made to me by one of ODM's senior campaign strategists (interviewed on September 27, 2007) with regard to the party's plans to put forward local candidates in all areas of the country, including in Central Province, in the 2007 election. The reason, he noted, was that the party must "maintain a national outlook and image."

in coethnic areas, unlike swing areas where the battle on the ground is often more evenly fought with rival parties.

Thus, while I expect parties to invest in both persuasion and mobilization, presidential aspirants should primarily focus their campaign efforts on persuasion, seeking to reach potential fence-sitters in areas where out-group voters are concentrated. This does not mean that when the presidential candidates hold rallies outside their ethnic strongholds they appeal only to uncommitted voters or aim only to win over fence-sitters. The high-level of support in areas where coalition partners are concentrated means that rallies in such areas will serve also to increase turnout among the party faithful. The point is not that rallies held in ethnic strongholds are designed solely to mobilize and those held in other areas solely to persuade. Rather, the key idea is that if candidates seek to increase their vote share through persuasion, they will direct such efforts outside their ethnic strongholds.

Persuasion Targeting

If presidential aspirants seek to increase vote share by courting swing voters, which groups should they target? Because in Kenya only a small number of ethnic communities typically have a coethnic in the race, there are a great number of potential strategies for how each party might allocate campaign effort across groups that do not. Thus, for example, a presidential aspirant might focus his or her efforts narrowly on communities where he or she already enjoys strong support, particularly allied groups that make up the candidate's broader coalition, reinforcing the efforts of regional allies to boost support among such groups. Alternatively, the candidate might adopt a broader strategy, appealing to voters more widely, including among groups where rivals hold the initial advantage.

I propose that in highly-diverse societies like Kenya, a broad approach is preferable to a narrow one. Decisions about persuasion targeting, like decisions about how to allocate resources between mobilization and persuasion, are made under conditions of uncertainty. Specifically, parties lack information about the responsiveness of voters in different out-group communities. Party leaders may estimate that their prospects of converting fence-sitters will be greater in areas where the party's candidate already enjoys significant support and/or where the party is backed by many prominent local leaders. Yet, it is not implausible to think that presidential aspirants may also be able to pick up votes in areas where baseline support is lower, a point conveyed to me in interviews with campaign strategists from both major parties in 2007.[17] Therefore, if candidates are risk-

---

[17] See footnote 2.

averse and are uncertain about the likely return on investment from targeting various types of voters, the preferable strategy will again be to diversify outreach efforts across groups that do not have a coethnic in the race rather than concentrating narrowly on voters in groups expected to be most responsive to the candidate's appeals.[18]

The tendency toward broad-based strategies is reinforced by the strategic nature of campaigning: candidates allocate resources with an eye toward undercutting rivals' efforts (e.g., Box-Steffensmeier, Darmofal, and Farrell 2009; Carsey, Jackson, Stewart, and Nelson 2011; Banda and Carsey 2015). One might expect that on the campaign trail each presidential candidate would prioritize areas where he or she holds an initial advantage, devoting less time to areas where opponents do. This, however, would leave one's rival(s) free to court voters in other areas unchecked. If candidates seek to blunt the advances of their opponents, then they will allocate campaign effort not only to areas where the effort to convert potential fence-sitters might seem especially promising, but also to areas where prospects may be more limited.

In sum, presidential candidates should target voters in all ethnic groups, save for those where party leaders have good reason to believe that their efforts will be a complete waste of time—their own and their rivals' ethnic strongholds. In some instances, they may also avoid allied groups that make up their rivals' broader coalitions, when bloc voting is especially high in these communities. Yet, more often, parties will not avoid targeting opponents' coalition groups, since, as shown in Chapter 3, voters within such communities update their voting intentions during the campaigns at rates similar to other more divided groups. One implication of these arguments is that if the leading parties all pursue broad-based strategies, they will converge on the same communities rather than courting rival ethnic factions. At the same time, parties will naturally devote more effort to larger ethnic groups simply by virtue of their greater numerical importance.

One additional qualification is necessary. To this point the argument has assumed that presidential candidates enter the race with near-universal support from coethnic voters. As shown in Chapter 2, however, this is not always that case, particularly for minor-party candidates. The extent of a candidate's coethnic support affects campaign strategies in two ways. First, when a candidate's coethnic support is lower, there will likely be a greater number of potential swing voters within his or her own ethnic community. As a result, candidates will have greater incentives to invest in persuasion within their ethnic strongholds, increasing the

---

[18] In addition, campaigning is also subject to diminishing returns (Jacobson 1990; Green and Zelizer 2017). If, as seems likely, the effects of holding presidential rallies in one group's ethnic area decline with each additional event, then candidates will be wise to spread their efforts across communities.

amount of time they allocate to campaigning in these areas. At the same time, opponents may conclude that members of the candidate's group may be available for conversion, increasing the likelihood of incursions on the candidate's home terrain. In short, candidates who enter the race without the full support of their ethnic communities will spend more time in their ethnic strongholds and will face a greater challenge from rivals on their home turf. However, to the extent that these candidates invest in persuasion outside their own communities, the arguments above still apply. I expect, in other words, that candidates who do not enjoy universal coethnic support will employ broad-based strategies outside their own areas even as they work to shore up coethnic support.

Summary of Expectations

The above discussion implies four testable hypotheses related to campaign strategy:

H1–*Swing targeting*: Presidential candidates will concentrate campaign effort in areas inhabited by groups that do not have a coethnic leader in the race, devoting less effort to areas inhabited by groups that do.

H2–*Convergence*: Presidential candidates will converge on the same set of out-groups.

H3–*Mobilization*: In targeting local-level mobilization efforts, parties will contact voters in their coethnic strongholds at higher rates than they contact members of other groups due to the greater ability to recruit lower-level allies in areas where coethnic voters are concentrated.

H4–*Coethnic support*: Presidential candidates with weaker initial coethnic support will devote more campaign effort to coethnic areas (as will their opponents), relative to candidates who start the race with more universal coethnic support.

It is important to note the contrast with standard core mobilization models that predominate in the ethnic politics literature. These models uniformly predict that parties should focus their campaign efforts on voters in the one or more ethnic communities that make up their respective bases (Horowitz 1985, 1991; Reilly 2001; Reilly and Reynolds 1999; Sisk 1994). Core mobilization models have particular relevance to Kenya, where prior literature suggests that the effort to shore up support within the parties' ethnic coalitions is central to electoral competition (e.g., Kagwanja and Southall 2009). Given the prominence of this alternative understanding of campaign strategy, the tests below explore whether the data better fit the swing-targeting approach offered here or the core mobilization model developed in prior literature.

Analysis of Campaign Rallies

The analysis of presidential rallies proceeds in three steps. I begin by testing the swing-targeting model in which the parties' respective core bases are defined simply as coethnic communities and swing groups are defined as all ethnic groups that do not have a coethnic in the race. I then test the alternative hypothesis, drawn from core mobilization models, that parties target campaign effort toward their existing ethnic coalitions, seeking to solidify support and ensure high levels turnout within these groups. Finally, I examine the extent to which the leading presidential aspirants converge across out-groups.

The analysis focuses on the campaign strategies of the main competitors (those that received 5 percent or more of the vote) in presidential elections in 2007, 2013, and 2017.[19] Table 4.1 lists the candidates included in the analysis, along with their ethnic groups, party affiliations, and the ethnic coalitions represented by their parties. I operationalize each candidate's ethnic coalition as the groups in which the candidate's support stood at 60 percent or more at the start of the main period of campaigning (typically about three months prior to the election), based on pre-election survey data shown in Tables A3.1–A3.3 the appendix. While the 60 percent threshold is an arbitrary one, it corresponds well with how ethnic coalitions are generally understood in Kenya.[20] For example, by this coding the PNU coalition

Table 4.1 Main presidential candidates, 2007–2017

Candidate	Party	Ethnic group	Ethnic coalition
2007:			
Mwai Kibaki	PNU	Kikuyu	Kikuyu, Meru, Embu
Raila Odinga	ODM	Luo	Luo, Kalenjin, Luhya, Kisii
Kalonzo Musyoka	ODM-K	Kamba	Kamba
2013:			
Uhuru Kenyatta	Jubilee	Kikuyu	Kikuyu, Kalenjin, Meru, Embu
Raila Odinga	CORD	Luo	Luo, Kamba, Luhya, Kisii, Mijikenda
2017:			
Uhuru Kenyatta	Jubilee	Kikuyu	Kikuyu, Kalenjin, Meru, Embu
Raila Odinga	NASA	Luo	Luo, Kamba, Luhya, Kisii, Mijikenda

Notes: Candidates receiving 5% or more of the official vote are included. Ethnic coalitions are defined as groups in which the candidate held 60% or more support in surveys conducted at the start of each campaign (see appendix).

[19] The analysis for 2017 examines the campaigning prior to the original election held on August 8, not the subsequent re-run mandated by the Supreme Court.

[20] For example, Maupeu (2008, p. 207) reports that ODM in 2007 was "commonly viewed in Kenya as an agreement to join majority forces between the Luos, the Luhyas, and the Kalenjins."

headed by Kibaki in 2007 includes the Kikuyu, Meru, and Embu; the ODM coalition led by Odinga includes the Luo, Kalenjin, Luhya, and Kisii; and ODM-K headed by Musyoka is confined to the Kamba, the only major ethnic group in which the candidate enjoyed >60 percent support at the start of the race. One limitation of this approach is that because it relies on pre-election polling to define ethnic coalitions, smaller ethnic groups (less than 1 percent of the population) cannot be coded, since pre-election polls typically contain too few observations to allow for reliable estimates for these groups.

Two features of the elections examined here are worth noting. First, in all three elections the main competitors came from different ethnic communities, as is commonplace in Kenya's presidential contests (see Chapter 1). Second, support among coethnic voters for each of the main contenders was typically near-universal at the start of the race. Surveys show that the major candidates generally entered the campaigns with 90 percent or greater support among coethnic voters (see appendix). The one exception is Musyoka, the minor-party candidate in 2007, who entered the race with roughly 60 percent support among coethnic Kambas.

To analyze campaign targeting, I collected data on the location of campaign rallies held by the candidates from newspaper coverage in Kenya's two major dailies, *The Nation* and *The Standard*.[21] I then geocoded each campaign event and plotted the rallies over demographic data. Figure 4.1 provides an illustration based on the 2007 election. Because Kenya's census is not sufficiently detailed for this

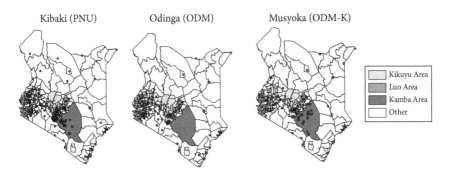

Figure 4.1 Presidential rallies held by leading candidates, 2007 election

Notes: Figures show the number of rallies (indicated by circle size) held by each candidate in the four months prior to the 2007 election, based on content analysis of newspaper coverage. Kikuyu, Luo, and Kamba areas are defined as parliamentary constituencies in which each group made up 50 percent or more of the population.

[21] For each election year, I examined articles published during the four months prior to the election. For 2007 and 2013, I collected relevant articles from print editions of *The Nation* and *The Standard*. For 2017 I used only *The Nation*, obtained through Lexis/Nexis, based on a keyword search for all article containing "Kenyatta" or "Odinga." These methods yield a dataset with information on 271 individual rallies in 2007, 129 in 2013, and 182 in 2017. Additional details on the data and concerns about bias are presented in the Online Appendix.

analysis, I use data from 12 separate national opinion polls conducted between November 2006 and January 2009 (with a total sample of 39,065 respondents) to estimate the ethnic composition of parliamentary constituencies, which serve as the unit of analysis in the tests that follow (details on the construction of these estimates can be found in the Online Appendix). I use the 210 constituency boundaries in place at the time of the 2007 election for all analyses because ethnic information is not available for the larger set of 290 constituencies created in 2010. One challenge is that in diverse constituencies it is not possible to determine which group(s) a candidate sought to reach. This problem, however, is mitigated by the relative homogeneity of parliamentary constituencies in Kenya. The average size of the largest ethnic group across all constituencies is 81 percent, and most constituencies (178 out of 210) contain a majority ethnic group. In most cases, then, it is possible to determine with a reasonable degree of certainty which groups the candidates sought to reach.

While parliamentary constituencies serve as a convenient unit of analysis, an inherent limitation is that the approach assumes that all residents within a constituency are being targeted and that rallies are meant to reach only residents of a single constituency. In practice, of course, a single campaign event may aim to attract only certain types of residents and may also attract voters from neighboring constituencies. There is, however, little reason to expect that these limitations will systematically bias the analysis for or against the main hypotheses. And in additional analysis presented in the Online Appendix, I show that the key findings hold when I use districts (a larger geographic division) rather than constituencies as the unit of analysis.

It is important to note that the data on campaign rallies is noisy due to variation in how the newspapers cover rally events. Typically, a single article will mention a small number of rally events. For example, among the 104 articles collected for the 2017 election, the mean number of rally events mentioned per article was 1.8. However, articles occasionally provide greater detail, mentioning the locations of a larger number of unique rallies, often smaller events held in the course of a single day's travel in a particular part of the country. For example, an article about Kenyatta's campaigning in Nyamira County on June 7, 2017 noted the location of six distinct rally events.[22] In other cases, it was clear that additional rallies were held beyond those for which locations are provided. However, when articles do not offer details on the locations, it is impossible to include those events in the data set. There is no reason to think that variation in the number of rallies mentioned by each article will bias the data (I do not expect that reporters systematically mention more events when candidates campaign in swing areas, for example). However, the overall sample size for each candidate in each election

[22] Mbula, Ruth. "Uhuru goes on vote hunt in Nyamira." *The Nation* (online). July 7, 2017.

year is relatively small. For this reason, the estimates provided below should not be taken as a perfect reflection of how candidates allocated effort across different ethnic areas. The value of the findings, rather, comes from the fact that a consistent picture of swing targeting is found across multiple candidates in multiple elections despite the imprecision of the measures used here.

Swing Targeting

I use regression analysis to estimate the relationship between ethnic demography and campaign targeting. For each election, I estimate a separate model for each candidate using negative binomial regression models, which are appropriate for event count data with overdispersion (Long and Freese 2006). In each model the dependent variable is the number of rallies held by the candidate in each constituency during the four months prior to the election. I define the key independent variable—*swing share*—as the aggregate population share of groups that do not have a coethnic leader in the race. All models control for the number of registered voters per constituency, constituency size (in square kilometers), population density, the number of major towns per constituency (defined as towns larger than 5,000 people in the 1999 census), and distance from Nairobi.[23] I also include a dummy variable for Westlands constituency in Nairobi which may be an outlier because it contains Uhuru Park, the city park where candidates hold rallies geared for broadcast on national television and radio, not local audiences.

The results, shown in Table 4.2, confirm H1: for all candidates in all election years, the number of rallies increases with *swing share* at the constituency level. The coefficient for *swing share* is significant at conventional levels (p<.10) for all candidates save for Kalonzo Musyoka, the minor-party candidate in 2007 who entered the race with weaker coethnic support than any of the other candidates in the races examined here. The deviation by Musyoka in 2007 is consistent with H4, which proposes that candidates will spend more time targeting coethnic voters when they enter the race with lower initial coethnic support.

To examine the substantive effects of *swing share*, Table 4.3 shows the predicted number of rallies for each candidate when *swing share* equals its minimum (0) and maximum (1), holding covariates at their mean or median values. In all cases, an increase in *swing share* from 0 to 1 is associated with a large and substantively meaningful increase in the predicted number of rallies at the constituency level (again with the exception of Musyoka in 2007). In 2007, an increase in *swing share* from 0 to 1 is associated with an increase from 0.35 to 0.68 for Kibaki, 0.08 to 0.69 for Odinga, and 0.29 to 0.40 for Musyoka, though these results are only

---

[23] For all urban constituencies in Nairobi and Mombasa, I code the number of major towns as 1.

Table 4.2 Models of swing targeting

	2007			2013		2017	
	(1) Kibaki	(2) Odinga	(3) Musyoka	(4) Kenyatta	(5) Odinga	(6) Kenyatta	(7) Odinga
Swing share	0.61**	2.09***	0.29	1.59***	1.03**	1.11***	0.99**
	(0.29)	(0.44)	(0.47)	(0.48)	(0.40)	(0.34)	(0.42)
Controls	Yes	Yes	Yes	Yes	Yes	Yes	Yes
Observations	210	210	210	210	210	210	210
Pseudo R^2	0.16	0.16	0.03	0.11	0.12	0.09	0.11

Notes: Negative binomial regressions. The dependent variable in all models is the number of rallies held by the candidate in each constituency. *Swing share* is a measure of the population share of groups without a coethnic candidate in the race. Controls include: the number of voters (measured in 2007), area, population density, distance to Nairobi, a count of major towns (>5,000 population), and a dummy for Westlands constituency. Robust standard errors in parentheses. ***p<0.01, **p<0.05, *p<0.1.

Table 4.3 Predicted number of rallies (with 95% confidence intervals)

Candidate	Swing share = 0	Swing share = 1
2007		
Kibaki	.35 [.18, .52]	.65 [.50, .80]
Odinga	.08 [.02, .14]	.66 [.45, .88]
Musyoka	.27 [.07, .47]	.36 [.22, .51]
2013		
Kenyatta	.09 [.02, .15]	.42 [.26, .58]
Odinga	.16 [.06, .26]	.45 [.29, .61]
2017		
Kenyatta	.22 [.09, .35]	.67 [.49, .85]
Odinga	.13 [.04, .22]	.36 [.24, .48]

Notes: Predicted valued based on models in Table 4.2, estimated with covariates held at mean or median values. 95 percent confidence intervals are shown in brackets.

statistically significant for the first two candidates. In 2013 and 2017, the predicted number of rallies for both major candidates is roughly three times greater in constituencies where members of swing groups make up 100 percent of the electorate relative to those with no swing. While in absolute terms these differences may seem small, it is important to bear in mind that because the dataset does not include information on all rally events, the actual number of rallies held across core and swing areas—and the absolute difference between the two—is greater than the estimates provided here suggest. Additional tests in the Online Appendix show that these results are robust to: (1) using a different unit of analysis (districts rather than constituencies); (2) alternative measures of ethnic demography (based on data from Demographic and Health Surveys); and (3) the inclusion of variables for proximity to Kenya's major roads.

To unpack the finding that candidates consistently target campaign effort toward swing areas, I test whether candidates avoid their rivals' ethnic strongholds, their own ethnic strongholds, or both. I re-estimate the models in Table 4.2 for each candidate with a measure of the candidate's own coethnic share (*coethnic share*) and a measure of opponents' coethnic share (*opponents' coethnic share*) at the constituency level. For example, for Kibaki in 2007, the model includes a measure of Kikuyu share and a measure of the combined population share of Luos and Kambas, the ethnic groups of Odinga and Musyoka. If, as proposed, candidates avoid both their rivals' ethnic strongholds and their own, the coefficients on *coethnic share* and *opponents' coethnic share* should be negative.

The results in Table 4.4 show that presidential candidates consistently avoid areas where opponents' ethnic groups are concentrated and generally avoid their own ethnic strongholds, though the later effect is less uniform. The coefficient on *opponents' coethnic* share is negative in all models and significant for all candidates except Kibaki in 2007.[24] The coefficient on *opponent's coethnic share* is consistently negative across most models, but is only significant in the 2007 race.

Table 4.4 Models of swing targeting—alternate specification

	2007			2013		2017	
	(1) Kibaki	(2) Odinga	(3) Musyoka	(4) Kenyatta	(5) Odinga	(4) Kenyatta	(5) Odinga
Coethnic share	−1.12***	−1.15**	1.22***	−0.66	−0.59	−0.51	0.19
	(0.41)	(0.45)	(0.41)	(0.51)	(0.44)	(0.39)	(0.33)
Opponents'	−0.39	−2.94***	−3.51***	−4.31***	−1.80***	−2.36***	−2.79***
coethnic share	(0.32)	(0.58)	(0.67)	(1.66)	(0.56)	(0.82)	(0.74)
Controls	Yes	Yes	Yes	Yes	Yes	Yes	Yes
Observations	210	210	210	210	210	210	210
Pseudo R^2	0.16	0.18	0.18	0.11	0.13	0.11	0.15

Notes: Negative binomial regressions. The dependent variable in all models is the number of rallies held by the candidate. *Coethnic share* is a measure of the population share of each candidate's coethnic group at the constituency level. *Opponents' coethnic share* is the coethnic population share of each candidate's main rival(s) in the election. Controls include: the number of voters (measured in 2007), area, population density, distance to Nairobi, a count of major towns (>5,000 population), and a dummy for Westlands constituency. Robust standard errors in parentheses. ***p<0.01, **p<0.05, *p<0.1.

[24] Additional analysis shows that while Kibaki did avoid areas inhabited by coethnics of his main rival (Odinga), he held several rallies in areas inhabited by Musyoka's coethnics (Kambas). This result is consistent with the expectation (H4) that because Musyoka's coethnic support was weaker at the start of the race, his opponents had greater incentives to hold rallies in his home ethnic area.

The results also indicate one anomaly: in the 2007 election Musyoka was *more* likely to hold rallies in his core ethnic area than in swing areas, as can be seen by the positive and significant effect of *coethnic share* on the number of rallies held by the candidate in 2007. This exception is again consistent with the expectation (H4) that because Musyoka's coethnic support was weaker at the start of the race, he (and his opponents) had greater incentives to hold rallies in his home ethnic area.

Coalition Mobilization?

While the results presented so far are consistent with the swing-targeting approach outlined in this book, it is worth examining whether the data fit with core mobilization models that expect that in settings like Kenya parties will target their campaign efforts toward the one or more ethnic communities in which they enjoy substantial support at the start of the race in order to unify their respective coalitions and ensure high turnout. Given the prominence of the core mobilization model both in the ethnic politics literature and in descriptions of electoral contests in Kenya, it is important to test whether there is any support for this understanding of electoral politics.

To do so, I generate a variable—*core coalition share*—that is the aggregate population share of groups in each candidate's core coalition at the constituency level (see Table 4.1 for coalition definitions). For example, for Kibaki in 2007, this variable is defined as the sum of Kikuyu, Meru, and Embu population shares at the constituency level. I re-estimate the models of campaign targeting where *core coalition share* is the key independent variable, again using the same set of control variables as in Table 4.2. Additionally, all models include measures of the coethnic share of each candidate's main rival(s), since results in Table 4.4 establish that candidates consistently avoid opponents' coethnic strongholds. Thus, for example, in the model for Kibaki in 2007, I include measures of the Luo and Kamba population shares. Specified in this way, the models test whether candidates are more likely to target areas where coalition groups, including coethnics, are concentrated, relative to areas where voters from groups that do not have a coethnic in the race predominate.[25]

The results show that there is no support for the core mobilization model for any candidate in any election. The estimates in Table 4.5 indicate that the coefficient on *core coalition share* is never significant, meaning that candidates *never* prioritize reaching voters in their ethnic coalitions over other groups that do not have a coethnic in the race. And in some instances, the coefficient is negative and

---

[25] As a secondary test of the core mobilization model, I interact *core coalition share* with a dummy variable for constituencies with historically low turnout to examine whether there is any support for the notion that within regions where coalition groups reside, parties focus their effort on increasing turnout among those at risk of staying home on election day. There is no consistent evidence in favor of this alternative view (results in Online Appendix).

Table 4.5 Models of core coalition targeting

	2007		2013		2017	
	(1) Kibaki	(2) Odinga	(3) Kenyatta	(4) Odinga	(5) Kenyatta	(6) Odinga
Core coalition	−0.68*	−0.53	−0.02	−1.05***	0.07	0.10
share	(0.38)	(0.33)	(0.46)	(0.33)	(0.31)	(0.29)
Controls	Yes	Yes	Yes	Yes	Yes	Yes
Observations	210	210	210	210	210	210
Pseudo R^2	0.20	0.15	0.11	0.15	0.10	0.15

Notes: Negative binomial regressions. The dependent variable in all models is the number of rallies held by the candidate in each constituency. *Core coalition share* is a measure of the population share of groups associated with each candidate's ethnic coalition. See text for explanation of how coalitions are defined. Controls include: the number of voters (measured in 2007), area, population density, distance to Nairobi, a count of major towns (>5,000 population), and a dummy for Westlands constituency. Models also control for the coethnic population share of each candidate's main rival(s) (e.g., Luo share and Kamba share for Kibaki in 2007). Robust standard errors in parentheses. ***p<0.01, **p<0.05, *p<0.1.

significant—for Kibaki in 2007 and Odinga in 2013—indicating that the candidates in these cases spent *less* time targeting voters from their core coalitions than other voters. These results are robust to alternative ways of operationalizing the parties' ethnic coalitions.[26]

Convergence

While the results presented so far are consistent with the swing-targeting approach, they tell us nothing about how parties allocate their campaign efforts across the many ethnic groups that do not have a coethnic leader in the race. The third step in the analysis is therefore to examine whether the parties converge or diverge in their pursuit of out-group voters. To do so, I calculate the share of each party's rallies held in the geographic areas of groups that did not have a coethnic in each race. For this analysis, each group's ethnic area is defined as the parliamentary constituencies in which the group makes up 50 percent or more of the population.[27] If the candidates converge on the same out-group communities,

[26] In additional tests (results not shown), I alternatively define core groups as those groups in which each presidential candidate had 50% or greater or 75% or greater support at the start of the race. The results presented here hold under these alternative specifications.

[27] The results presented here are unchanged if ethnic areas are defined using a higher threshold, e.g., 60% or 75% (see Online Appendix).

we should observe that they devote relatively similar shares of their campaign efforts to the areas where Kenya's major ethnic groups are concentrated.

It is important to bear in mind that because the data used to study campaign strategies are noisy, there are limits to the precision with which I can track fine-grained differences in how much effort is devoted to particular ethnic areas. Despite this limitation, the data, plotted in Figure 4.2, show that while there is some variation across groups, candidates uniformly choose broad-based strategies, courting voters across swing communities. As a result, they typically converge on the same communities, rather than targeting distinct, non-overlapping coalitions.

Another way to examine convergence more formally is to investigate the spatial correlation of presidential rallies across constituencies. A positive correlation indicates that the candidates allocate effort to similar areas, while a negative correlation indicates that candidates target different types of constituencies. Results in Table 4.6 show a high degree of overlap. For the two leading candidates in the 2007 election, Kibaki and Odinga, the correlation is 0.64. This value remains high (0.46) even when Nairobi is excluded, indicating substantial overlap in rural areas where constituencies are more ethnically homogenous.[28] In 2013, the spatial correlation between the two leading candidates was again relatively high: 0.39 overall and 0.31 when Nairobi is excluded. In 2017 the overall correlation was somewhat lower (0.09) but was again relatively high (0.34) when Nairobi is excluded. In sum, the results indicate that the leading candidates court the same groups of voters, not distinct, non-overlapping coalitions.

Household Contact

The above results highlight the importance of reaching voters outside the candidates' ethnic strongholds during campaigns. I argue, however, that parties do not neglect the job of mobilizing coethnics within their strongholds; rather, this task is delegated to lower-level actors. To test this proposition, I turn to survey data on campaign contact at the household level from the 2007 election.[29] Respondents in a large national survey (n=3,600) were asked: "Did a candidate or agent from any party come to your home during the campaign before last year's election?"

---

[28] The correlations with the minor-party candidate, Musyoka, are lower (but still positive), which is unsurprising given that Musyoka allocated more effort to his coethnic region than either Kibaki or Odinga.

[29] These data come from a survey that was conducted as part of an evaluation of Kenya's national civic education program (see Finkel, Horowitz, and Mendoza (2012)). Because the sample frame was designed to oversample particular groups, it was necessary to re-weight the data. To determine how the sample should be weighted, I compared the data to a random-sample survey conducted by the Afrobarometer in 2005. It was necessary to weight by province, urban/rural location, and gender. On other variables—age, education, and community group membership—the data closely resembled the Afrobarometer sample.

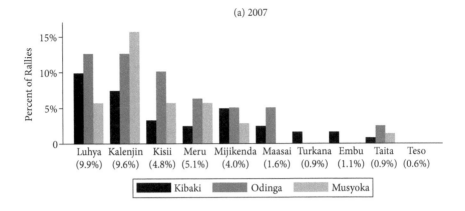

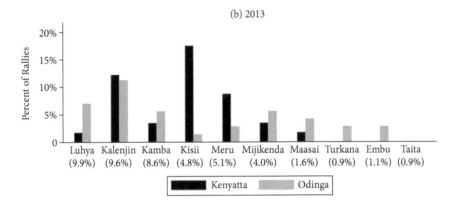

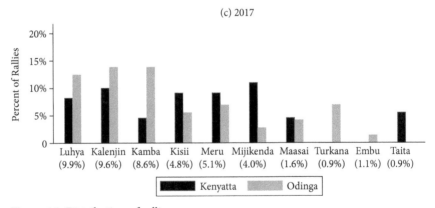

Figure 4.2 Distribution of rallies across groups

Notes: Figures show the share of rallies held by each of the leading presidential candidates in the ethnic areas (defined as parliamentary constituencies in which each group made up 50% or more of the population) of the ten largest groups that did not have a coethnic leader in each race. The x-axis shows the share of registered voters in each ethnic area as a percentage of the national total (based on 2007 registration data).

Table 4.6 Spatial correlation between major-party candidates'
rallies

Election year	All constituencies	Excluding Nairobi
2007	.64	.46
2013	.39	.31
2017	.09	.34

Notes: Table shows the correlation between the number of rallies held by two
leading candidates in each race across constituencies.

A follow-up question recorded all parties mentioned by those who gave an affirmative answer. I examine household contact by each of the three main parties: PNU headed by Kibaki, ODM led by Odinga, and ODM-K headed by Musyoka. The data show that 40 percent of respondents were contacted by PNU; 41 percent by ODM; and 13 percent by ODM-K during the 2007 campaigns.[30]

To examine the ethnic targeting of the parties' canvassing efforts, I estimate separate logit models of campaign contact for each of the three leading parties. The dependent variable is a dichotomous measure of household contact. The key independent variable in each model is an indicator that takes a value of 1 for respondents in constituencies in which the presidential contender's own ethnic groups makes up a majority (Kikuyus for PNU, Luos for ODM, and Kambas for ODM-K). To ensure comparability between these results and the analysis of presidential rallies, I include the same constituency-level covariates from the previous tests: the number of voters, the size of the constituency, population density, and a dummy variable for Westlands constituency.[31] I add a control for the margin of victory in the previous parliamentary elections in 2002 to account for the possibility that local-level actors may invest more effort in grassroots contact when they expect local races to be competitive. Because these tests use individual-level data, I also control for respondent characteristics, specifically, the number of community groups to which respondents belong and whether respondents serve as leaders in one or more of these groups.[32] I also include basic

[30] PNU was a coalition that included several smaller parties. For these tests, I define voters who were contacted by PNU as those who reported having been reached by PNU or any of its main allies (KANU, DP, FORD-K, FORD-P, Safina, FORD-A, and NARC-K). The substantive findings of the tests do not change when PNU's coalition partners are excluded.

[31] I exclude distance to Nairobi and the count of major towns—variables that are less relevant to local-level canvasing.

[32] To measure membership in community groups, the survey asked respondents whether they belonged to each of the following groups: a church or religious group, a youth or sports group, a trade union, a women's group, a cultural or school organization, a burial society, a civic organization, a tribal or clan association, a business or professional society, a political party, and other. The measure of group membership is the sum of positive answers. The measure of leadership comes from a question that asked whether respondents were presently or had ever been a leader in one or more of these groups.

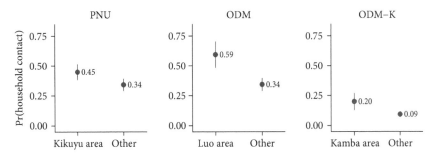

Figure 4.3 Predicted probability of household contact, 2007 election

Notes: Figure shows the predicted probability of household contact by each party during the campaign, based on logit models shown in the appendix. Estimates are calculated with covariates held at their mean or median values. Ethnic areas are defined as constituencies in which the group makes a 50 percent or more of the population. Error bars show 95 percent confidence intervals. Standard errors are clustered by constituency.

demographic variables: gender, age, and education, and whether respondents reported that they were registered to vote in the 2007 election. Standard errors are clustered by constituency.

Figure 4.3 plots the predicted probabilities of being contacted by PNU, ODM, and ODM-K respectively, holding all covariates constant. All three parties contacted voters in their respective coethnic areas at higher rates than voters in other areas. In substantive terms, these differences are meaningful. For PNU the difference is an 11 percentage point increase (from 0.34 to 0.45, p<.01); for ODM it is a 25 point increase (from 0.34 to 0.59, p<.01); and for ODM-K it is an 11 point increase (from 0.9 to 0.20, p<.01). In sum, these findings confirm that while presidential aspirants spend relatively little time in their own ethnic strongholds during campaigns, parties do not ignore the need to mobilize coethnic voters. This job is left to lower-level actors.

Alternative Explanations

Next, I address a series of alternative explanations related to institutions, cross-cutting identities, and local diversity. First, it is important to explore whether the broad, inclusive strategies chosen by candidates are driven by Kenya's electoral institutions rather than the factors proposed above. From 1992 to 2010 Kenya's constitution stipulated that to win the presidential race in the first round a candidate needed to gain at least 25 percent of the vote in five of Kenya's eight provinces. If the leading candidate did not satisfy the "five of eight" rule, a second-round run-off would be held between the top two candidates. A new constitution adopted in 2010 made two modifications to the electoral code (Kramon and Posner 2011). First, the "five-of-eight" rule was replaced by a requirement that the election winner must gain at least 25 percent of the vote in half or more of the 47 counties that replaced administrative districts. Second, the election code was changed to stipulate that the election winner must garner 50 percent or more of the national vote or face a second-round run-off between the top two candidates. In the past, only a plurality was required. It is possible that these institutional requirements, not the factors identified above, lead presidential candidates to opt for broad campaign strategies.

The available data suggest that institutional factors have little explanatory power in Kenya simply because they are not binding constraints on the major candidates. Consider the 2007 election. Survey data collected prior to the campaigns shows that Kibaki had already cleared the 25 percent mark in at least five provinces by the start of the campaign (see Online Appendix), and there is no evidence that Kibaki concentrated his campaign efforts on the two provinces where his support hovered near the 25 percent mark, Western and North Eastern. Kibaki held 10 percent of all rallies in Western Province, but held a similar or larger share of rallies in provinces where he was well above the 25 percent mark, and held only four rallies (3% of the total) in North Eastern. Likewise, institutional requirements are unable to explain the targeting decisions made by the opposition candidates in 2007. The leading contender, Odinga, had cleared the 25 percent mark by a wide margin in six of eight provinces well before campaigning got under way. To be sure, he would not want to see his support erode in these provinces, but it seems unlikely that his campaign decisions were driven by concerns about falling below the 25 percent threshold, given that his support was well above the required level at the start of the race. Similarly, institutional explanations offer little insight into Musyoka's choices. The candidate was nowhere near the 25 percent threshold at the start of the race in any province other than Eastern, where coethnic Kambas are concentrated. It is unlikely, therefore, that Musyoka's strategy was driven by the five of eight rule, given that he had little chance of realistically clearing the 25 percent bar outside of Eastern province. More plausible is that the candidates held rallies across out-group areas because they lacked information needed to assess the relative responsiveness of voters in swing groups and sought to blunt their rivals' advances in swing areas.

The available data also suggest that in subsequent races the requirement to gain at least 25 percent of the vote in half or more of Kenya's 47 counties had little effect on campaign strategies. While survey data are not sufficiently rich to generate county-level estimates of pre-election support for the candidates in 2013 or 2017, election returns provide a useful proxy. Election results show that the two main competitors in 2013 and 2017—Kenyatta and Odinga—cleared the 25 percent bar in half of all counties with relative ease. Kenyatta cleared the mark in 32 countries in both 2013 and 2017, eight above the required 24. Odinga cleared the bar in 29 and 27 counties in 2013 and 2017 respectively, a slimmer margin, but still with room to spare in both elections. Given this, it seems unlikely that their campaign strategies would have been driven by concerns about satisfying electoral requirements. Moreover, the data on campaign rallies held by the leading contenders shows that the presidential candidates did not target competitive counties over less marginal areas, suggesting that institutional requirements have little influence on the strategies adopted by the major parties.[33] Finally, it is important to remember that broad, inclusive strategies are observed prior to the implementation of the 2010 consitution, suggesting that other factors are at work.

Regarding the requirement that the election winner must obtain 50 percent or more of the overall vote in races since 2010, here too there is reason to doubt that this rule is driving campaign strategies. First, because the penalty for failing to clear the hurdle is a re-run of the election, not an electoral defeat, candidates should be expected to focus their attention on maximizing their overall vote share during the campaign and give less consideration to the spatial distribution of their support. Second, it is again useful to recall that broad-based campaign strategies precede the adoption of this rule, suggesting that other factors account for the targeting strategies documented in this chapter. Thus, while it is plausible that the 50% +1 rule has increased the premium on constructing broad and diverse elite coalitions (Cheeseman et al. 2019), there is less evidence that it has altered campaign tactics.

A second alternative explanation points to the possibility of cross-cutting identities that might bridge ethnic divisions or subordinate identities that may weaken the extent of bloc voting within communities. Kenya lacks the kinds of cross-cutting cleavages that have been shown to temper ethnic politics elsewhere in Africa (Dunning and Harrison 2010; Koter 2013). However, sub-tribal divisions are important in some communities, and it is possible that presidential aspirants focus their campaign efforts on groups that are more internally divided. This argument is most relevant to the Luhya community, which has historically been riven by sub-tribe divisions (MacArthur 2008). However, while this explanation may help to explain why the Luhya are an attractive target for campaign persuasion, it does not provide a general framework for conceptualizing core and swing.

A third alternative explanation is that parties target ethnically-diverse areas and that these areas happen to be places where ethnic groups without a coethnic in the election are concentrated. One reason to doubt that ethnic diversity is driving the main findings, however, is that, as noted above, most parts of the country are

---

[33] Data from the 2013 race, for example, shows that Kenyatta and Odinga held a similar number of rallies in competitive counties (defined here as those in which the final margin between the two was less than 20 percentage points) as in less competitive areas. Thus, the average number of rallies in competitive counties for Kenyatta was .75 vs. 1.16 in non-competitive counties. For Odinga, the average number was 1.40 vs. 1.27 in competitive vs. non-competitive counties.

relatively homogenous. Nonetheless, to test whether the results presented above are driven by ethnic diversity, I rerun the models of presidential rallies in Table 4.2 and include a measure of ethnic fractionalization estimated at the constituency level. The results (presented in the Online Appendix) demonstrate that ethnic diversity is not consistently associated with the number of rallies held per constituency, and the main results on *swing share* remain significant when this measure is included in the models. This is unsurprising given that most swing areas—as defined in this book—are fairly homogenous.

Do These Arguments Apply to Earlier Races?

Finally, this chapter explores whether the swing-targeting approach holds for earlier elections after the return to multiparty competition, when the party system was more fragmented. Some accounts of the 1992, 1997, and 2002 races suggest that shoring up coethnic support may have been a more central priority than in the later races examined in this chapter (Throup and Hornsby 1998; Elischer 2013; Cheeseman, Lynch, and Willis 2014). Data limitations make it difficult to examine campaign strategies in Kenya prior to 2007. For earlier races I again collected articles on campaign rallies during the months prior to each election from Kenya's two main newspapers. Unfortunately, the number of rallies reported in the newspapers for these contests is much smaller. Moreover, in Kibaki's case, an additional challenge relates to the 2002 election in which a road accident cut short his time on the campaign trail, yielding a very small sample that is likely not representative of the overall campaign strategy that he would have implemented had he been able to travel throughout the campaign period.

Despite these limitations, it is possible to gain some insight into campaign strategies prior to 2007 by examining two candidates—Kibaki and Kenyatta—who competed in both earlier and later races. The available data suggest that coethnic mobilization was *never* the primary goal for either candidate, even in earlier periods. Table 4.7 presents the share of rallies held in coethnic constituencies (those in which coethnics make up 50% or more of the population) by Kibaki in the four races in which he competed from 1992 to 2007, and for Kenyatta in the 2002, 2013, and 2017 elections.[34] It also shows estimated coethnic support for each candidate in these races (based on data presented in Chapter 2). The results indicate that Kibaki never made coethnic mobilization his top priority. While he did devote more than a third of his time on the campaign trail to Kikuyu

---

[34] I use the 210 constituency boundaries in place at the time of the 2007 election for these analyses because constituency-level ethnicity estimates are not available for the smaller number of constituencies used in earlier races or the larger number created after 2010.

Table 4.7 Share of rallies held in coethnic areas

Candidate	Election year	Share of rallies in coethnic area	Coethnic support
Kibaki	1992	0.10	0.50
Kibaki	1997	0.39	0.95
Kibaki	2002	0.04	0.70
Kibaki	2007	0.12	0.95
Kenyatta	2002	0.25	0.30
Kenyatta	2013	0.12	0.96
Kenyatta	2017	0.13	0.92

Notes: Tables shows the share of rallies held in constituencies where coethnic voters are a majority based on newspaper content analysis from each race. Also shown are estimates of the candidates' coethnic support in each election cycle, based on data from Chapter 2.

constituencies in 1997, he still held roughly two-thirds of his rallies elsewhere. And in those years in which he was challenged by a competitor from his own community (Matiba in 1992 and Kenyatta in 2002), Kibaki nonetheless spent nearly all of his time campaigning outside of the Kikuyu homeland. The same is true for Kenyatta. Even in 2002, when he was battling to steal Kikuyu votes away from Kibaki, he still only devoted a quarter of all rallies to Kikuyu areas. In 2013 and 2017, when his hold on the Kikuyu vote was stronger, he devoted very little time to Kikuyu strongholds. These patterns, while only suggestive, indicate that when candidates are working to bolster coethnic support, they may allocate more campaign effort to coethnic areas. Yet, even in such elections, candidates do not focus exclusively or even primarily on these areas.

Conclusion

This chapter draws on data on the location of campaign rallies in Kenya's multiparty era to test the swing-targeting model developed in this book. Though the data is noisy, a consistent pattern is observed. Presidential aspirants generally devote little campaign effort to the pursuit of voters in their own—or rivals'— coethnic strongholds. Outside of these areas, the parties target their efforts widely and compete intensely for the same out-group voters. To explain these patterns, the chapter emphasizes uncertainty about the responsiveness of voters arrayed across ethnic areas, the desire to blunt rivals' advances, and the ability to delegate mobilization in their strongholds to lower-level actors.

The arguments and evidence assembled in this chapter contrast with canonical literature on electoral politics in diverse societies, which generally predicts that where parties draw their main support from distinct ethnic segments of the electorate, they will concentrate their energies on mobilizing their respective core bases rather than courting voters across ethno-partisan lines. This perspective has particular relevance to Kenya, where parties are often described as coalitions that advance the interests of rival ethnic factions. The data in this chapter indicates that campaign politics in Kenya do not conform to such visions.

5

Persuasion on the Campaign Trail

The pursuit of out-group voters affects not only where candidates hold rallies but also what they say on the campaign trail. For presidential hopefuls the central task is at once to project an inclusive image while also casting doubt on the ethnic favoritism intentions of rivals. In the parlance of Kenyan politics, each party seeks to convince voters that its leader is a *nationalist*, concerned about the welfare of all citizens, and that opposing leaders are *tribalists*, interested only in representing the interests of their narrow ethnic bases. To do so, candidates rely on a mix of positive and negative messages, both aimed primarily at potential fence-sitters in swing communities. Positive messages about the candidate's own accomplishments and proposals signal the leader's inclusive intentions. Negative appeals about rivals are crafted with an eye toward limiting competitors' reach beyond their ethnic strongholds. Campaign appeals, of course, are not intended only to convert swing voters; they serve also to shore up support and motivate voters in core groups. This chapter's focus on how the pursuit of the swing affects campaign messages complements prior research in which efforts to mobilize core voters have been studied more extensively (e.g., HRW 2008; KNCHR 2008; CIPEV 2008; Barkan 2008b; Chege 2008; Kagwanja 2009; Klopp and Kamungi 2008).

The argument in this chapter breaks with conventional approaches in three ways. First, it is widely assumed that in settings like Kenya where ethnicity is politically salient to voters, candidates are better served by narrow particularistic appeals than broad, universal promises (Horowitz 1985; Rabushka and Shepsle 1972; Wantchekon 2003). This chapter, by contrast, shows that where candidates must court a diverse electorate, they opt mainly for universal appeals. Second, it shows that the dichotomy between narrow clientelist appeals and broad programmatic pledges is overdrawn (e.g., Kitschelt 2000). In settings like Kenya where voters are highly attuned to localized issues, candidates are compelled to make targeted appeals to specific groups and localities on the campaign trail. Yet, the need to curry favor with a diverse electorate means that they do so in a universal fashion. Third, standard accounts expect that candidates turn to divisive ethnic rhetoric only when they endeavor to whip up the base, and refrain from such strategies when they seek support broadly from multiple ethnic communities (Horowitz 1991; Reilly 2001, 2006). Here, I show that parties may employ divisive appeals—in the form of negative messages that demonize rivals as ethnic chauvinists or worse—even when the primary task is to court voters across ethnopartisan lines.

Multiethnic Democracy: The Logic of Elections and Policymaking in Kenya. Jeremy Horowitz, Oxford University Press.

Empirically, this chapter draws on a rich collection of nearly 120 hours of audio recordings of campaign speeches from Kenya's 2007 election. Recordings were obtained from three sources. First, a local human rights group, the Kenyan National Commission on Human Rights (KNCHR), employed a staff of approximately 20 people who were assigned to monitor rallies and record speeches during the campaign. Second, I employed 15 research assistants who were based throughout Kenya. Each research assistant was asked to record major rallies held in his or her geographic area. Finally, a small amount of material was obtained from a local media organization. In total, the sample includes recordings from 99 campaign rallies—51 held by PNU and 48 by ODM. While the analysis is based on recordings from a single election year, it illustrates how broad-based campaign strategies influence campaign messages. All quotes provided in this chapter are in English, often translated from Swahili or vernacular languages. See Online Appendix for details on translation.

Studies of campaign communication typically rely on content analysis of televised advertising or newspaper coverage of campaign events (Goldstein and Freedman 2002; Sides 2006; Boas 2010; Davis 2004; Ferree 2011; Bleck and van de Walle 2011, 2013; Taylor 2017). In Kenya, however, it was important to collect original recordings of the candidates' speeches. As noted in prior chapters, the use of paid campaign advertising is much less prevalent in Kenya than in long-standing democracies. Moreover, there are limits to what can be learned from media coverage in a setting like Kenya where media outlets avoid reporting content that might be considered inflammatory (Weigton and McCurdy 2017). The analysis in this chapter builds on studies that explore aspects of campaigning in Kenya (Gadjanova 2017; Harneit-Sievers and Peters 2008; Cussac 2008; Lynch 2008; MacArthur 2008) but provides a more extensive characterization than possible in work drawn from anecdotal sources or newspaper coverage alone.

While campaign recordings provide a valuable resource, there are limitations to what can be learned from studying them. First, the recordings provide insight into only one aspect of campaign communication which on its own cannot capture all the nuances of the messages conveyed by parties and their supporters. Some evidence suggests that the crudest ethnic language in Kenya is reserved for less public means of communication, such as text messages, which can be sent anonymously (KNCHR 2008). Second, the recordings are drawn mainly from presidential rallies. Local rallies held by candidates for parliamentary or local council seats are not covered. Third, by necessity, the coding scheme used in this chapter focuses only on explicit appeals. Efforts to develop a consistent strategy for coding implicit appeals proved to be unworkable in the Kenyan context, where nearly everything the candidates do and say on the campaign trail can be viewed through an ethnic lens. Given the risk of inferring ethnic meaning where none was intended, I opted for the more conservative strategy of focusing on explicit content. This means that the innuendos and subtle references that Kenyan politicians are famous for do not enter into the analysis.

Despite these limitations, there is value in focusing on the messages that the parties employ at major public rallies. The parties invest considerable resources—time and money—in organizing campaign events, a reflection of the importance they attach to them. Moreover, large-scale rallies garner the bulk of media attention, and the messages conveyed at these rallies have the greatest national reach. And, while the messages from large public rallies may be more tame than those employed in other contexts, unabashed appeals to ethnic interests, resentments, and antipathies are fully on display in the data. Finally, unlike messages spread by supporters through informal channels, the parties have direct control over the content of appeals made at their rallies. For all of these reasons, the parties are careful to craft messages that they believe will serve their electoral goals. Studying these appeals provides a useful window into their aims and goals.

This chapter is structured as follows. The next two sections develop the argument that links campaign goals to rhetorical strategies and provide an overview of the main themes on the campaign trail in the 2007 race. The chapter then turns to more structured content analysis. The results provide evidence of symmetrical strategies used by incumbent and challenger: both employ a mix of positive and negative appeals; both rely more heavily on universal appeals than particularistic ones; and both use particularistic messages in a universal way. And, while the specific themes used to demonize opponents vary across incumbent and challenger, the goal of negative appeals remains the same—to raise doubts about the favoritism intentions of one's rival(s).

The Logic of Campaign Appeals

Much of the existing literature suggests that in multiethnic democracies parties will rely on narrow, communal appeals in place of broad, nationally-oriented promises. Standard accounts assume that leaders distribute state-controlled resources to clients in exchange for support (Bratton and van de Walle 1997; Chabal and Daloz 1999; Berman 1998; Ekeh 1975; Joseph 1987), and that ethnicity serves as the organizing principle for patronage (Fearon 1999; Chandra 2004; Posner 2005). This literature implies a clear model of campaign communication: if politicians build and maintain support by targeting material resources to ethnic clients, campaigns ought to be filled with promises to provide resources to supporters in the one (or more) ethnic communities that make up their core ethnic coalitions.

There is considerable anecdotal evidence consistent with these expectations. Beckett's (1987, p. 91) description of post-independence elections in Nigeria, for example, notes that "electoral politics were ethnic politics . . . Electoral appeals consequently were couched in terms of ethnic advancement (or survival) and amenities for communities." Chazan (1982, p. 469) characterizes political competition in

Ghana during the late 1970s in much the same way: "Elites of different ethnic origins rallied the support of other segments of their ethnic groupings...not only to protest against measures perceived as detrimental to their well-being, but also to acquire gains at the expense of other similarly organized elites." Barkan (1987, p. 221) likewise reports that in Kenya's early post-independence elections, the two leadings parties—KANU and KADU—rarely competed for the same voters; instead, "both coalitions sought to mobilize the series of ethnically homogenous areas to which they laid claim into a series of one-party fiefs." Moreover, Wantchekon's (2003) experimental study of campaign appeals in Benin shows that voters are more responsive to promises of targeted transfers than nationally-oriented programs, suggesting that parties should be better off using particularistic appeals.

In contrast to these accounts, I argue that in Kenya the need to attract support from multiple ethnic communities leads parties to avoid portraying themselves as representatives of a limited set of ethnic groups. A candidate who offers distributional promises to core ethnic voters will have little appeal to members of other communities. As a result, parties design campaign appeals with an eye toward increasing support from voters in many groups. To do so, parties seek to convince voters of their inclusive intentions, assuring voters in all groups that their community will be treated fairly and that none will be left out. Moreover, because presidential candidates often (though not always) enter the race with near universal support from coethnic voters, there is little need to reassure their most dependable supporters that their interests will be represented; this is well understood from the outset. For parties, then, there is little to gain (and much to lose) from messages tailored toward narrow ethnic clientele.

While parties seek to convey an inclusive image, they must also address voters' localized concerns. In developing countries like Kenya, voters are particularly attuned to local considerations: whether roads are passable in the rainy season, whether the local school has enough teachers, whether the nearby well is functioning, and so forth (Barkan 1979, 1984; Barkan and Holmquist 1989; Lindberg 2010). This means that parties cannot help but employ particularistic appeals: promises to pave the roads in a certain area, hire more teachers in local schools, and drill boreholes in specific localities. However, it is important not to equate this type of particularism with a strategy of narrow communal mobilization. While particularism is often viewed as an alternative to nationally-oriented policies (e.g., Kitschelt 2000; Keefer 2007; Wantchekon 2003), this need not be so. In Kenya parties employ particularistic promises as part of a nationally-oriented electoral strategy, offering targeted pledges across localities and ethnic communities. The benefit of adopting a *universal approach to particularism* is that it allows parties to address voters' local concerns while also maintaining an inclusive image. Moreover, voters generally will be indifferent between particularistic and universal policies (Nathan 2016). It makes little difference whether the nearby road gets paved as a part of a nationwide initiative or a targeted effort to upgrade infrastructure in one's area; whether more teachers are hired for the local school as part of a national program or a targeted allocation; or whether more wells are drilled as part of a national scheme or a more narrow one favoring the area.

While positive appeals play an important role in campaigns, so too do negative claims about opponents. A common thread in much prior literature is a focus on how negative messages are used by parties to shore up support among coethnic voters in multiethnic societies—for example, by priming distributive concerns among white voters in the U.S. (Mendelberg 2001; Valentino, Hutchings, and White 2002; Huber and Lapinski 2006; Valentino, Neuner, and Vandenbroek 2018); unifying Hindu voters across caste divisions in India (Wilkinson 2004); bolstering support among Serbs in Yugoslavia (de Figueiredo and Weingast 1999; Gagnon 2004); or rallying coethnic voters in Africa (Klopp 2002; Klaus and Mitchell 2015). By contrast, I emphasize here the ways in which negative appeals are used to court voters *outside* of the parties' core ethnic strongholds. As shown in the prior chapter, the primary goal of presidential campaigning in Kenya is to reach potential fence-sitters in many ethnic communities and to convert them to one's cause. This is done both by burnishing one's own inclusive credentials and by creating doubts about the ethnic intentions of one's rivals. Thus, negative ethnic messages are used by both incumbent and challenger in an effort to demonize and discredit the other. The specific content, however, of such appeals varies across parties and election cycles, reflecting the varying opportunities and constraints in specific electoral contests.

Campaign Appeals in the 2007 Election

To recall, the 2007 election pit the incumbent president, Kibaki, against a resurgent opposition coalition headed by Odinga (see Chapter 2). At the start of the campaigns, Kibaki was in a greatly diminished position due to the collapse of the NARC coalition that brought him to power in 2002. Pre-election polls showed that 48 percent of registered voters nationally intended to vote for Odinga, relative to 39 percent for Kibaki three months before election day.[1] The uphill battle for Kibaki, however, was not merely that the ethnic arithmetic favored Odinga, who headed a larger and more diverse coalition.[2] To win, Kibaki would need to overcome widespread beliefs that his administration favored the Mt. Kenya communities—his own Kikuyu and the closely-related Meru and Embu. Data

---

[1] Survey conducted by Steadman (now Ipsos) in September 2007 (n = 2,020), about three months before the December 2007 election.

[2] See also Cheeseman (2008) and Kagwanja (2009) for overviews of the 2007 campaigns.

from a survey conducted in October 2007, roughly two months before the election, showed that outside of the Kikuyu, 61 percent of registered voters reported that they thought Kibaki would represent the interests of "only some tribes" if re-elected for a second term.[3] Thus, for Kibaki and his allies in PNU, a key task on the campaign trail was to counter perceptions of the president as an ethnic chauvinist. For Odinga, the path to victory was more straightforward: the view among many voters that Kibaki's government served the interests of "only some communities" provided an opening for a campaign built around allegations of ethnic favoritism and promises to rectify it.[4]

For Kibaki and PNU the strategy on the campaign trail was to highlight the president's performance record and the benefits delivered to members of all ethnic groups. Coming to power in 2002, Kibaki inherited a country that had been ravaged by the effects of a stagnant economy and a corrupt political elite. By the end of his first term the fruits of Kibaki's efforts were undeniable. The economy had grown at a steady clip, primary schooling was once again free for all students, and the country's infrastructure was on the mend. Even opposition supporters acknowledged these accomplishments.[5] On the campaign trail, therefore, Kibaki sought to remind voters of the myriad improvements brought about by his nationally-oriented reforms and to promise more of the same. PNU's campaign slogan, *kazi iendele* (let the work continue), reflected the party's emphasis on performance as the core of its appeal.

The following examples illustrate how PNU, and especially Kibaki, sought to highlight the national character of his accomplishments. Nearly every speech Kibaki gave included a discussion of his administration's success in expanding access to primary school (coupled with a promise to remove secondary fees if re-elected), revitalizing the economy, and improving national infrastructure.

I want to let you know that we have a plan to construct high schools everywhere. And those children that we have right now who are in primary, who are continuing with secondary school—we want all the children to go and learn in

---

[3] Survey conducted by Steadman (now Ipsos) in October 2007 (n=2,736). The question asked: "If Kibaki and his group emerges as the winners during the forthcoming General Elections, do you think he will represent equally the interest of all tribes or just some tribes only?"

[4] In interviews conducted in Nairobi, ODM officials noted that because of widespread perceptions that Kibaki had favored his own community and other allied groups, the party could not avoid addressing the issue of ethnic favoritism on the campaign trail. Yet, leaders also stressed that the party sought to avoid demonizing the broader Kikuyu community, focusing its allegations on elite actors that had benefited.

[5] Survey data from December 2007 show that among those who felt close to one of the major opposition parties, ODM or ODM-K, 44% said that Kibaki's performance on economic conditions was better or much better than under the prior president, Moi. On education, 54% gave Kibaki higher marks than Moi on cost and 37% on quality. On infrastructure ("upgrading roads and bridges"), 47% thought Kibaki had done a better job than Moi. Data is from a national survey commissioned by the Afrobarometer and Oxford University (n=1,206).

secondary school. They learn secondary one, secondary two, secondary three and four...We have money ready...Because we need such development. And we need every Kenyan wherever they are in Kenya.

(Kibaki, Malava Constituency, Western Province, Dec. 5)

We as Kenyans have decided to repair the roads going from here to everywhere. In the whole of Kenya, all regions. If you want to go to North Eastern or to the Lake Victoria areas, the Coast, or even Sudan, we are making the roads...The roads from Ethiopia to Coast and Lamu are already being constructed. That is a good thing, which will bring development in this country.

(Kibaki, Dandora, Nairobi, Oct. 31)

When I took the leadership of this nation, Kenya was very behind...Industries had collapsed and had died. If you calculate, they are now active. They have expanded and they have increased in resources, and they will continue to increase the growth of this nation...They are adding value to us, on the side of milk, maize, flowers and many other things...All of them are bringing income to all the citizens...in the whole republic of Kenya.

(Kibaki, Masii Mwala, Eastern Province, Oct. 23)

In an effort to counter PNU's credit-claiming, the opposition campaigned on a litany of alleged failures by the incumbent regime, related to constitutional reform, corruption, job creation, inflation, and over-crowded schools. A core message was that the benefits of economic growth had been confined to the small urban elite surrounding Kibaki: while a few well-connected families benefited from growth, most Kenyans remained poor and struggled with the rising cost of basic commodities. On education, one of Kibaki's centerpiece reforms, the opposition argued that the introduction of free primary education had led to over-crowded classrooms that compromised education quality.

Odinga relied on a stock formulation—"he has failed his exams"—that he repeated at nearly every rally, exemplified by the first and third quotes below. These claims were frequently paired with allegations of corruption by Kibaki and his inner circle, referencing a string of high-level scandals and Kibaki's association with the former President, Daniel arap Moi, and other members of the prior regime, as exemplified by the third quote.

Kibaki has failed. He promised a constitution in 100 days. Has he delivered? In five years he said he will finish corruption. Has he done it?...He said he will finish tribalism. Has he done it? He said the economy will grow and there will be jobs. Has it happened? Have the youths found jobs? Aren't they still at home? And the price of basic commodities has gone? (Crowd: Up) The price of paraffin has gone? (Up) The price of soap has gone? (Up) The price of bread, the price of flour, bus fare has gone? (Up) And the salary is? (Down)...That is why I am saying he has failed and he should go home and let Raila continue with the work.

(Odinga, Garsen, Coast Province, date unknown)

Yesterday you saw the outcomes of the class eight exams. They say some schools from this area have had improvements. But it's the private schools that did well. They are not the government ones, right? For what reasons? You find the children are many but teachers are few. From next month, we will hire 60,000 teachers, okay? That is so that we can raise the standards of free primary education.

(Odinga, Bungoma, Western Province, Dec. 21)

Right now he [Moi] is the Chief advisor of Mr. Kibaki on political issues. He is a professor in stealing...Recently we got a report concerning him from America...It says that Moi, together with all his sons and some of his friends, stole up to 130 billion, and they are keeping the money in foreign banks in countries like Australia, USA, and Britain. Here our children go hungry; the mothers have got no food...We have said that Kibaki failed the exams because all the people involved in corruption are with him.

(Odinga, Coast Province, Nov. 29)

Central to the opposition's campaigns were charges of ethnic favoritism and the promise to implement a devolved form of government (*majimbo* in Swahili) that would ensure more equal division of government resources across ethnic groups. ODM leaders alleged that ethnic favoritism was rampant under Kibaki's regime, affecting government appointments, as well as the distribution of funds for infrastructure, social services, and local development. In some areas these appeals were paired with claims about marginalization and discrimination, alleging that Kibaki's regime had mistreated or abused specific communities, for example, by forcibly removing Kalenjin squatters from government lands in the Mau Forest, by deporting Muslims to Somalia, or by taking land that belonged to Maasai people in the Rift Valley.

The opposition offered *majimbo* as the solution to ethnic favoritism, promising that 60 percent of government revenue would be channeled to districts, equalizing access to official funds and allowing communities to control their own development initiatives.[6] The central claim, sometimes made explicitly and sometimes in more veiled tones, was that *majimbo* would put an end to the marginalization and discrimination that groups experienced under Kibaki's leadership. Typically, *majimbo* appeals emphasized the centralization of government revenue and expenditures, arguing that allocations to localities were dependent on the discretion of senior leaders, particularly those at the Treasury, which is responsible for producing Kenya's annual budget. Odinga frequently referenced the Finance

---

[6] For background, see Anderson (2005).

Minister, Amos Kimunya, a Kikuyu appointed by Kibaki in 2006 to head the Treasury, implying that Kimunya favored Kikuyu areas at the expense of other parts of the country. No line of attack was more incendiary than ODM's repeated allegations of ethnic favoritism and its promise to implement *majimbo* as a solution. The quotes here illustrate the standard tropes used by Odinga and other ODM allies (additional examples are provided in the Online Appendix).

> When they are planning the budget, there's no one there from Kimilili [the rally location]. And from the first to the twentieth, all are from one tribe. So they only remember their own roads, hospitals, water, and electricity projects. That leads to disproportionate development...Some areas are so much better developed that you might think you are abroad, while others, you think that Livingstone hasn't discovered it yet.   (Odinga, Kimilili, Western Province, date unknown)

> This road of Garsen-Hola-Bura-Garissa...is dying here and is being resurrected in Nyeri, Kibaki's area. It's only Nyeri and Meru that have their roads constructed...Starting next year, ODM will be in government, and this road will be constructed up to Garissa.   (Odinga, Garsen, Coast Province, Nov. 29)

> All he [Kibaki] is doing is getting money from you and making roads elsewhere. He gets money for electricity and takes it elsewhere. He takes water from here and takes it elsewhere...We want to change this, and say that what belongs to Keiyo remains in Keiyo, what belongs in Marakwet remains in Marakwet, what belongs in Uasin Gishu remains in Uasin Gishu.
>   (Odinga, Keiyo South, Rift Valley Province, Dec. 16)

> The funds will come from Nairobi and then you yourselves get it and plan for it. Not that you wait for Mr. Kimunya to remember you. Mr. Kimunya does not know the roads in Garsen; he only knows those in Nyandarua [a Kikuyu area].
>   (Odinga, Garsen, Coast Province, Nov. 27)

> *Majimbo* will create equality...When you go to buy soap, oil, sugar, soda, cigarettes and even one for the road, that money is taxed, like it or not. But that money helps others. It does not cater for roads, water, or hospitals. Why do you pay here in Mombasa, and roads are being put on the other side? Is that right? We want to change that. The money should be taken from every corner and divided in an orderly way.   (Odinga, Mombasa, Coast Province, Dec. 22)

To counter these claims, PNU appealed to fears that *majimbo* would require those living outside of their "ethnic homelands" to return to their group's area, re-igniting fears of inter-communal violence sparked by prior elections in 1992 and 1997 (HRW 1993; Throup and Hornsby 1998; Kagwanja 1998; Anderson and Lochery 2008). PNU characterized Odinga and ODM as tribalists who sought to divide the country along ethnic lines, raising the specter of ethnic war if Odinga came to power. PNU portrayed Odinga as a violent and blood-thirsty leader, pointing to his involvement in a failed 1982 coup attempt and the time he spent studying in communist East Germany as evidence of his radicalism. The party also claimed that Odinga would seek retribution for past injustices if he came to office. Odinga had been imprisoned for nearly a decade as a result of his involvement in the 1982 coup attempt and his subsequent efforts to bring about a multiparty system in the late 1980s. PNU hinted that Odinga would exact revenge against the former president, Daniel arap Moi, and his ethnic community, the Kalenjin. PNU also played on the historical enmity that has at times existed between Kikuyus and Luos (e.g., Ajulu 2002), suggesting that if Odinga came to power, he would seek revenge against Kikuyus for alleged past mistreatment.

Kibaki personally showed little interest in attacking the opposition, preferring instead to emphasize his own accomplishments and promises for his second term. The first quote below provides an illustration of a rare moment when the president did criticize ODM's *majimbo* plan and the relatively mild language he used to do so. More often, it was lower-level party members in PNU who made the more pointed attacks on Odinga, as in the other quotes below.

You are asking about *majimbo*. Let him [Odinga] go and dream about *majimbo* …Every Kenyan is allowed to stay where he or she wants…You can go anywhere and buy a piece of land so that you can farm, stay, and do other things there…He is coming to destroy us, and there is no way that he will do it. You are used to staying in peace. Now you are being divided by *majimbo*. If you want to marry, you get a wife from any place you want. That is why you can buy a piece of land anywhere, build a house, and make a family. Whoever is coming up with *majimbo* is the one whose thoughts are in the past. Pray to God so that they do not win.   (Kibaki, Kisii, Nyanza Province, Oct. 15)

ODM means "one dangerous man." This man [Odinga] is dangerous. At the time when Idi Amin of Uganda took over, people came and welcomed him, clapping for him. But a few years down the line they cried. In Ethiopia, when Mariam [Mengistu Haile Mariam] took over, people clapped for him. They thought he was brave. But a few years down the line they cried. In Germany they elected Hitler. When Hitler started killing them, they couldn't believe that it was the same person they elected. So let's not elect our own Hitler in our country!
                          (Unknown, Mukurweini, Central Province, Oct. 13)

He [Odinga] wants to divide the country by introducing *majimbo*…What they are calling federalism is not federalism…What he is talking about is tribalism. The last time we talked about *majimbo*, what really happened? In Likoni people were killed. We talked of *majimbo* in Molo, and people were killed. We talked of *majimbo* in Subukia, and people were killed. And they [ODM] want to introduce something that is killing people. Kibaki says Kenya will be one country. And

when his rival [Odinga] takes over, Kenya will be divided. It will be a divided and
lost country, like Somali, Ethiopia, and Sudan.

(Mutahi Kagwe, Othaya, Central Province, date unknown)

I want to assure you that Raila Odinga...has never gone to church...People
who do not go to church are called pagans. And for them to make their gods
happy, they give them sacrifices and the sacrifice is people's blood. And the
reason why Raila has brought all these problems, the things about *majimbo*, is to
make his gods happy.   (Unknown, Laikipia, Rift Valley Province, Dec. 23)

Senior allies in both coalitions played important roles on the campaign trail. The
presidential candidates were almost always accompanied at rallies by prominent
figures from the region, as well as lower-level candidates from the area. Regional
allies help to signal the candidates' inclusive intentions both by appearing on the
party ticket and by vouching for party leaders. These allies also played the role of
hatchet men (and occasionally women), leveling some of the more bellicose
attacks against rivals.

The following examples are from ODM's senior regional leaders, including
William Ruto, who served as ODM's point person among Kalenjins in the Rift
Valley, Najib Balala, who played the same role with Coastal communities, and
other allies like Martin Shikiku (Luhya), Joseph Nyagah (Embu), and William Ole
Ntimama (Maasai).

President Kibaki has called all his fellow tribesmen to the strong ministries in
Kenya. If you look at the Ministry of Security, there are his people from the top
post to the last. Ministry of Finance, Ministry of Education, Ministry of Defense –
does Kenya belong to his tribe?...You can see their relatives are right here, and
they can't support us because they are waiting for victory so that they can grab
our lands, even our beaches. Will you allow that?

(Najib Balala, Lamu, Coast Province, date unknown)

We have nothing to do with these people from the mountain [Mt. Kenya]...
Kibaki is an enemy, an enemy, an enemy...How can he not be an enemy? He
sent home our grandchildren, saying their days are over. He burned peoples'
houses in Mau...I want to ask you, can any man from the mountain vote for
anyone else? Can he?...So, women, somebody who cannot vote for you, even if
rivers flow upstream, can you vote for him?

(William Ruto, Eldoret, Rift Valley Province, Oct. 26)

Everything we buy in our shops is taxed – match boxes, oil, sugar, bread. And all
the taxes are taken to Nairobi...All those people who deal with the collected
taxes are Kikuyus: Minister of Finance, Kimunya; his deputy, the Permanent
Secretary; the Financial Secretary; the Governor of the Central Bank – all of them
Kikuyu....There are no Luhyas in those Ministries.

(Martin Shikiku, Khayega, Western Province, Nov. 11)

Did Kibaki give [us] ministers? (Crowd: No) Did he give you ministers? (No) Permanent secretaries? (No)...Do you even have a PC or DC? You are being used badly, people of Tigania Igembe. So from now on, let's hold each other and be one thing, because I know when I am near there, my people of old Meru North and Tigania and Meru, this area of Igembe, you will be given big, big, big jobs with our forthcoming president...I want Raila to give the big seats to people of Meru North. Do you agree?   (Joseph Nyagah, Maua, Eastern Province, Oct. 28)

Raila does not want our land...Those who want to steal our land come from Mt. Kenya. He [Odinga] wants to protect it. So let's elect him so that our land will be safe...He will make sure the Maasai land remains with the Maasai.
(William Ole Ntimama, Narok South, Rift Valley Province, Dec. 4)

Content Analysis of Campaign Speeches

To explore campaign messages more systematically, the analysis draws on 117 hours of recordings obtained from rallies held by the two main parties, PNU and ODM. Because the parties spent the vast majority of their time on the campaign trail in areas primarily inhabited by ethnic groups that did not have a coethnic candidate in the presidential race, most recordings were obtained from swing regions. Comparing the distribution of recordings to the data on the location of campaign rallies from the previous chapter indicates a reasonably good correspondence between the two. Table 5.1 compares the share of recordings collected from core coethnic areas and swing areas with the share of presidential rallies held in each type of area, for each party. The table shows a relatively close match, providing assurance that the data used in this chapter is not skewed by sampling. All speeches were translated to English prior to coding.

The content analysis coding scheme uses the *individual statement* as the unit of analysis. All statements that fell into one or more of the categories described below were included. Statements varied in lengths from very short mentions of a

Table 5.1 Recording sample versus estimated number of rallies (percentages)

	PNU		ODM	
	Recordings	Rallies	Recordings	Rallies
PNU core ethnic area	15	12	2	3
ODM core ethnic area	0	0	3	5
ODM-K core ethnic area	6	12	0	0
Swing areas	79	75	95	92

Notes: Core ethnic areas for each party are defined as parliamentary constituencies in which the party leader's coethnics make up 50 percent or more of the population.

particular issue to longer statements, examples of which are shown throughout this chapter. The advantage of using a simple count, rather than coding for the length of statements, is that it provides a comparable measure that is easily applied across parties and speakers. All coded messages are categorized according to tone in order to distinguish *positive* messages about the speaker or his/her party from *negative* messages about rivals. Each message was further coded as follows.

Positive messages were coded as *particularistic* or *universal* appeals. Speakers employ a mix of both types of appeals, often with regard to the same issue area and in the same speech. For example, PNU speakers routinely emphasized *both* the national reach of education reforms and the specific benefits to local communities in the course of a single campaign event, often blurring the lines between particularism and universalism. Likewise, ODM speakers devoted considerable attention to devolution (*majimbo*), emphasizing both the national character of the proposed reforms (all regions would gain greater authority and resources) and the specific ways in which devolution would benefit the locality or ethnic community where each rally was held. Because this book makes the argument that broad, inclusive appeals are *more common* than prior literature suggests, I used a conservative coding approach that will, if anything, bias the results against this claim. I coded an appeal as particularistic if it made *any* reference to localized benefits, even if the national character of the policy or promise was also emphasized. Positive messages included both retrospective performance claims and forward-looking promises, and were coded accordingly. Each appeal was also coded by sector (e.g., education, health, economic development, etc.).

Negative messages about rival leaders and parties were coded into five categories:

o Candidate characteristics (e.g., not trustworthy, corrupt, incompetent)
o Allegations of corruption
o Performance criticisms (coded by sector)
o Allegations of ethnic favoritism, including general claims that an opponent had or would favor some groups over others
o Allegations that the opponent posed a security threat

Messages that fell outside of these defined parameters were not included. Thus, for example, I did not code greetings, get-out-the-vote appeals, messages urging voters to engage in party-line voting, and so forth. I also excluded appeals related to local races for parliamentary or councilor seats.

In total, the dataset includes 1,145 coded messages, divided relatively evenly between PNU (43%) and ODM (57%) speakers. For both parties, the largest share of coded messages came from the party's presidential nominee: for ODM, more than half (51%) of all coded messages are from Odinga, while for PNU, the proportion from Kibaki (25%) is smaller. This disparity reflects differences in the leaders' rhetorical styles: Kibaki tended to stick to a smaller number of key messages and to make shorter speeches, while Odinga often covered more ground and spoke for longer. The appendix provides details on the speakers included in the dataset for each party.

With regard to tone, the data demonstrate a marked contrast between PNU and ODM: 82 percent of PNU's messages were positive, relative to 53 percent of ODM's messages. This is consistent with the notion that PNU sought to make the election a referendum on Kibaki's first-term performance and emphasize the potential benefits that a second term would bring, while ODM was more frequently on the attack, seeking to undermine PNU's performance claims and portray the incumbent as an ethnic chauvinist.

I present the results, along with illustrative quotes, below. The goal is not to provide a comprehensive overview of campaign messages. Rather, the analysis focuses primarily on the strategies parties use to appeal to ethnic interests related to the allocation of government benefits, potential threats posed by rival leaders, and inter-group resentments. I first demonstrate that both parties opted more for universal appeals than particularistic ones. Second, I show that particularism was deployed in a universal fashion. Third, I turn to the parties' negative messages, documenting the distinct content of each party's attacks on the other.

Universalism Rules

Both parties relied more heavily on universal appeals than targeted, particularistic promises, with 65 percent and 69 percent of positive appeals being universal messages for PNU and ODM respectively.[7] Figure 5.1 plots these appeals across the main sectors mentioned in their speeches. The mix of universalism and particularism varied across sectors. For PNU, education appeals tended to emphasize universal programs, specifically the implementation of free primary education during Kibaki's first term and the promise to introduce free secondary education if re-elected. In other areas—especially infrastructure and district creation—appeals were more often localized, which is unsurprising given the nature of these goods. Likewise, for ODM, variation is observed across sectors: particularism was more common in appeals related to devolution and infrastructure and less so for general representational appeals (those that referred to the candidate's representational intentions, typically promises to represent all groups fairly) and those related to economic conditions and education.

---

[7] As the incumbent, PNU's positive appeals tended to emphasize accomplishments realized during Kibaki's first term. As the challenger, ODM's positive message mainly focused on forward-looking promises.

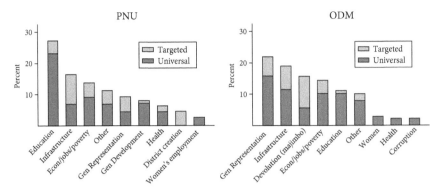

Figure 5.1 Positive appeals, by party and sector

The Universality of Particularism

While particularistic appeals were less common than universal ones, nearly a third of all positive messages for each party emphasized the local benefits of a specific proposal or accomplishment. Table 5.2, which presents the distribution of particularistic appeals by target ethnicity (inferred from the local composition of the constituencies where rallies were held), shows the broad, inclusive character of targeted appeals for both parties.[8] The use of particularistic appeals was not confined to the parties' core coethnic areas or to those areas where coalition groups were concentrated. In PNU's case, only a small share of its particularistic messages was directed at Kibaki's coethnic Kikuyu or other aligned groups like the Meru. Likewise, for ODM, a very small share was directed toward Odinga's Luo ethnic community, and while the party did offer many particularistic promises to coalition groups like the Kalenjin and Mijikenda, it also offered targeted promises to Kikuyus and Merus—groups outside its core coalition. Based on these findings, it would be hard to sustain the notion that the parties used promises of targeted transfers to galvanize support primarily among voters in their respective ethnic coalitions. Rather, the data indicate that those communities that received a larger number of particularistic appeals were simply those where the parties held a larger number of rallies.

The following quotes illustrate the types of particularistic appeals seen on the campaign trail in 2007. Though PNU tended to highlight national achievements

[8] Ethnic targeting was coded according to the ethnic composition of the parliamentary constituency where each event was held, using the ethnicity data introduced in Chapter 3. Each rally was coded according to the group that made up 50 percent or more of the constituency population (or as targeting constituencies where there was no ethnic majority). I lacked sufficient information to identify the location of two rallies.

Table 5.2 Particularistic appeals across ethnic areas

PNU	Number of messages	% of total
No majority	139	29
Luhya	79	16
Kamba	66	14
Kikuyu	55	11
Kalenjin	47	10
Meru	36	8
Maasai	30	6
Borana	10	2
Kisii	10	2
Mijikenda	8	2

ODM	Number of messages	% of total
No majority	209	33
Kalenjin	156	25
Mijikenda	64	10
Kikuyu	54	8
Meru	49	8
Luhya	46	7
Luo	30	5
Maasai	10	2
Kisii	10	2
Turkana	8	1

Notes: Ethnic areas are defined as constituencies in which the ethnic group makes up 50 percent or more of the population.

more than local accomplishments or promises, the party's appeals also emphasized localized concerns and the delivery of specific goods to particular communities.

We have expanded water industries in many parts of this region ... We are going to open many more, and we have opened six of them and this is going to develop your region, especially to get clean water in your homes – children will get clean water, which is available, mothers will not have to wake up early in the morning to look for water 10 miles ... In each region of Ukambani we have constructed all these water catchment areas ... Today we have opened four, and we shall continue. (Kibaki, Masii Mwala, Eastern Province, Oct. 23)

I have seen that this area needs a new district, so that we can bring officers and when they are near here, they will serve you better. Those employed in those offices will represent all the Government's departments so that you don't have to go all the way to Meru. There will be veterinary and agricultural officers present so that they can serve you. (Kibaki, Meru area, Dec. 10)

> I would like to point out a few things about the roads that will be constructed here at the Coast. Let me name a few. The government is improving the Likoni-Ukunda road at the cost of 340 million shillings... The contract and the designing of the Ukunda by-pass will be awarded very soon... This will be done after a week or so, and they will commence their work as soon as possible. The government is also designating Mariakani-Kinango-Kwale road for upgrading. The design is all ready, and we are prepared with the money to construct and even upgrade it to a tarmac road.   (Kibaki, Msambweni, Coast Province, Nov. 5)

One unique aspect of PNU's rallies is that as the incumbent president Kibaki was often presented with requests from lower-level politicians serving as spokesmen for their localities. Requests invariably focused on local demands, such as creating a new district, upgrading a local hospital, or paving a local road. While Kibaki tended to stick to a standard stump speech on the campaign trail, he uniformly responded positively to such requests, as in the following two examples.

> I will answer the two questions that I have been asked. First, there is this road from Sigalagala to Butere... We will look into that, and we are capable of doing that work. And we will do that work immediately, after we start the New Year. Now, the second [request]. There is one division, and two are needed – the south and north divisions. And these divisions need DOs [District Officers], and that is easy work. We will find one DO.   (Kibaki, Ikolomani, Western Province, Dec. 3)

> You have asked for a Teachers Training College... We shall be willing to help. Whenever you have started building, we shall help you. You had asked for electricity too, and we shall do that too, and that is a very important job too. Right now you have asked for a district. For now it will be impossible to grant a full district, but we can offer you a sub-district. This is because the population hasn't grown, but when it does, we will be willing to do so... About the roads, we have already started, and there are two other sections that we will build, is that okay? You have talked about electricity. I know it is very vital to this area, and we shall see to it together with the roads.   (Kibaki, Iten, Rift Valley, date unknown)

The following quotes from various senior-level PNU leaders exemplify the way in which allies stumped for the party in their own regions. In each case, the speaker addresses respondents in his own ethnic area, emphasizing specific benefits and development projects that have been realized and/or more general considerations about communal representation.

> We also thank you [Kibaki] for senior appointments of our people... Personally, you have elected me as the Chairman of Kengen [Kenya Electricity Generating Company]. Without my presence these people cannot get electricity, and these

people here are happy because they have received rural electrification, which has spread to many parts of Kitui, in areas we never expected.

(Titus Mbathi, Kitui, Eastern Province, Oct. 24)

Others are saying that we are not employing our youth, but look at the police, the national youth service, and even the teachers for our schools – 80 percent of them come from our own people.   (Moody Awori, Funyula, Western Province, Dec. 10)

I want to thank you, Mr. President, for all the things you have done for the Meru people in general ... for improving our hospitals, our dispensaries, health centers, and increasing medicine such that we now get better services. We also thank you for making many roads – renovating the road from Meru to Maua, our road from Makutano, through Embu coming to Meru going to Nanyuki, renovating and starting the construction of the Meru-Mikinduri-Maua road.

(David Mwiraria, Meru, Eastern Province, Dec. 10)

Like PNU, ODM leaders relied on particularistic appeals, emphasizing the same issues raised by PNU: education, infrastructure (especially roads), and the local economy, as in the following examples.

We are saying that we will improve our roads. From Mombasa to Nakuru to Busia will be a dual carriage way, OK? This will bring many jobs for the youth. Then electricity will be brought to the interior so that the youth can start small-scale industries.   (Odinga, Nakuru, Rift Valley Province, Nov. 4)

We as a party have a very special program here in Lamu ... I promise that next year after becoming leader, construction will start ... We will put up a road that goes around the whole of Lamu ... We want Lamu to be the second port of Kenya. We will build big roads and a railway line to Nairobi until South Sudan ... We want to open up Lamu properly and put up an airport, so that planes can leave directly to abroad ... We will ensure that the residents of Lamu will be given title deeds to own land ... We will find a way to ensure a lot of wealth is found here in Lamu, so we can end poverty.

(Odinga, Lamu, Coast Province, date unknown)

Attack Mode

As noted above, when PNU attacked its rival, the primary strategy was to stoke fears related to security threats posed by Odinga. By contrast, when ODM went on the attack, its strategy was to criticize Kibaki's performance record and to artic-ulate allegations of ethnic favoritism (see also Kagwanja and Southall 2009; Kagwanja 2009; Chege 2008; and Cussac 2008). Figure 5.2 plots the negative appeals used by each party, confirming that while there were some areas of

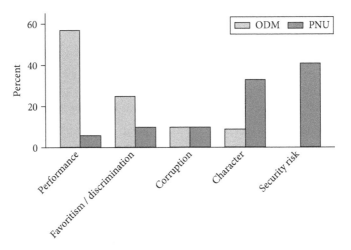

Figure 5.2 Negative appeals, by party

overlap—particularly on allegations of corruption—the parties demonized each other in distinct ways. These findings highlight the ways in which negative messages draw upon long-standing tensions but also reflect the particular context of the election and its competitors. Thus, in the 2007 race, parties drew on enduring themes (e.g., fear of "Kikuyu dominance") but also tailored messages to particular opportunities presented by the specific actors in the race and by recent political events. In ODM's case, Kibaki's failure to maintain a diverse elite coalition and his promotion of several Kikuyu leaders to prominent government positions left the president vulnerable to claims of ethnic favoritism. For its part, PNU's strategy was largely a response to the opposition's embrace of *majimbo* in the 2007 election. This suggests that while long-standing inter-group tensions provide the raw material for divisive campaigns, whether leaders play to them depends also on the particular configuration of candidates and alliances contesting the election (see also wa Gīthīnji and Holmquist 2008; Kanyinga 2009; Malik 2016).

Conclusion

This chapter draws on a large collection of campaign speeches from rallies held in the months prior to Kenya's 2007 presidential election. The analysis shows that the pursuit of a diverse electorate disincentives the use of narrow ethnic patronage appeals directed toward core supporters in the parties' ethnic strongholds. Where candidates enter the campaigns with strong coethnic support, as they often do in Kenya, the challenge is to transcend ethnic bases, not reinforce them. Universal appeals that highlight broad, national accomplishments or policy reforms are therefore preferred to narrow, targeted promises. Thus, candidates often focus on national efforts to improve infrastructure, increase access to social services, or create jobs and grow the economy. This does not mean that candidates fully eschew targeted appeals. Promises to deliver specific benefits to localities or groups are commonplace, particularly in battleground areas. Such appeals, however, are offered in a universal fashion, part of the candidates' larger efforts to bolster their support among out-group voters. The analysis also shows that candidates typically link national policy reforms with benefits realized in specific localities. In this way, the chapter suggests that the stark division between programmatic appeals that highlight national policies and particularistic appeals that offer promises to specific localities or groups is overdrawn in the literature. The data from Kenya shows that the programmatic and the particularistic often go hand-in-hand, serving as complements rather than substitutes. Finally, the chapter illustrates how parties use negative messages that demonize opponents in ethnic terms in order to heighten distrust of rivals and limit their appeal to swing voters.

6

From Electoral Politics to Policymaking

Education Reform in Kenya

This chapter examines the linkages between electoral politics and policymaking in Kenya. The imperative of courting voters from multiple ethnic groups during election campaigns creates an incentive for politicians to propose—and adopt—universal policies that distribute benefits widely. Presidential candidates win office at the national level by appealing to a diverse electorate and anticipate the need to do so in future elections. As a result, universal policies that establish an inclusive record and make distributive promises to out-group voters credible are preferable to those that concentrate benefits narrowly.

To demonstrate the electoral value of universal policies, this chapter examines the education sector. Education languished in Kenya during the 1980s and 1990s, as in much of Africa, due to chronic budget deficits that led to cuts in service provision. Since the return to multiparty politics, presidential aspirants have made education reform central to their electoral appeals, and successive leaders have implemented a number of reforms—most notably the reintroduction of free primary education (FPE)—that have dramatically increased access to formal education among children from all ethnic groups. On the campaign trail, incumbents tout their accomplishments in the education sector, highlighting the inclusive nature of universal policies, while challengers compete by offering equally expansive reform proposals.

The empirical analysis in this chapter focuses on primary-school enrollments and school construction for the 45 years from 1970 to 2015, a period that spans both single-party and multiparty eras. Education is particularly well suited for this analysis because education policies have well-documented distributive effects across ethnic communities in Africa and because education represents one of the largest budgetary items for African governments.[1] Given the history of ethnic favoritism in the education sector during Kenya's single-party era (Franck and Rainer 2012; Kramon and Posner 2016), I expect that if the argument is correct, the data should provide evidence of favoritism during the single-party era but not after the transition to multiparty politics.

---

[1] In Kenya the education sector has been among the top budgetary items in every year since independence, receiving on average 17 percent of the annual government budget between 1963 and 2015 (*Statistical Abstracts*, various years).

Multiethnic Democracy: The Logic of Elections and Policymaking in Kenya. Jeremy Horowitz, Oxford University Press.
© Jeremy Horowitz 2022. DOI: 10.1093/oso/9780198852735.003.0006

The analysis proceeds in three steps. First, I show that after accounting for other relevant factors, the gross primary enrollment rate in districts where the president's ethnic group makes up a majority was 9–13 percentage points higher than in other parts of the country during the single-party era but that enrollment rates equalized after the transition to multiparty competition. Second, the chapter shows that this narrowing of the enrollment gap can be attributed to government policies, particularly the adoption of free primary education, rather than other economic and social factors. Third, the chapter shows that the main results also hold for school inputs, measured by primary-school construction. While data on school construction is more coarse, the findings support the conclusion that multiparty electoral competition in Kenya is associated with more inclusive policies, offering evidence of ethnic favoritism during the single-party era but not after.

These findings contribute to a growing literature that examines whether the transition to democracy tempers ethnic favoritism in diverse societies. The results in this chapter differ from two recent studies by Franck and Rainer (2012) and Kramon and Posner (2016), both of which show the persistence of ethnic favoritism in the education sector after the transition to democracy across Africa and in Kenya. The difference likely stems from the type of data used in these prior studies, both of which rely on cohort analysis of individual-level survey data that is not well suited for tracking the short-term effects of policy changes like FPE. While the data used in this chapter has its own limitations, it allows for an examination of the more immediate effects of policies implemented in the multiparty era.[2] This chapter also offers a distinct account of how democracy alters patterns of ethnic favoritism. A prominent study of road expenditures in Kenya by Burgess et al. (2015) argues that democracy reduces ethnic favoritism by constraining the president's discretionary powers. I contend that executives in Kenya, like much of Africa, retain considerable discretion. This chapter proposes instead that democracy attenuates ethnic favoritism because electoral competition increases the value of universal policies.

This chapter does not assert that Kenyan leaders have implemented universally-targeted education reforms *solely* because they seek to reap electoral

---

[2] Franck and Rainer (2012) and Kramon and Posner (2016) draw on data from DHS surveys conducted at regular intervals in Kenya since 1989. While these surveys have many advantages for tracking education outcomes over time, one limitation is that there is a significant temporal lag that stems from the sampling strategy, which includes women 15–59 and a random sample of their partners. The most recent DHS dataset from Kenya used in both studies was conducted in 2008/09. The youngest respondents in that survey would have been 10 years old in 2003 when the free primary education (FPE) reforms discussed in this chapter were implemented, four years above the typical starting age for primary school. As a result, the DHS data contain few respondents who would have been able to benefit from FPE at the time the reform was adopted, making it poorly suited for tracking the short-term effects of FPE. DHS surveys also do not record whether respondents attended public or private schools, which have become increasingly prevalent in Kenya since the early 2000s (Nishimura and Yamano 2013).

rewards. Like post-independence leaders across Africa, Kenya's modern leaders may favor expanding educational access simply because they seek to improve the well-being of citizens across the country, without regard to ethnic backgrounds. Moreover, given many African countries' dependence on foreign aid, donors— who prioritize need-based allocation criteria over political considerations—may restrict distributive targeting (Dreher et al. 2019; D'Arcy 2013; though see Jablonski 2014). Thus, this book does not propose a mono-causal explanation of policymaking. Rather, the goal of this chapter is to demonstrate that multiparty elections generate an incentive for the adoption of inclusive policies in a context where electoral competition is more often thought to reinforce patterns of ethnic patronage.

The chapter is organized as follows. The next section develops the argument linking electoral strategies to universal policies. Next, it documents a close connection between campaign strategies and education reforms in Kenya's multiparty era. It then describes the data and presents the results. Finally, to bolster confidence in the proposed explanation, the chapter addresses alternative explanations related to institutional reforms, executive constraints, and especially donor pressure.

The Electoral Benefits of Universal Policies

Elected leaders face a choice between using government resources to reward their existing supporters, court potential new supporters, or both. The standard view in the ethnic politics literature is that the priority is to reward the base: politicians in diverse societies are expected to serve as faithful representatives of communal interests and are naturally bound to engage in ethnic patronage. The literature traces the incentive to "favor one's own" variously to elite preferences that stem from in-group attachments (Ekeh 1975; Hyden 1980, 1983; Berman 1998; Ake 1993a), social pressure within ethnic communities (Bates 1983; Berman 1998), and electoral incentives (Horowitz 1985, 1991; Rabushka and Shepsle 1972; Reilly 2001; Reilly and Reynolds 1999; Fearon 1999). Consistent with these approaches, several recent studies from Africa and Kenya in particular provide evidence of ethnic favoritism in various sectors, including education and health provision (Franck and Rainer 2012; Kramon and Posner 2016), roads (Barkan and Chege 1989; Burgess et al. 2015), foreign aid targeting (Jablonski 2014), and local development spending (Harris and Posner 2019).

There is, however, less agreement about whether the transition to multiparty competition alters patterns of ethnic favoritism. Core mobilization models propose that parties are better off channeling rewards to the party faithful, reinforcing ethno-partisan alignments (e.g., Horowitz 1985, 1991). This approach echoes more general core-mobilization models found in the broader distributive politics literature (e.g., Cox and McCubbins 1986; Nichter 2008; Diaz-Cayeros et al. 2016). Swing-targeting models, including the approach developed in this book, suggest that electoral incentives lead incumbents to direct resources toward voters who are up-for-grabs rather than toward their core bases (e.g., Lindbeck and Weibull 1987). While core mobilization models remain dominant in the literature on Africa, a smaller body of research supports the swing-targeting approach (e.g., Casey 2015).

The argument outlined here starts from the assumption that neither core-mobilization nor swing-targeting models are universally applicable. Rather, the task is to link theoretical expectations to the specific context under study through a careful examination of electoral dynamics. Thus, in Kenya, where presidential contenders concentrate their campaign efforts on reaching a diverse set of swing voters—rather than focusing their energies on turning out voters in their ethnic bases—the swing-targeting approach should have greater relevance.

How does the pursuit of a diverse electorate at election time affect the policy choices made by incumbent leaders? The simple proposition offered here is that where campaigning entails appealing to voters from a broad set of ethnic communities, universal policies offer a useful strategy for building and maintaining electoral support. A key challenge faced by candidates in multiethnic democracies is that voters may view promises to share resources across group lines as cheap talk, especially where voters have come to expect that politicians will favor their own groups, as in Kenya (Posner 2005). Politicians work to overcome credibility deficits with out-group voters by adopting universal policies that demonstrate their commitment to inclusive resource distribution schemes. Universal policies establish clear, unambiguous rules for deciding how resources are allocated, typically through formula-based programs or new entitlements.

Universal policies also allow incumbents to make good on campaign promises and avoid punishments for failing to do so. As shown in the previous chapter, inclusive promises are a mainstay of campaigning in Kenya. Presidential candidates routinely pledge to implement nationally-oriented programs that improve infrastructure, expand public services, and increase economic opportunities. Election winners face the prospect of being punished next time around if they fail to follow through on these promises (Stokes 2001; Tavits 2007; Stasavage 2005b). Given the broad-based nature of many campaign appeals in Kenya, universal policies should be an important aspect of any leader's subsequent policy agenda.

Universal policies may also increase support for the incumbent party *between* election rounds (Harding 2020; Harding and Stasavage 2013; Travaglianti 2017; Dionne and Horowitz 2016; Ferree and Horowitz 2010). Control of the policy-making agenda means that incumbents are uniquely positioned to use policy choices to alter voters' beliefs about which party will best represent the interests of their ethnic communities. Observing that the incumbent has built roads in one's area—or improved schools, drilled water wells, expanded the electricity grid, and so forth—may lead voters to update their beliefs about the incumbent's favoritism intentions in advantageous ways and help to inoculate incumbents against the inevitable charges of ethnic favoritism from opponents on the campaign trail.

Electoral Competition and Education Reform in Kenya

Education reform provides an illustration of how the imperative of cultivating cross-ethnic support affects policy choices in Kenya.[3] As an opposition candidate in the 1997 election, Mwai Kibaki pledged to remove primary school fees during an unsuccessful presidential bid, a commitment reiterated in the run-up to his victory in the 2002 election. This promise was part of the candidate's broader effort to boost his support outside his narrow ethnic support base. As documented in earlier chapters, Kibaki struggled in 1992 and 1997 to extend his reach beyond coethnic Kikuyus and the closely-related Meru and Embu. Thus, in the 2002 race Kibaki and his allies aggressively courted a broad and diverse coalition and adopted a campaign platform that would have wide appeal across ethnic communities. Given the focus on winning over out-group voters, FPE was an attractive strategy since, as a universal entitlement, it would provide benefits to voters in all groups. Moreover, the FPE pledge in 2002 provided a useful contrast with Kibaki's main rival, Uhuru Kenyatta, who as Moi's hand-picked successor represented the old order under which service delivery had deteriorated (Oketch and Rolleston 2007). While Kibaki repeatedly asserted that the Kenyan tax base was sufficient to pay for FPE, Kenyatta claimed that adopting free primary education was not feasible given the country's economic struggles.[4]

After winning the 2002 election, Kibaki quickly made good on the pledge, pushing through FPE in time for the 2003 school year which was set to begin just days after the election. While the FPE roll-out was criticized for having been implemented without adequate preparation and for contributing to overcrowding, the public response to FPE was overwhelmingly positive.[5] Survey data collected at the end of Kibaki's first term shows that approval of his government's performance on education was both high in absolute terms and relative to other

[3] This follows a general pattern of education reform across Africa. Harding and Stasavage (2013) provide evidence suggesting that multiparty elections create incentives for politicians to implement policies that expand access.

[4] Nation Correspondent. "NARC Pledges to Use Taxes in Alleviation of Poverty." *The Nation.* Dec. 3, 2002. Nation Team. "Education Won't Be Free, Says Uhuru." *The Nation.* Dec. 7, 2002, p. 3. Vincent Bartoo. "Uhuru Campaigns in Nandi, Says Narc Manifesto Impossible to Achieve." *East African Standard.* Dec. 7, 2002.

[5] There was much criticism at the time regarding insufficient planning to accommodate the influx of new students (e.g., World Bank 2009; Nicolai, Prizzon, and Hine 2014; Mukudi 2004).

areas.[6] Table 6.1 shows that the Kibaki government received low marks on areas that Kenyans routinely cite as their top priorities: unemployment, economic reform, corruption, and crime and insecurity.[7] However, on education, 85 percent were either satisfied or very satisfied, well above the mean for the other 13 items included on the survey (39%). Even opposition supporters, who were generally critical of Kibaki's performance in other areas, gave the president high marks on education: 77 percent of those who registered an intention to vote for opposition candidates in 2007 approved of Kibaki's performance in education. Moreover, as shown in Table 6.2, among those who rated Kibaki's performance in fulfilling his 2002 campaign pledges positively (62% of the sample), education reform was by far the most frequently cited reason for the positive assessment, with 62 percent of those giving a positive response mentioning education.[8]

Table 6.1 Approval ratings for Kibaki's government, September 2007 (percentages)

	All respondents	Incumbent supporters	Opposition supporters
Education	85	97	77
Health management	73	88	63
Prisons reform	67	82	58
Public transport	49	68	39
Agriculture sector	49	70	35
Economic reform	43	70	26
Terrorism	33	49	25
Crime and insecurity	31	52	17
Land reform and ownership	30	49	20
Corruption	28	53	12
Housing, slum & squatter settlements	21	36	12
Unemployment	17	30	9
Constitutional review process	17	33	7

Notes: Survey data come from a nationally-representative poll (n=2,020) conducted by Steadman (now Ipsos) in September 2007. The table shows the percentage of respondents who were "very satisfied" or "somewhat satisfied" with the government's handling of each issue. Incumbent supporters are defined as those who stated an intention to vote for Kibaki in the 2007 election; opposition supporters are those who stated an intention to vote for Odinga or Musyoka.

[6] Survey data come from a nationally-representative poll (n=2,020) conducted by Steadman (now Ipsos) in September 2007. The question asked, "Please tell me how satisfied you are with the way the government is dealing with each of the issues I read out." Answer options were: very satisfied, somewhat satisfied, somewhat dissatisfied, and very dissatisfied.

[7] The most frequent responses to a question that asked, "In your opinion, what are the most important problems facing Kenya today?" were unemployment (24%), poverty (16%), insecurity (12%), corruption (11%), and inflation (7%).

[8] The question was: "Would you rate the President's performance in fulfilling the campaign pledges he made to Kenyan people as very good, good, poor, or very poor? Why do you say so?" [Up to 3 responses.] Whether these positive assessments of Kibaki's education reforms helped him at the polls in 2007 remains an open question. See Harding and Stasavage (2013) for a discussion.

Table 6.2 Reason(s) cited for saying Kibaki kept his 2002 campaign promises (percentages)

Free / improved education	62
Constituency Development Fund	20
Improved economy	17
Improved infrastructure	16
Improved health care	14
Good governance	13

Notes: Survey data come from a nationally-representative poll (n=2,020) conducted by Steadman (now Ipsos) in September 2007. Table shows the top reasons provided by respondents who rated the president as "very good" or "good" in fulfilling prior campaign pledges.

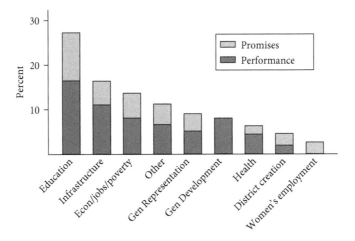

Figure 6.1 PNU campaign appeals by sector, 2007 election

On the campaign trail for re-election in 2007, Kibaki made education a central part of his appeal to voters. As noted in the prior chapter, Kibaki was fighting an uphill battle in 2007 to dispel views that his administration favored the Kikuyu and other allied communities. Against this backdrop, education reform—which benefited voters in all ethnic communities—proved especially useful. Content analysis of speeches at major campaign rallies shows that education was the top issue area mentioned on the campaign trail by Kibaki and other senior PNU leaders in 2007 (see prior chapter for a description of the campaign speech data). Figure 6.1, which disaggregates all positive appeals made at rallies by retrospective claims about performance and prospective promises, shows that for Kibaki and his allies more than a quarter of all positive appeals related to education, well above other sectors like infrastructure or the economy.

Kibaki and his allies in PNU made it a point to convey the inclusive nature of education reforms, noting that children in all parts of the country benefited from free primary education and promising that if re-elected he would expand access to secondary education in his second term. For example, at a rally in Iten (a Kalenjin area), he said, "I want our children to go to secondary school from Form 1 up to Form 4...We want the Marakwets [a Kalenjin sub-tribe] to be the same with all Kenyans...We want all the children to be the same in Kenya."[9] In Malava (a Luhya area), Kibaki similarly stressed the broad reach of his education reform agenda: "Those children that we have right now that are in primary who are continuing with secondary school, we want all the children to go and learn in secondary school...Because we need such development, and we need every Kenyan wherever they are in Kenya."

In subsequent elections, universal education reforms remained a common feature of electoral campaigns. In the 2013 election, Uhuru Kenyatta, the eventual winner, made the ambitious promise to provide incoming primary students with solar-powered laptops, continuing the program until all primary students were equipped nationwide.[10] While the Kenyatta government subsequently struggled to make good on this promise, by the end of Kenyatta's first term in 2017, the government claimed to have distributed nearly a million tablet computers to students at more than 14,000 primary schools (about 40% of all public primaries).[11] During Kenyatta's re-election bid in 2017, he promised that secondary education would be made free after the election.[12] Not to be outdone, the main opposition leader, Raila Odinga, also promised free secondary education, claiming that if elected, he would implement the program sooner than Kenyatta.[13]

In sum, since the transition to multiparty competition, presidential aspirants in Kenya—both opposition and incumbent—have used education reform as a strategy for gaining electoral support, highlighting the ethnically-inclusive nature of universal policy initiatives. Does campaign rhetoric translate into concrete benefits that are widely shared? Or are such high-minded appeals merely false promises?

Data and Methods

To test whether the transition to multiparty competition altered patterns of ethnic favoritism in Kenya's education sector, I examine two indicators:

---

[9] Excerpts are from recordings of campaign rallies collected by the Kenya National Commission on Human Rights. See Chapter 5 for details.

[10] Ngirachu, John. "Jubilee Unveils Its Manifesto with Land Reform Plan." *Daily Nation*. Feb. 4, 2013, p. 3.

[11] Source: https://www.delivery.go.ke/flagship/dlp. Accessed July 13, 2017.

[12] Lucas Barasa and Kalume Kazungu. "Uhuru Lifts Night Curfew in Lamu, Promises Free Primary Education." *The Nation* (online). May 25, 2017.

[13] Benson Amadala. "I'll Transform Kenya in 90 Days, Says Raila Odinga." *The Nation* (online). June 4, 2017.

primary-level enrollment and primary school construction. The data for both spans the single-party era (1970–1991) and the multiparty period (1992–2015). The tests compare district-level outcomes for each variable between the president's *coethnic districts*—those in which the president's ethnic group makes up a majority of the population—and other parts of the country. *Coethnic districts* are defined as Kikuyu-majority districts during the presidencies of Jomo Kenyatta (1970–1978), Mwai Kibaki (2003–2013), and Uhuru Kenyatta (2013–2015), and Kalenjin-majority districts during the presidency of Daniel arap Moi (1979–2002). Data on the ethnic composition of districts comes from the 1962 census, compiled by Burgess et al. (2015).[14]

The first set of analyses focuses on primary enrollment. I examine district-level gross primary enrollment rates, defined as total annual enrollment divided by the school-aged population at the district level.[15] Because district boundaries change over time, I aggregate the enrollment data to the original 41 districts that existed at independence in 1963.[16] The main analysis covers the period from 1970 to 2015.[17] The enrollment data comes from annual *Statistical Abstracts* produced by the Kenya National Bureau of Statistics (KNBS). Annual estimates of the school-age population at the district level are generated from decennial census reports with linear interpolation between census years.[18]

To explore the effects of having a coethnic in the presidency on gross primary enrollments, I employ a difference-in-difference framework, using a linear model in which the dependent variable is gross primary enrollment measured annually at the district level from 1970 to 2015. The main specification is as follows:

$$enrollment_{dt} = \gamma_d + \alpha_t + \beta_1(coethnic\ district_{dt}) + \beta_2(multiparty_t)$$
$$+\beta_3(coethnic\ district_{dt} \times multiparty_t) + \theta(X_{d1963} \times [t - 1963]) + u_{dt},$$

where *enrollment*$_{dt}$ is a measure of gross primary enrollment in district d at time t. *Coethnic district*$_{dt}$ is an indicator for districts in which the president's ethnic group makes up a majority during each year. *Multiparty*$_t$ is an indicator for years in which opposition parties are allowed to compete in presidential elections

---

[14] I date the start of Moi's presidency as 1979, the first full year he was in office (he assumed the presidency following Kenyatta's death in August 1978).

[15] There are both practical and conceptual reasons for using gross enrollment rather than net enrollment, which is the total enrollment of primary-age children divided by the school-aged population. Practically, calculating net enrollment is more difficult because it requires information about the share of enrolled students who are in the appropriate age bracket, data that is not publicly available in Kenya. By contrast, gross enrollment can be calculated with information on aggregate enrollment, which is available. Conceptually, gross enrollment is also preferable because I seek to examine overall changes in enrollment, not limited to students who fall in the primary-age bracket.

[16] In 2010 Kenya's districts were replaced by counties; to simplify the presentation, I use "districts" throughout the chapter to refer to the unit of analysis.

[17] Prior to 1970 the *Statistical Abstracts* present the data at the County Council level, which reduces the number of annual observations.

[18] Kenya employed a 7-6-3 educational system until 1985, when it switched to 8-4-4. The target age for primary school was 6–12 prior to 1985 and 6–13 thereafter.

(1992 and after). The interaction term, *coethnic district*$_{dt}$ x *multiparty*$_t$, tests whether the enrollment gap between coethnic districts and others declines after the transition to multiparty competition. X_{d1963} is a vector of district-level demographic and economic variables (population, area, urbanization rate, earnings, employment, and cash crops) from government sources compiled by Burgess et al. (2015). Because time-series data for these variables is not available, I follow Burgess et al. (2015) and use baseline measures taken from around the time of independence in 1963 and interact each with a linear time trend $[t - 1963]$ to allow their impact to vary over time. Models include district and year fixed effects $(\gamma_d + a_t)$ and cluster standard errors at the district level.

There are three main limitations in the data on primary enrollments. First, because the analysis seeks to draw inferences about individuals from aggregate data, ecological fallacy is a concern. The problem comes from the fact that while districts in Kenya are relatively homogeneous, they are not perfectly so. In more diverse areas, there is no way to know whether changes in enrollment rates over time are shared equally by the various groups in the district or concentrated in some communities. While there is no simple way to account for this problem with the available data, I draw on individual-level survey data for the period after 1992 to corroborate the findings regarding the effects of free primary education on enrollment, the main mechanism through which multiparty electoral competition affected enrollment (see Online Appendix). Second, because the number of districts (counties after 2010) changes over time, constructing a panel requires matching new units to the prior units. Fortunately, new districts after 1990 were created by carving out divisions from the original set of 41 districts, making it possible to aggregate the data back to the original units. The 47 counties that were created in 2010 also nest within the original 41 districts. Third, the ethnic composition of districts may change over time. The research design relies on the fact that the ethnic composition of the main areas of interest—Kikuyu-majority and Kalenjin-majority districts—remains relatively stable over time (see appendix).

Results

To explore whether ethnic communities benefit from having a coethnic president in power, I first plot in Figure 6.2(a) enrollment rates in Kikuyu-majority, Kalenjin-majority, and other districts. For much of the period, gross enrollment rates exceed 1, which occurs when aggregate enrollment is greater than the number of primary school-age children.[19] Enrollment rates were higher in

---

[19] This happens in Kenya both because a large number of students routinely fail to advance to the next grade at the end of each year and because students outside the primary-age range enroll in primary school (World Bank 2009). Available data show that repetition rates are relatively high in Kenya. In 1999 and 2003 the primary repetition rates were 13.2% and 9.8% respectively (World Bank 2009, p. 140). Data from

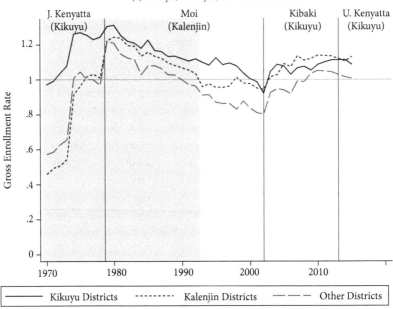

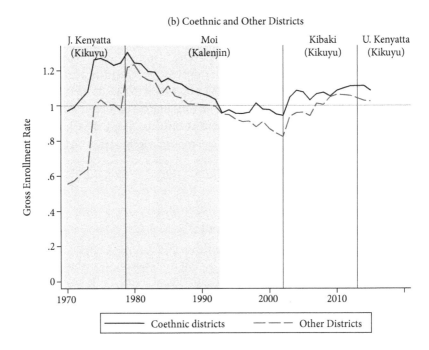

Figure 6.2 Primary school gross enrollment rates, 1970–2015

Notes: The single-party era is shaded, and vertical lines indicate presidential transitions. Gross enrollment rates are defined as total enrollment / primary school-age children (based on decennial census data, interpolated for intercensal years). Figure (a) shows enrollment rates for Kikuyu-majority districts, Kalenjin-majority districts, and all others. Figure (b) shows enrollment rates for the president's coethnic districts (Kikuyu for 1970–1978 and 2003–2015; Kalenjin for 1979–2002) relative to others.

Kikuyu-majority districts than in other areas for most of the period under study, until about 2005. Enrollment rates in Kalenjin-majority districts were initially lower than in other areas but caught up by the late 1970s and were then above other areas (though not Kikuyu areas) for much of the following decades. The effects of government policies related to school fees are evident: sharp enrollment increases are observed when school fees were removed or reduced in 1974, 1978, and 2003, while declines are observed following the re-introduction of fees in the mid-1980s.[20]

Figure 6.2(b) shows the key outcome of interest: presidents' coethnic districts relative to all others across the same time period. The figure indicates that enrollment rates in coethnic districts were above other districts in most years. However, this gap should not necessarily be taken as evidence that groups benefit from having a coethnic in power. One might expect that enrollment rates for groups that had a coethnic in the presidency, particularly the Kikuyu, would potentially be higher throughout the post-independence era as a result of greater access to education during the colonial period, higher levels of economic development, higher population density, proximity to Nairobi, and other group-level factors.[21] I therefore turn to a regression framework to test whether the enrollment gap between coethnic districts and others persists after accounting for various group-level differences.

Results are presented in Table 6.3. Model 1 shows that after accounting for district and year fixed effects, gross enrollment was 13 percentage points higher in coethnic districts during the single-party era.[22] The gap disappears after the introduction of multiparty elections, as shown by the sum of the coefficient on *coethnic district* and the interaction term *coethnic district x multiparty period*. These results are robust to the inclusion of demographic and economic controls in Model 2 and to the inclusion of district-level time trends in Model 3 (though this model cannot be estimated with other covariates).[23]

While these specifications cannot address all possible confounds, the plausibility of a causal interpretation is bolstered by the inclusion of district-level time trends in model 3, which allays concerns that the results could be a function of distinct growth trends across districts unrelated to having a coethnic leader in

the 2005/06 Kenya Integrated Household Budget Survey (n=59,096) show that in 2005/06, 36 percent of those enrolled in public primary schools were not of primary-school age (6 to 13). Of primary-attenders who were not of primary age, most (77.1%) were in the 14–17 age range.

[20] For an overview on education policy in Kenya, see Eshiwani (1993), Bogonko (1992), and Oketch and Rolleston (2007).

[21] See Alwy and Schech (2004) on the persistence of ethnic inequalities in education.

[22] Similar results based on individual-level data are interpreted as evidence of favoritism in Franck and Rainer (2012), Kramon and Posner (2016), and Li (2018). Simson and Green (2020) challenge this interpretation on methodological grounds.

[23] Additional tests in the Online Appendix show that these results are also robust to expanding the time period to 1965–2015 and aggregating the data to the 34 geographic units contained in the pre-1970 *Statistical Abstracts*.

Table 6.3 Gross primary enrollment rates, 1970–2015

	(1)	(2)	(3)
Coethnic district	0.13***	0.13***	0.09***
	(0.03)	(0.02)	(0.03)
Multiparty period	0.53***	0.63***	−0.28***
	(0.04)	(0.07)	(0.02)
Coethnic district x multiparty period	−0.19***	−0.18***	−0.10***
	(0.05)	(0.05)	(0.03)
Coethnic district + (coethnic district x	−0.06	−0.05	−0.01
multiparty period)	(0.03)	(0.04)	(0.03)
Observations	1,840	1,840	1,840
Year and district fixed effects	Yes	Yes	Yes
(controls) x trend	No	Yes	No
District time trends	No	No	Yes

Notes: Ordinary least squares (OLS) regression on annual district-year gross primary enrollment (number of enrolled students / school-aged population) panel dataset of 41 districts for the period of 1970–2015. Coethnic district is equal to 1 for districts in which the president's ethnic group makes up 50 percent or more of the population in each year. Multiparty is equal to 1 for years in which opposition parties are allowed to compete in presidential elections (1992–2015). Column 2 includes initial controls interacted with a time trend. These controls are district population (1962), district size (square km), urbanization rate (1962), district formal total earnings (1966), formal employment (1963), and value of cash crop exports (1965). Robust standard errors clustered at district level in parentheses.
***p<0.01, **p<0.05, *p<0.1.

power (see Simson and Green 2020 on this point), and by the results in the next section that draw on data from a narrower time frame for which a richer set of time-varying controls is available to explore the effects of FPE.

Free Primary Education and the Equalization of Access

The results presented so far indicate that the primary enrollment gap between districts where presidents' groups are concentrated and other parts of the country narrowed after the transition to democracy. Can these changes be attributed to government policy choices rather than other time-varying factors? In this section, I provide evidence that they can by examining the effects of the introduction of free primary education by President Kibaki in 2003. While all ethnic groups benefited from FPE, the benefits were disproportionately large outside of the president's own ethnic community. These effects helped to close persistent inter-group disparities in primary education access that have existed in Kenya since the colonial era (Alwy and Schech 2004).

To explore the effects of FPE, Figure 6.3 plots trends in gross primary enrollment rates for the 10-year period before and after its adoption in early 2003. The figure plots these data for Kikuyu-majority districts, relative to other districts.

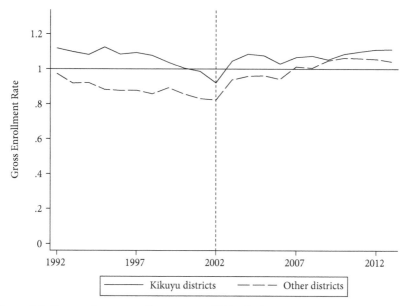

Figure 6.3 Gross primary enrollment rates, 1992–2013

It shows that enrollments were declining during the ten years prior to the reintroduction of FPE both in Kikuyu-majority districts and elsewhere. The adoption of FPE produced a large, immediate increase in enrollment in both areas. And, over the longer term, FPE appears to have restored enrollments in Kikuyu areas to their level from the early 1990s, while in other areas FPE produced a sustained increase over prior rates.

To explore the effects of the 2003 fee removal more carefully, I estimate a difference-in-difference model of gross primary enrollment rates using district-year observations for a narrower window of five years before and after the 2003 transition to FPE (1998–2007). The model includes an indicator variable, *FPE*, that takes a value of 1 for years following the re-introduction of FPE (2003–2007), an indicator for Kikuyu-majority districts, and the interaction of the two. The narrow time-frame for the analysis helps to limit concerns about time-varying confounds. Nonetheless, I include district-level controls for economic conditions (total earnings, wage employment, and a proxy for total economic activity taken from satellite readings of nighttime light).[24] I also include controls for school

---

[24] Wage employment data measures the number of people employed in the formal sector (including casual and part-time workers but not self-employed or those receiving irregular wages). These data are from annual *Statistical Abstracts*. Earnings data (the total in Kenyan Shillings of formal sector wages) are measured annually (from *Statistical Abstracts*) and extrapolated for years after 2006, when disaggregated data is no longer reported. Nighttime light data come from the National Oceanic and Atmospheric Administration (NOAA). Luminosity is measured as the average nighttime brightness of pixels by district, measured annually.

inputs: a district-level measure of the number of primary schools (interpolated for years when data is not available), and annual Constituency Development Fund (CDF) expenditures on education and school bursaries.[25] Finally, the model includes demographic controls for population size (interpolated from decennial census data), area (in sq. km.), population density, and an indicator for the eight districts that are categorized as Arid or Semi-Arid Lands (ASAL). The model includes random effects to account for time-invariant district-level factors that might affect enrollments. The model includes a time trend and clusters standard errors by district.

The results are shown in Table 6.4. Model 1 indicates that FPE produced no discernable increase in average annual enrollment rates in Kikuyu-majority districts (as shown by the sum of the coefficients for *FPE* and its interaction with *Kikuyu district*) for the five years after its introduction relative to the five years

Table 6.4 Gross primary enrollment rates, 1998–2007

	(1)	(2)	(3)
FPE	0.13***	0.12***	0.11***
	(0.02)	(0.02)	(0.02)
Kikuyu district	0.27***	0.17***	0.10
	(0.08)	(0.06)	(0.06)
FPE x Kikuyu district	−0.09**	−0.11*	−0.09**
	(0.04)	(0.05)	(0.04)
FPE + (FPE x Kikuyu district)	0.04	0.01	0.02
	(0.04)	(0.05)	(0.04)
Controls	No	Yes	Yes
District random effects	No	No	Yes
Observations	410	400	400

Notes: Ordinary least squares (OLS) regression on annual district-year gross primary enrollment (number of enrolled students / school-aged population) panel dataset of 41 districts for the period of 1998–2007. FPE is equal to 1 for years in which primary education was free (2003–2007). Kikuyu district is equal to 1 for districts in which Kikuyus make up 50 percent or more of the population. Column 2 includes controls for: economic conditions (total earnings, wage employment, and a proxy for total economic activity based on the NOAA nighttime lights images); school inputs (the number of primary schools (interpolated for years when data is not available), Constituency Development Fund (CDF) expenditures on education, and school bursaries); and demographic factors (population size (interpolated from decennial census data), area (in sq. km.), population density, and an indicator variable for the eight districts that are categorized as Arid or Semi-Arid Lands (ASAL)). Column 3 includes district random effects. The sample size in columns 2 and 3 drops to 400 due to missing data on primary schools for Nairobi district. Robust standard errors clustered at district level in parentheses. ***p<0.01, **p<0.05, *p<0.1.

[25] The number of schools comes from District Development Plans (renamed County Integrated Development Plans in 2013), produced every three to five years from 1974 to 2013, interpolated linearly for years in which plans were not produced. Data on CDF allocations for education and bursaries come from annual CDF reports.

before. However, in non-Kikuyu areas average annual gross enrollment rates were 13 percentage points higher after the introduction of FPE than before. Model 2 shows that these results are robust to the inclusion of the controls described above, and Model 3 shows that they are robust to the inclusion of district random effects. I also show that the main findings hold when I vary the timeframe for analysis or when I use individual-level data rather than district-level enrollments (see Online Appendix). Additional analysis in the Online Appendix suggests that the benefits of FPE were lower in Kikuyu-majority areas relative to other parts of the country due to enduring socio-economic differences: because Kikuyus have traditionally been better off on average than members of other communities, school fees prior to 2003 likely posed less of a barrier for Kikuyu families.

These aggregate enrollment shifts led to disproportionately large increases in government transfers for primary education to non-coethnic areas, relative to Kikuyu-majority districts. To fund the anticipated spike in enrollments from the adoption of FPE in 2003, the government instituted a capitation grant of 1,020 Kenyan Shillings (about US$13 at 2003 exchange rates) per primary student that was allocated to district authorities (Nicolai, Prizzon, and Hine 2014). While modest, this funding approach tied resource allocations to enrollments. In absolute terms, the introduction of FPE led to an increase of 44,761 more students a year per district for the five years after FPE relative to the five prior years in non-Kikuyu areas, implying an average annual transfer of an additional $570,702 per district in non-Kikuyu areas. The average annual enrollment increase in Kikuyu districts was 20,551, resulting in an average of $262,025 in new funding per year. In per capita terms, this represented an annual increase of $0.73 per person in non-Kikuyu districts, relative to $0.32 in Kikuyu-majority districts.

School Construction

This section provides additional evidence that policies related to primary education changed after the introduction of multiparty elections by examining school construction. These results are important for two reasons. First, observing the same pattern for school inputs as for enrollment rates increases confidence that a meaningful policy shift occurred. Second, prior work on ethnic favoritism in Kenya's education sector (Kramon and Posner 2016) points to the preferential allocation of funds for school construction as the primary mechanism that explains why students from the president's ethnic group benefitted from having a coethnic in power in the decades after independence.

Data on school construction come from District Development Plans (DDPs) issued every three to five years since 1974 (renamed County Integrated Development Plans after 2010). The DDPs provide information on the number of primary schools at the district level at the time each plan was created.[26] Nationally, the number of government-operated primary schools increased from 5,631 to 19,326 during the period under study (1974–2013), an average increase of nearly 350 new schools per year.

Figure 6.4(a) plots the number of primary schools per 1,000 residents for Kikuyu-majority, Kalenjin-majority, and other districts. The figure shows that the number of schools per capita was relatively similar across ethnic areas in the first year for which data is available (1974). The number of schools per capita then rose in Kalenjin-majority areas, starting in the latter portion of Jomo Kenyatta's presidency and accelerating in the early years of Moi's presidency. The per capita number of primary schools declined throughout much of this period in Kikuyu-majority areas and remained stable in other areas. Since the reintroduction of multiparty competition in 1992, the gap between Kikuyu-majority and other areas narrowed, while the gap between Kalenjin-majority and all other areas persisted and then grew in the most recent period for which data is available. Figure 6.4(b) contrasts the president's coethnic districts with all others. It shows a gap between the president's ethnic area and other parts of the country resulting from the higher number of schools in Kalenjin-majority areas throughout Moi's presidency, a gap that was larger during the single-party era than the multiparty period.

While these data may be suggestive of favoritism in the allocation of funds for new school construction, particularly during the early years of the Moi presidency, as noted above, there are important regional differences in population density, ease of travel, and other factors that might imply some regions should require more schools per capita to serve the local population effectively. Thus, to test whether groups benefit from having a coethnic president, I again employ a regression framework to account for non-political differences that might affect school construction.

The dependent variable for this analysis is the number of schools per 1,000 residents in each district-year. The key independent variable, *coethnic district*, again takes a value of 1 for districts where the president's ethnic group made up a majority of the population at the time of each DDP.[27] I interact *coethnic district* with an indicator for the *multiparty period*. The primary limitation with this data is that the number of districts increases after 1990, and due to missing observations in later years, the data cannot be aggregated to the original 41 districts. Unfortunately, covariates are not available at the varying levels of aggregation in the years after 1990. Therefore, instead of accounting for possible confounds

---

[26] A small number of reports (30 of about 540, roughly 6%) could not be located. After 1989 the number of districts increased in Kenya. In 2010, districts were replaced by counties and the number was reduced to 47. Data for Nairobi is not available in most years (district development plans were not created).

[27] Ethnic coding is based on the original 41 districts. Thus, for example, any district that split off from a Kikuyu-majority district after 1989 is coded as Kikuyu-majority.

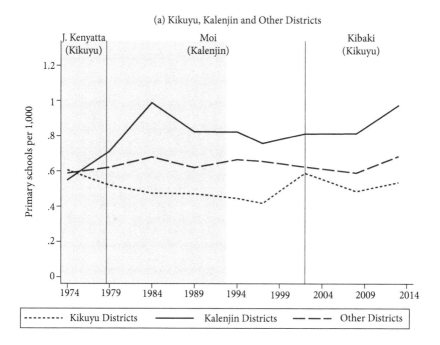

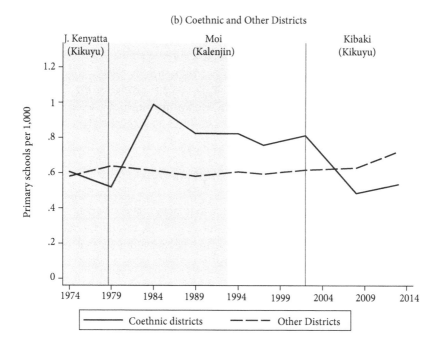

Figure 6.4 Primary schools per 1,000 residents, 1974–2013

Notes: The single-party era is shaded, and vertical lines indicate presidential transitions. Figure (a) shows the number of primary schools per 1,000 residents for Kikuyu-majority districts, Kalenjin-majority districts, and all others. Figure (b) shows the number of primary schools per 1,000 residents for the president's coethnic districts (Kikuyu for 1970–1978 and 2003–2015; Kalenjin for 1979–2002) relative to others.

Table 6.5 Primary schools per 1,000 residents, 1974–2013

Coethnic district	0.14**
	(0.06)
Multiparty period	0.17
	(0.10)
Coethnic district x multiparty period	−0.12**
	(0.06)
Coethnic district + (Coethnic district x multiparty)	0.01
	(0.03)
Observations	489
Year and district fixed effects	Yes

Notes: Ordinary least squares (OLS) regression on number of schools per 1,000 residents with district-level observations in 1974, 1979, 1984, 1989, 1994, 1997, 2002, 2009, and 2013. Coethnic district is equal to 1 for districts in which the president's ethnic group makes up 50 percent or more of the population in each year. Multiparty is equal to 1 for years in which opposition parties are allowed to compete in presidential elections (1992–2013). Robust standard errors clustered at district level in parentheses.

***p<0.01, **p<0.05, *p<0.1.

directly, I include district and year fixed effects to capture time-invariant district characteristics and over-time shocks to the overall number of schools per capita.[28]

Results shown in Table 6.5 provide evidence of favoritism during the single-party era but not the multiparty period. Model 1 indicates that during the single-party era, coethnic districts had on average 0.14 more public primaries per 1,000 respondents than other districts.[29] This is a substantively meaningful difference, equal to an additional 73 primaries per district on average across the time period. The results show that the disparity between coethnic districts and others disappears after 1992.[30]

Alternative Explanations

While the findings are consistent with the argument that the pursuit of a diverse electorate leads incumbents to adopt inclusive policies, several alternative explanations merit consideration. I examine the possible influence of institutions,

---

[28] District fixed effects are based on the original 41 districts.

[29] These results are similar to those in Kramon and Posner (2016). When I restrict the analysis to match the time period covered in their study (1974 to 2002), the results are nearly identical. The authors find that having a coethnic in power is associated with 0.17 more schools per 1,000 residents on average, while I find that the disparity is 0.16. The slight difference is likely because the sample used here is larger (320 vs. 232 district-years).

[30] These results are robust to an alternative specification that uses district weights to account for the increasing number of districts after 1989.

donor pressure, and executive constraints, demonstrating that these rival explanations cannot account for policy shifts in the multiparty era.

Institutions. Two institutional reforms are worth exploring. First, from 2007 to 2013 Kenya was governed by a power-sharing arrangement that brought together the incumbent president, Kibaki, and his main rival, Odinga, in a grand coalition. Second, in 2010 a new constitution was adopted that devolved substantial power and resources to lower-level governmental units (Kramon and Posner 2011). Given the prominence of institutional approaches in the literature, it is worth examining whether the outcomes observed here can be attributed to features of Kenya's constitutional framework. There is some evidence that the power-sharing regime may have affected patterns of resource allocation (Jablonski 2014), and others have noted that devolution has improved public service access (Kanyinga 2016). However, the major initiative related to primary school enrollment, the introduction of FPE in 2003, was implemented prior to the power-sharing period or the 2010 constitutional reforms. And, as noted above, the effects of FPE were immediate and sustained throughout the years before power-sharing or devolution. Moreover, subsequent reforms, including subsidized secondary education, have been promised by incumbent leaders, though the power-sharing arrangement ended with the 2013 election. Thus, neither power-sharing nor devolution can account for the initiation or expansion of universal education reforms in the multiparty era. And, as detailed in Chapter 4, the broad-based campaigns observed in Kenya's multiparty era cannot be attributed to electoral rules, suggesting that institutions hold little explanatory power in this case.

Donor Pressure. A second alternative explanation is that donor pressure may be responsible for the move toward inclusive education policies since the 1990s. Kenya has long been favored by foreign donors, who have at times used aid leverage to encourage policy changes, particularly during the early 1990s when Western donors played a role in pushing for democratic reforms (Brown 2007). Moreover, donors, including the World Bank, UNICEF, and several bilateral aid missions, were instrumental in supporting the transition to free primary education, particularly in the years immediately after its introduction (World Bank 2009). In addition, there is some evidence that restrictions placed on World Bank funds make it difficult for leaders in Africa to target Bank-funded projects for political purposes (Dreher et al. 2019).

However, it is important to recall that the initial pledge to introduce FPE was made by an opposition candidate, not an incumbent leader, suggesting that donor pressure probably had little influence, at least on the initiation of FPE. Second, donor funds make up a relatively small share of the education budget in Kenya, contributing between 2 percent to 7 percent of the sectoral budget in the years immediately before and after the introduction of FPE (Colclough and Webb 2010). Given this, it seems unlikely that government leaders would adopt and maintain the policy solely to placate foreign donors. Finally, based on dozens of interviews with government representatives, donor agencies, and NGOs in Kenya, Colclough and Webb (2010) conclude that with regard to education reform, the interests of the donors and the government coincided after Kibaki came to power but that the government was largely responsible for formulating key policies, with the donors playing a limited support role. While it is clear that donor funding was important in sustaining education reforms, there is no evidence that donor pressure led Kibaki or subsequent leaders to initiate major reforms or to prioritize increasing access rather than adopting other types of initiatives aimed at quality improvements (Colclough and Webb 2012).

Executive Constraints. A third alternative argument from Burgess et al. (2015) questions not whether democracy reduces ethnic favoritism but the mechanism by which it does so. The authors propose that democracy increases constraints on the executive that restrict the potential for discretionary targeting of government resources across ethnic communities. They argue that in Kenya, "flows of information, a vocal civil society and an independent parliament all severely curtail the ability of the executive to blatantly discriminate between different districts in choosing where to place roads projects" (p. 1846). There is, however, reason to doubt this explanation. First, while there is no denying that media and civil society groups now operate more freely, substantial barriers remain that make it difficult for such actors to monitor government favoritism. The government does not publish data on budgetary allocations by sector across districts, and obtaining systematic information on outcomes like road construction, education provision, or other sectors is difficult, limiting the ability of civil society groups or the media to track expenditures.

Second, though the legislature has become more independent since 1992 (Barkan 2008a; Opalo 2014), effective oversight of the executive requires both formal authorities and the incentive to constrain the executive (Tsebelis 2002). However, throughout the multiparty era, the incumbent president in Kenya has always enjoyed majority support in parliament, weakening the incentives of Members of Parliament (MPs) to impose restrictions on the executive. Indeed, the president's allies in parliament are precisely those who would stand to benefit from ethnic favoritism. MPs in Kenya, and other similar settings, must demonstrate their capacity to bring home "development" to their constituencies (Barkan 1995; Lindberg 2003). Parliamentary elections in Kenya are highly competitive, often at the nominations stage if not in the general election, incentivizing sitting MPs to work hard to bring home resources in order to enhance their re-election prospects. Thus, targeting resources toward the Kikuyu homeland during Kibaki's time in office, for example, would greatly aid lower-level Kikuyu politicians seeking to claim credit for delivering desired local benefits. Many legislators, therefore, have an incentive to keep patterns of ethnic favoritism in place, not to restrain the president's use of discretionary authority. In addition, the informal powers that accrue to the president by virtue of his control over appointments, patronage allocations, and ballot access limit the ability of legislative actors to constrain the executive despite changes in the formal rules, calling into question whether changing patterns in policymaking can be attributed to legislative oversight (Mueller 2008).

Finally, analysis of budgetary oversight suggests that despite the substantial authorities that now rest with the Kenyan legislature, the body plays little substantive role in the budgeting process. A report by the International Budget Partnership (2015, p. 13), for example, found that:

> The National Assembly has considerable powers under the 2010 constitution. On balance, however, it is not yet using those powers to manage the process and ensure Treasury compliance, nor to make substantive inputs in areas that do not affect its own interests. Its overall contribution to the budget-making process is limited in terms of both the breadth and quality of deliberation over trade-offs in the budget, and the substance of the changes made.

In sum, there is little evidence that the transition to multiparty competition was accompanied by a substantive shift in executive constraints. By contrast, it is clear that the transition did increase the importance of appealing to voters in a diverse array of ethnic communities during elections, raising the political value of delivering widely-shared benefits.

Conclusion

This chapter shows that where electoral politics entails the competition for voters arrayed across many ethnic communities, the transition to democracy can encourage leaders to adopt inclusive policies in place of those that target resources to ethnic clientele. In linking electoral competition to policymaking, this chapter argues that the need to court out-group voters in multiple ethnic communities makes universal policies an attractive strategy. An observable implication is that in sectors where ethnic favoritism has been the norm during non-democratic periods, we should observe that the adoption of multiparty elections is associated with a reduction in favoritism. Data on primary education enrollments and school construction in Kenya support these claims.

To conclude, I address several questions related to the generalizability of these findings and the limitations of the analysis. First, one might argue that because primary enrollment rates among Kikuyus were above those for other communities at the start of the multiparty era, education reforms introduced by a Kikuyu president would inevitably benefit non-coethnics disproportionately. While this is true for certain kinds of reforms, such as FPE, it is important to remember that elected officials could have pursued alternative policies that would have concentrated benefits on core ethnic supporters. For example, Kibaki's government might have focused on expanding scholarships that could be allocated with discretion, or targeting funding for school construction or additional teachers to particular areas—strategies that were common during the single-party era. What is striking, then, is not only that subsequent governments in the multiparty era have opted for universal entitlements but that in doing so they have eschewed the targeted strategies of the past.

Second, one might question whether the findings reported in this chapter represent a meaningful shift in policymaking, given that the analysis is based on a single sector. While there are still only a handful of quantitative studies of ethnic favoritism in Kenya, it is clear that the trends documented here are part of a broader movement away from particularistic policymaking. As noted in the introduction to this book, policy-makers since the transition to multiparty competition have introduced several formula-based programs and constitutional reforms that have restricted leaders' ability to engage in discretionary targeting, including the Local Areas Transfer Fund (LATF), the Constituency Development Fund (CDF), and provisions in Kenya's 2010 constitution that call for a minimum of 15 percent of national revenue to be transferred to county governments. In addition, studies from other sectors provide evidence of ethnic favoritism during the single-party era but not under multiparty competition (Burgess et al. 2015; Klaus and Hassan 2020), though the broader literature is divided on this score.

This book does not argue that all forms of ethno-partisan favoritism have (or will) disappear in Kenya or other similar settings after the transition to multiparty politics. Favoritism has many sources—some that are beyond the electoral arena. Leaders may "favor their own" because communal attachments and identities bind more strongly within groups than across them (Ekeh 1975; Berman 1998). They may face social pressures from coethnics and co-partisans to channel resources toward core groups (Bates 1983). They may also fear that the failure to reward the partisan base will lead to its erosion over time (Diaz-Cayeros, Estévez, and Magaloni 2016). Thus, the electoral incentives outlined in this book are only one influence on patronage decisions, and may not in all cases prove decisive. Moreover, this book focuses on presidential elections and national-level dynamics. Lower-level actors—such as Governors, Members of Parliament, and local bureaucrats—may have divergent incentives, given differences in the ethnic composition and competitiveness of local vs. national elections. Recent work by Harris and Posner (2019), for example, shows that ethnic favoritism at lower levels remains pervasive in Kenya (see also Hoffman et al. 2015). Thus, the move toward more inclusive policymaking at the national level may coincide with the persistence of ethnic favoritism at lower levels.

Third, a related question is whether the education reforms discussed in this chapter can be attributed to the transition to competitive politics rather than the preferences of particular leaders, especially Kibaki. Answering this question is difficult for the obvious reason that Kenya has only had a small number of leaders in the multiparty era. Yet, it is noteworthy that at least with regard to education reform, nearly all major candidates in recent elections have embraced broad, inclusive reforms and incumbents—including Kenyatta who as a candidate in 2002 argued that Kenya could not afford free primary education—have routinely campaigned on promises of national reforms that expand access among all groups. While it is possible that these various leaders all favor education access for reasons unrelated to electoral calculations, more likely is that presidential aspirants have come to appreciate the electoral benefits of inclusive policies regardless of whether they prioritized such policies previously.[31]

Finally, this chapter points to the 2003 introduction of FPE as the principal education reform in the multiparty period. Yet, as noted, similar reforms were implemented in 1974 and 1978 during the single-party era, potentially casting doubt on whether electoral competition can explain why incumbents opt for universal policies in the education sector. While these prior experiences demonstrate that democracy is not the only route to inclusive education reforms, there is good reason to think that recent reforms will be more sustainable since they are reinforced by electoral incentives. Evidence from across the continent (and globally) confirms that democratic competition creates incentives to expand access to primary education and increase budgetary allocations for education, especially at the primary level, and that these reforms can produce electoral benefits (Ansell 2008; Stasavage 2005a, 2005b; Harding and Stasavage 2014; Travaglianti 2017). These broader findings are relevant to Kenya's experience. Earlier reforms in the 1970s proved vulnerable when the country's economy eroded in the 1980s. At the helm of a stable single-party system, the country's political leaders, and the president in particular, were relatively isolated from whatever popular discontent may have arisen from the reintroduction of school fees during the 1980s. The same cannot be said of Kenya's current leaders, who, given the intensity of electoral competition, have strong incentives to maintain the gains made since 2003 and to expand both access and quality over time. Thus, while democracy clearly is not required for reform, electoral competition alters incentives in ways that encourage the initiation and maintenance of inclusive programs.

---

[31] See Stasavage (2005b) for an example from Uganda of how electoral competition may alter leaders' priorities, encouraging the adoption of universal reforms.

7

Electoral Competition and Policymaking in Ghana

To demonstrate that the swing-targeting approach developed in prior chapters has relevance beyond Kenya, this chapter turns to Ghana, a country that makes for an especially useful comparative case. While Ghana is similar to Kenya in many respects, the electoral context differs in three important ways: the party system is more institutionalized; elite coalitions are less central to electoral competition; and ethnicity is often thought to be less salient to voters. This chapter shows that despite these critical differences, the swing-targeting approach offers insight into patterns of electoral competition and policymaking in Ghana. It offers support for the book's central propositions—namely, that core and swing can be conceptualized in ethnic terms, that the pursuit of swing voters leads parties to opt for broad campaign strategies, and that incumbents select universal policies in order to facilitate their efforts to court out-group voters beyond their core ethnic strongholds.

The defining feature of Ghana's electoral landscape since the return to a multiparty system in 1992 is that competition in presidential elections centers around two main parties—the National Democratic Congress (NDC) and the New Patriotic Party (NPP)—each of which draws its strongest support from a distinct ethnic base. The NDC can reliably count on near-universal support from Ewe voters (about 13% of the population), while the NPP routinely garners high levels of support from the Ashanti (15%) and other closely related groups like the Akyem (3%) and Akuapem (3%) that are part of the larger Akan linguistic group. The durability of these linkages means that parties enter campaigns secure in the knowledge that they can count on backing in their respective strongholds. Other communities are more divided and fluid in their electoral orientations. It is these groups that decide electoral outcomes, and competition for voters in them is at the center of campaign politics. As in Kenya, parties work to convey their inclusive intentions on the campaign trail, and incumbents use policy choices to signal their commitment to the equitable allocation of government resources, a strategy designed above all to aid in the pursuit of voters outside their ethnic strongholds.

This chapter first describes Ghana's electoral landscape and demonstrates that ethnicity plays an important role in structuring core and swing. Though ethnicity is not the only factor that comes into play when voters make electoral choices, it

Multiethnic Democracy: The Logic of Elections and Policymaking in Kenya. Jeremy Horowitz, Oxford University Press.
© Jeremy Horowitz 2022. DOI: 10.1093/oso/9780198852735.003.0007

would be difficult to explain enduring features of Ghana's partisan landscape without taking account of how ethnicity influences voter behavior. The chapter then shows that the leading parties adopt broad-based electoral strategies aimed at currying favor with voters in multiple ethnic groups, animated above all by the competition for voters in swing communities that are less tightly linked to either of the two main parties. Finally, it demonstrates that electoral calculations incentivize the adoption of universal public policies. In tracing through the connection between electoral strategies and policymaking, the chapter focuses on the NPP's rise to power in the 1990s and the health sector reforms party leaders pursued after winning the presidency in 2000.

Core and Swing in Ghana's Fourth Republic

Ghana returned to multiparty politics in the early 1990s after a long period of single-party rule. The transition to the Fourth Republic, as the post-1992 constitutional order is known, was presided over by the incumbent president, Jerry Rawlings, the larger-than-life figure who many credit with turning Ghana around after an extended period of misrule and economic decline in the 1960s and 1970s. Rawlings, a former air force lieutenant who seized power in military coups in 1979 and again in 1981, ruled as the head of a military regime—the Provisional National Defense Council (PNDC)—until the restoration of multiparty competition in 1992. Rawlings won the first two multiparty presidential elections in 1992 and 1996 as the leader of the NDC, the party he founded in advance of the 1992 contest. The first alternation in power in the multiparty era occurred in 2000 when the NPP's candidate, John Kufuor, prevailed over Rawlings' designated successor John Atta Mills. The NDC and the NPP have alternated in office since, with the NPP winning reelection in 2004, the NDC returning to power in 2008 and 2012, and the NPP winning in 2016. This pattern of alternation, a rarity in Africa, has won Ghana high praise for its democratic credentials (Gyimah-Boadi 2009; Abdulai and Crawford 2010).

Ethno-partisan alignments in the Fourth Republic are well documented. As noted, the NDC holds a near-monopoly on Ewe voters concentrated in the Volta Region. The NPP draws its strongest support from Ashanti (also Asante) voters clustered in Ashanti Region and other Akan-speaking groups like the Akyem and Akuapem. Other ethnic communities have been more split, particularly in recent elections, and have exhibited greater fluidity across elections. This is true of Akan-speaking groups like the Brong and Fante, as well as northern groups like the Mole-Dagbani, the Gurma, and the Grusi. Thus, Nugent (2001b, p. 3) notes that while the Ashanti and Ewe have consistently been allied with distinct parties, "in the rest of the country the historic pattern has been one of shifting patterns of allegiance."

To study voter alignments, scholars typically rely on district-level election returns. Because ethnic communities are geographically concentrated, these data allow for a rough estimation of bloc voting across Ghana's major ethnic communities. Here I draw on two types of data to explore ethno-partisan linkages with greater precision. First, I employ ecological inference (EI) tools to estimate voting behavior for Ghana's larger ethnic communities using district-level election returns and census data (details of the EI methods are provided in the appendix).[1] Second, I draw on data from a national exit poll conducted during the 2008 election (Hoffman and Long 2013). While both types of data suffer from various limitations, the results improve upon analysis that relies solely on district-level election returns, allowing for a more careful examination of ethno-partisan ties in the Fourth Republic.

Figure 7.1 plots support for the NPP in presidential elections from 1992 to 2016 using the EI data. I generate estimates for the major ethno-linguistic categories employed in the 2000 census. Studies of voter behavior in Ghana often treat Akan-speaking groups as a single community. This, however, obscures important variation in the strength of ethno-partisan attachments within Akan sub-groups. I therefore disaggregate the Akan into the Ashanti, Fante, and Brong and a residual "Akan-other" category that includes several smaller sub-groups.

The EI estimates show that there is considerable variation in the extent to which ethnic groups are durably linked to either of the major parties and in the

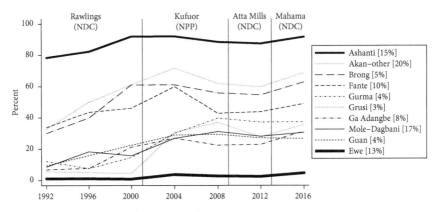

Figure 7.1 NPP support (EI estimates), 1992–2016

Notes: Estimates are based on ecological inference methods described in the appendix. Population figures from the 2000 census are shown in brackets in the legend. Vertical lines show presidential transitions.

---

[1] I generate estimates for the major ethno-linguistic categories listed in the 2000 census. While these categories encompass many smaller sub-groups, it is not possible to estimate voting trends for sub-groups given the limitations of census data, which is only disaggregated to the district level. The one exception is the Akan, which, because of the relatively large size of some sub-groups, can be partially disaggregated.

magnitude of group-level shifts over time. Bloc voting among the Ashanti and Ewe has been nearly uniform since 1992, while members of other groups have been more divided and more prone to shift partisan orientations from one election to the next. Major Akan-speaking groups, especially the Brong and Fante, have been fairly evenly divided between the major parties throughout the Fourth Republic, and support within these groups has shifted significantly across elections. Other major groups, including those concentrated in the North (Mole-Dagbani, Gurma, and Grusi) and the Ga Adangbe concentrated in and around the capital city, Accra, initially leaned toward the NDC at the start of the multiparty period. Over time, support for the NPP has increased among all of these groups, resulting in a two-party system in which national support is more evenly divided across the two major parties.

The results in Figure 7.1 corroborate standard accounts of elections since 1992. The data show that Rawlings enjoyed wide backing across ethnic communities in the 1992 and 1996 elections; that the NPP's victory in 2000 was fueled by growing support from all major "unaligned" groups; and that the NDC's return to power in 2008 was the result of waning enthusiasm for the NPP among voters in these communities (Nugent 2001a; Jockers, Kohnert and Nugent 2010; Anebo 1997; Gyimah-Boadi 2001; Jeffries and Thomas 1993).

Survey data from the 2008 exit poll in Table 7.1 tell a similar story, but allow for a more disaggregated view of alignments among Akan-speaking groups. The NPP's strongest support in 2008 came from the Ashanti, Akyem, and to a lesser extent the Akuapem, while for the NDC the strongest support—as always—was

Table 7.1 Vote choice by ethnic group, 2008 election (percentages)

Group	Population	Sample	NPP	NDC	Other	Refused
Akan, of which …	49.1	2,121	67.3	21.9	6.5	4.3
Ashanti	14.7	755	82.9	10.5	4.1	2.5
Akyem	3.4	164	75.0	15.2	3.7	6.1
Akuapem	2.9	141	66.7	19.2	7.8	6.4
Brong	4.9	99	57.6	31.3	7.1	4.0
Fante	9.8	409	51.1	36.7	9.3	2.9
Other	13.4	553	57.5	27.7	8.1	6.7
Ga-Adangbe	8.0	239	32.2	52.3	9.6	5.9
Ewe	12.7	507	17.8	72.4	6.3	3.6
Guan	4.4	83	36.1	45.8	10.8	7.2
Gurma	3.9	129	36.4	49.6	9.3	4.7
Mole-Dagbani	16.5	585	35.0	54.9	6.8	3.3
Grusi	2.8	109	48.6	36.7	11.9	1.8
Mande	1.1	128	32.0	53.9	10.2	3.9
Other	1.5	121	40.5	44.6	5.0	9.9

Notes: Vote choice data is from the 2008 exit poll (see Hoffman and Long 2013). Population size is from the 2000 census.

from the Ewe. Other Akan-speaking groups, including the Brong and Fante, leaned toward the NPP in 2008 but were less united in their support than the Ashanti and Akuapem. Likewise, many other groups, including those concentrated in the North and the Ga Adangbe in the South, leaned toward the NDC but were considerably more divided than the Ewe.

This brief examination of ethno-partisan alignments shows that the electoral landscape in Ghana mirrors the Kenyan case: the major presidential contenders draw strength from distinct ethnic strongholds while voters in other groups are more divided and fluid in their alignments. There are, however, three differences that should be emphasized.

First, core and swing in Ghana do not depend on the ethnic identities of the main presidential candidates to the same extent as they do in Kenya. Ghana's more institutionalized party system means that the parties structure electoral competition more so than in Kenya. In Ghana, voters seeking to divine which party will better represent their ethnic interests look to party labels for information about how prospective candidates are likely to behave in office—which groups they will favor and which groups they will neglect if elected, as in institutionalized party systems elsewhere in Africa (see Ferree (2011) on South Africa). Given the long-standing association between each party and its core ethnic base, voters associate the parties first and foremost with their respective cores. Thus, Asante and Gyimah-Boadi (2004, p. 33) note that "the two main parties, the NDC and NPP, are largely perceived as Ewe and Ashanti/Akan based respectively." Using survey data, Fridy (2007, p. 300) confirms that voters distinguish the parties based on these perceived ethnic affiliations: "More than 70 percent of respondents identified the NPP as most popular amongst Akan speakers in the Ashanti region, and nearly 60 percent identified the NDC as most popular amongst Ewe speakers. Across the three constituencies surveyed, far more voters are taking this ethnocentric information about the parties behind the polling station security screens than anything resembling socioeconomic distinctions." These perceptions of the parties as representatives of distinct ethnic communities remain in place even when the parties put forward presidential candidates who are not from their respective core groups.

Yet, while Ghana's parties play a more important role in structuring electoral alignments than their counterparts in Kenya, the distinction should not be overdrawn. As in Kenya, the perceptions Ghanaian voters hold about the parties' ethnic affiliations have much to do with the ethnic identities of the parties' top leaders, past and present. For many voters, the NDC is inextricably linked to its founder, Jerry Rawlings. Though Rawlings was careful to cultivate an image as an inclusive leader while in power, the NDC is seen by many as a vehicle first and foremost for the advancement of Rawlings' ethnic group, the Ewe (Chazan 1982; Nugent 2001b; Asante and Gyimah-Boadi 2004). These perception—correct or not—remain cemented in voters' minds, shaping beliefs about the NDC even as

Rawlings' influence in the party has waned and it has put forward non-Ewe candidates for the presidency in all races since 2000.[2] Nearly a decade after Rawlings stepped down from the presidency, Arthur (2009, p. 51) notes that "many Ghanaians believe that the leaders of the PNDC, which became the NDC and ruled Ghana for nineteen years, were predominantly Ewe people. The perception of Ewe dominance has created the impression, rightly or wrongly, that the NDC belongs to the Ewe ethnic group" (see also Jockers, Kohnert, and Nugent 2010). This connection persists in part because Rawlings continues to be an active presence in the NDC, notwithstanding occasional tensions with subsequent party leaders (Kelly and Bening 2013).

Similarly, views of the NPP as an "Ashanti party" have much to do with the ethnic identity of its top leaders, especially its presidential candidates. In the 1992 election, the first after the return to multiparty politics, the newly-founded NPP chose Albert Adu Boahen, a prominent historian of Ashanti and Akyem lineage, as its nominee.[3] In the 1996, 2000, and 2004 elections, the party nominated John Kufuor (also Ashanti), a longtime political actor who had competed unsuccessfully for the party's nomination in 1992. After Kufuor's two terms in office from 2000 to 2008, the NPP chose Nana Akufo-Addo (Akyem, a closely-related Akan sub-group to the Ashanti) as the party's flag-bearer in the 2008, 2012, and 2016 elections. In short, while parties are more institutionalized in Ghana, their strength in distinct ethnic strongholds has much to do with the ethnic identities of their top leaders, as in Kenya.

A second difference is that elite coalition building does not shape ethno-partisan alignments in Ghana as fully as it does in Kenya. Again, however, the distinction is a difference of degree and not of kind. In Ghana, as in Kenya, elite alliance building is a central strategy office-seekers employ in the effort to bolster their support among out-group voters. One merely needs to look at the vice-presidential candidates chosen by the NDC and NPP since 1992 to appreciate this point. It is no coincidence that, as shown in Table 7.2, both major parties have chosen running mates *only from northern ethnic groups or the Fante*—communities routinely characterized as swing groups.

As an example, consider Rawlings' choice of John Atta Mills, a Fante (also Fanti), as his running mate in 1996. Jeffries (1998, p. 193) notes that "part of the reasoning lay...in the calculation that the NDC needed desperately to win the Western and Central Regions...Mills could help to swing the vote partly by virtue of being a Fanti." The Fante are the second largest Akan-speaking group, after the Ashanti, and have a long history of tension with the Ashanti dating

---

[2] The NDC's presidential candidate in 2000, 2004, and 2008, John Atta Mills, was Fante. The party's candidate in 2012 and 2016, John Mahama, was Gonja, a sub-group of the Guan, a predominantly Muslim group from the North that is spread throughout the country. See Table 7.2.
[3] Boahen is of mixed heritage: his father is Akyem and his mother is Ashanti (Elischer 2013, p. 146).

Table 7.2 Ethnicity of presidential and vice-presidential candidates, NDC and NPP

Year	Party	Presidential candidate	Running mate
1992	NDC	J. Rawlings (Ewe)	K. Nkensen Arkaah (Fante)
1996	NDC	J. Rawlings (Ewe)	J. Atta Mills (Fante)
2000	NDC	J. Atta Mills (Fante)	M. Amidu (Northerner, Builsa (Mole-Dagbani))
2004	NDC	J. Atta Mills (Fante)	M. Mumuni (Northerner, Dagomba (Mole-Dagbani))
2008	NDC	J. Atta Mills (Fante)	J. Mahama (Northerner, Gonja)
2012	NDC	J. Mahama (Northerner, Gonja)	K. Amissah-Arthur (Fante)
2016	NDC	J. Mahama (Northerner, Gonja)	K. Amissah-Arthur (Fante)
1992	NPP	A. Adu Boahen (Ashanti/Akyem)	I. Alhassan (Northerner, Dagomba (Mole-Dagbani))
1996	NPP	J. Kufuor (Ashanti)	K. Nkensen Arkaah (Fante)
2000	NPP	J. Kufuor (Ashanti)	A. Mahama (Northerner, Dagomba (Mole-Dagbani))
2004	NPP	J. Kufuor (Ashanti)	A. Mahama (Northerner, Dagomba (Mole-Dagbani))
2008	NPP	N. Akufo-Addo (Akyem)	M. Bawumia (Northerner, Mamprusi (Mole-Dagbani))
2012	NPP	N. Akufo-Addo (Akyem)	M. Bawumia (Northerner, Mamprusi (Mole-Dagbani))
2016	NPP	N. Akufo-Addo (Akyem)	M. Bawumia (Northerner, Mamprusi (Mole-Dagbani))

Notes: Data compiled by author.

back to the colonial era (Shumway 2014), making Fante voters a prime target for efforts at persuasion and conversion.

The selection of northerners as running mates also reflects the importance of elite alliance building as an electoral strategy. Thus, after becoming the NDC's presidential nominee in 2000, Atta Mills chose a succession of northern running mates: Martin Amindu in 2000, Muhammad Mumuni in 2004, and John Mahama in 2008. Mahama, who ascended to the presidency upon Atta Mills' death in 2012, maintained this pattern of ethnic balancing by choosing a Fante running mate (Kwesi Amissah-Arthur) in 2012 and 2016. For the NPP, the pattern is equally clear: the party, which has nominated only Ashanti and Akyem (or mixed) candidates since 1992, has always chosen a northerner for the vice-presidential slot, save for 1996, when coalition politics led to the selection of a Fante leader (see Bob-Milliar 2012b). What makes northerners such attractive running mates? The answer, Iddi (2016, p. 64) notes, is that "the conventional wisdom in Ghana's elections is that northerners are likely to vote for a party that has a northerner on its presidential ticket."

Third, Ghana is often described as a country where ethnicity is less salient to voters than in Kenya, raising questions about whether core and swing can usefully be understood in ethnic terms. Accounts of voter behavior in Ghana routinely emphasize non-ethnic influences. Scholars stress the unique history of Ghana's two ideological traditions: the liberal tradition established by J. B. Danquah and Kofi Busia, independence-era political leaders who played important roles in founding some of Ghana's first major political parties, and the more radical/populist tradition established by Kwame Nkrumah, Ghana's first president (Whitfield 2009; Anebo 1997; Obeng-Odoom 2013). Others point to urban/rural divides (Nugent 2001a; Lindberg and Morrison 2005), performance evaluations (Hoffman and Long 2013), and economic interests (Kim 2018) to explain partisan orientations. Research that examines swing voters using micro-level survey data argues that performance evaluations define core and swing more so than ethnic identities (Lindberg and Morrison 2005; Weghorst and Lindberg 2013). Much of this literature notes the association between ethnicity and voter preferences but contends that these ethno-partisan alignments have nothing to do with ethnicity itself. For example, Weghorst and Lindberg (2013) argue that electoral choices made by Ashantis and Ewes, the two groups in which bloc voting has been most consistent over time, are best explained by performance evaluations, not ethnicity. Likewise, Whitfield (2009, p. 632) claims that ethnicity overlaps with class and ideology, and that these factors—not ethnic identities—produce bloc voting, arguing that "what might have begun as an ethnic affinity has developed into a party loyalty based on other factors."

Yet, while studies emphasizing non-ethnic factors undoubtedly capture important features of voter decision making in Ghana, it would be a mistake to discount entirely the role ethnic concerns. Research demonstrates that instrumental theories of ethnic voting help to explain patterns of voter behavior in Ghana, as in Kenya and other parts of Africa. Ninsin (2016), for example, argues that vote choice stems at least in part from the beliefs voters hold about which candidate or party will serve as the more faithful communal patron. He notes that because of widespread poverty in Ghana, "access to public goods such as piped water, health facilities, schools, tarred roads, and jobs are crucial for improving quality of life." As a result, "an election is about choices of immense public import because its outcome . . . shapes the distribution of public goods" (p. 118).[4] Tonah (2007, p. 69) similarly reports that voters are highly attuned to concerns about ethnic patronage: "there have always been complaints . . . about state power being allegedly controlled by a particular ethnic group and the largesse of office accruing mainly to members of the ethnic group of the leaders." Jockers, Kohnert, and Nugent (2010) observe that in the 2008 election, perceptions of ethnic favoritism by the incumbent NPP helped to cement Ewe voters to the NDC: "there was a common belief [among those in Volta Region] that public money had been diverted by a

---

[4] For accounts of ethnic politics prior to the Fourth Republic, see Chazan (1982) and Austin (1976).

corrupt national government to other regions that were better endowed with basic infrastructure like roads, schools, and hospitals... The reason given for why a change of government was necessary was that the power had to be taken away from 'those people in Kumasi' [the center of the Ashanti region] who allegedly did not care about Volta Region" (pp. 108–10). Quantitative research supports these assertions. Nathan (2016) shows that voters expect that the party associated with their ethnic community will deliver a greater share of material benefits to the group than parties associated with other ethnic groups, and that expectations regarding ethnic favoritism are strongly related to actual vote choices.[5] Ichino and Nathan (2013) show that expectations of ethno-partisan favoritism help to explain why local ethnic geography affects electoral preferences—patterns that would be difficult to explain without taking account of ethnicity.

In sum, this section shows that while parties in Ghana are more institutionalized, elite coalition building is less central, and ethnicity is perhaps less salient, a framework that distinguishes core and swing at least in part as a function of ethnicity has relevance to this case. This section emphatically does not argue that ethnic considerations are the sole or even most important influence on voter behavior for all Ghanaians. Rather, it claims that the durability of ethno-partisan alignments in Ghana's Fourth Republic means that the electoral landscape faced by presidential aspirants is remarkably similar to the Kenyan case: in both cases, candidates enter the race knowing that they can count on steadfast support from voters in their respective ethnic strongholds, and that if they seek to increase their vote share through campaigning, they will be well advised to concentrate their efforts on voters outside these strongholds.

Campaign Strategy

The swing-targeting approach advanced in prior chapters traces broad-based campaign strategies to uncertainty about the relative responsiveness of voters in swing communities, the strategic imperative of blunting rivals' advances, and the ability to delegate core mobilization to lower-level actors. This section first demonstrates that parties in Ghana's Fourth Republic consistently choose broad-based electoral strategies and then examines whether the factors identified earlier help to explain these patterns.

---

[5] Other survey data also demonstrates that expectations of ethnic favoritism are commonplace in Ghana. Price (1973) surveyed respondents in Ghana's capital, Accra, in the late 1960s and found that many Ghanaians expect "tribal affiliations to influence the treatment received by a citizen when he utilizes the services of a government agency" (p. 474) and expect "special treatment from civil servants who are their tribesmen" (p. 471). Langer and Ukiwo (2008) draw on survey data from three constituencies in 2005 to show that beliefs about ethnic favoritism are enduring.

It is well understood that elections in Ghana are won and lost based on how the parties fare among swing groups.[6] As Tonah (2007, p. 66) observes, "none of the country's ethnic groups can single-handedly decide the outcome of national elections...Candidates and their political parties are thus compelled to establish a nation-wide support base, build trans-ethnic group alliances and seek votes beyond their ethnic strongholds to be able to win national elections."

Studies attest to the broad reach of the parties' campaign efforts in Ghana. Jeffries (1998, p. 194) notes that during the 1996 campaigns, the NPP's candidate, John Kufuor, "toured the regions tirelessly," visiting 190 of the country's then 200 constituencies by election day. Reflecting on the 2000 election, Nugent (2001b, p. 3) argues that "each of the parties, both large and small, was at pains to project itself as a party of the entire country." Quantitative studies that track the location of campaign rallies as an indicator of ethnic targeting confirm these impressions, offering evidence of the broad reach of parties' efforts on the campaign trail (e.g., Taylor 2017).

Campaign appeals reflect the broad nature of these campaign strategies. The major parties typically focus on nationally-oriented issues: government performance, proposals for reform, allegations of corruption, programmatic promises, and so forth (Jeffries and Thomas 1993; Gyimah-Boadi 2001; Nugent 2001a; Ayee 2017). Based on content analysis of newspaper coverage of campaign rallies in the 2008 and 2012 elections, Taylor (2017) documents that the majority of the campaign appeals offered by the NDC and NPP relate to nationally-oriented programmatic promises, such as improvements in education and healthcare. The parties generally eschew narrow, targeted appeals that promise goods to specific ethnic groups or claim credit for delivering benefits to particular ethnic communities.

It is not difficult to see why party leaders opt for nationally-oriented appeals rather than narrow, targeted ones. As in Kenya, the fear of alienating potential swing voters leads parties to prefer inclusive approaches and universal policies. As Fridy (2012, p. 119) notes, "as somewhat uncomfortable allies to either the NPP or NDC base...non-Asante Akan speakers [the Fante, Brong and others] provide a strong disincentive for politicians on either side of the aisle for making narrow sectional campaign appeals, or governing in a way that could be perceived by voters in the important non-Asante Akan districts as parochial or 'tribalistic.'" Similarly, Abdulai and Hickey (2016, p. 52) observe that "the outcomes of elections tend to be determined largely by so-called swing ethno-

---

[6] It is important to bear in mind that parties also invest in mobilizing their existing supporters and that in Ghana's tight elections differential turnout rates can affect election outcomes. Thus, in the 2016 election, the NPP's victory was aided by unusually high turnout in its traditional strongholds and atypically low turnout in NDC areas. See Alexander Afram and Kafui Tsekpo. "Missing Numbers in Ghana's Election 2016: Low Turnout or a Bloated Register?" *Pambazuka News* (online), February 2, 2017.

regional groups. This situation compels ruling elites to avoid deep and explicit forms of exclusionary politics."

While the parties steer clear of targeted ethnic promises in favor of nationally-oriented messages, they do not hesitate to appeal to ethnic interests by calling into question their rivals' ethnic intentions. A central feature of campaigns in Ghana, as in Kenya, is the competitive effort to brand opponents as tribalists in order to limit their appeal among swing voters, a well-worn strategy that has been used since the earliest elections in the 1950s when Nkrumah and the Convention People's Party (CPP) sought to drive a wedge between the Fante and the Ashanti-based National Liberation Movement (Austin 1964). In more recent decades, Oelbaum (2004, p. 250) documents efforts by the NDC during the 1990s to portray the NPP as antagonistic to the interests of Brongs and Northerners by emphasizing supposed threats to these communities' interests and security, noting that "the NDC followed a pattern long familiar in Ghanaian politics, in which the ruling government attempts to diminish the credibility of opposition movements by tarring them with the brush of tribalism." Likewise, Taylor (2017, p. 963) notes that in 2008 and 2012, "a key piece of the NDC's strategy . . . was to portray the NPP as a party that represented only the interests of elite Akans, playing on the perceived history of Akan political domination over Ghana's other ethnic groups." The NPP is especially susceptible to allegations of ethnic favoritism both because of the expansionist history of the Ashanti empire in the pre-colonial period and because the Ashanti in modern times are better off economically than most other ethnic communities (Langer 2007). These historical factors and inter-group inequalities make Ashanti leaders in the NPP an easy target for allegations of ethnic favoritism (Briggs 2021).

Ghana's major parties compete for voters arrayed across the ethnic landscape rather than mobilizing rival multi-group coalitions. Thus, Jeffries (1998, p. 193) notes that it would be "seriously misleading" to think that electoral politics in Ghana is about "stitching together a coalition of ethno-regional blocs." Less clear is why they adopt these strategies rather than concentrating their efforts on cobbling together more limited coalitions. For the NPP, in particular, it would appear a natural strategy to bring together a coalition of Akan-speaking groups, which share linguistic and cultural similarities and collectively make up a near-majority of the population—49 percent according to the 2000 census. There is, moreover, historical precedent for a "Grand Akan" coalition of this type dating back to the 1969 election when the Progress Party headed by Kofi Busia was elected with strong support from all major Akan communities (Austin 1976; Twumasi 1975). Likewise, the NDC is frequently characterized as a coalition of the Ewe, Ga, and northern ethnic groups, a core support base that has been a steady foundation in all elections since 1992. Yet, neither party limits its campaign efforts to the pursuit of voters in these narrow coalitions.

The swing-targeting approach developed in this book suggests that information constraints lead party strategists in multiethnic settings to diversify their electoral approaches by campaigning widely. If NPP leaders, for example, knew with certainty that members of Akan-speaking groups like the Brong and Fante would be more responsive to the party's entreaties than Gas, Moles, or Guans, the party could safely target its campaign efforts toward those groups. Parties, however, face a formidable challenge in assessing the relative responsiveness of members of different target communities. Fridy (2012) captures this uncertainty well in characterizing the non-Asante Akan groups as "uncomfortable allies" for both the NPP and NDC. He observes that "districts heavily populated by speakers of Fante, Abron, Nzema, and all the other non-Asante Akan languages share some linguistic, cultural and climatic similarities with Twi-speaking voters populating the NPP's electoral core." However, he notes, "citizens of these districts...also have their fair share of historical pre-colonial and colonial-era rivalries with the Asante Empire" (p. 119). Given the uncertain receptivity of voters in these groups, if NPP leaders are risk-averse, diversification will be an attractive strategy. The same, of course, is true for the NDC.

The strategic nature of campaigning adds to the incentive to cast a wide net on the campaign trail. Because parties seek to blunt the advances of their rivals among voters outside their respective strongholds, they are compelled to campaign even in areas where the prospects of winning over new adherents may be low. This logic can be seen in the parties' competitive efforts to court the Brong and Fante. Just as the potential benefits of a "Grand Akan" coalition are obvious to the NPP, so too are the disadvantages for the NDC. The unification of a solid Akan voting bloc would potentially lock the NDC out of power for the foreseeable future. For this reason, the NDC is particularly keen to counter the NPP's advances among non-Ashanti Akan groups by courting voters in these communities during campaigns, nominating leaders from these groups to top party positions, using policies to reassure members of these groups of the party's inclusive intentions, and campaigning in the regions where they are concentrated. Similar dynamics can be seen in the North, where, as noted, both major parties vie for the hearts and minds of voters from ethnic groups in the region (Briggs 2012). Failure by the NPP, for example, to pursue northerners would leave the NDC free to press its advantage with the area's voters. Thus, even if the NPP rightly estimates that its chances of peeling away northern voters are limited (Bob-Milliar 2011), the party still has an incentive to court voters in these communities simply to offset the NDC's efforts in the region. As in Kenya, uncertainty and strategic imperatives compel parties to embrace broad-based strategies on the campaign trail, rather than working to stitch together a narrow coalition.[7]

---

[7] The analysis of campaign strategies in Kenya also emphasizes the delegation of mobilization to lower-level actors, which frees presidential candidates to concentrate their campaign efforts on winning over swing group voters. I lack sufficient data on the location of campaign rallies and household canvassing to test this aspect of the argument in Ghana.

From Electoral Politics to Policymaking

The swing-targeting model proposes that the competition for swing voters in multiethnic democracies encourages the adoption of universal policies that distribute benefits widely. These claims find support in Ghana, where accounts commonly emphasize the inclusive nature of distributive politics. For example, Nugent (2007, pp. 265–6) summarizes the record during the Fourth Republic as follows:

> The NDC's canny approach was to ensure that enough development projects came on stream *in every district in the country* (emphasis added) for it [the NDC] to be considered worth supporting... The NPP has so far continued to operate according to the same logic... Since its victory [in 2000], the NPP has underlined its willingness to treat NDC areas on a par with its political heartlands with a view to convincing the former that it can in fact be trusted.

To document the connection between electoral strategies and policymaking, this section focuses on the NPP's rise to power in 2000 and its subsequent decision to adopt Ghana's National Health Insurance Scheme (NHIS), which Carbone (2011, p. 392) describes as "one of the most remarkable, if not *the* most remarkable, social policy measures adopted during the country's two decades of democratic politics" (emphasis in the original).[8] The context in which the NPP initially proposed the NHIS parallels the political environment in which free primary education was introduced in Kenya. As in Kenya, the opposition struggled to construct a sufficiently broad support base in the first elections after the return to multiparty politics. Rawlings easily defeated the NPP in 1992 and 1996 (by margins of 28% and 17% respectively). In both races the NPP secured overwhelming support in its ethnic strongholds, particularly Ashanti and Akyem areas, but was not competitive nationally. To succeed at the national level, the NPP needed to improve its standing with voters outside the party's core ethnic strongholds. As in Kenya, this led party leaders to promise—and adopt—universal policies.

The NPP's success in 2000, with John Kufuor as its presidential nominee, reflected the party's efforts to project a national image. As Nugent (2001b, p. 3), notes, "The NPP, whose base was narrower to start with, worked very hard to spread its tentacles into every region." Kufuor's pledge to reform the health system

---

[8] While patterns of resource targeting have not been studied as extensively in Ghana as in Kenya, several quantitative studies support the conclusion that parties in the Fourth Republic shy away from favoring their core ethno-partisan supporters (Banful 2010, 2011; Briggs 2012; McDonnell 2016; Miguel and Zaidi 2003), though some evidence of favoritism in specific sectors has been documented (Franck and Rainer 2012; Briggs 2021; Abdulai and Hickey 2016).

provided a useful strategy in this regard since it would benefit voters in all communities. Moreover, the reform initiative provided a valuable opportunity for the NPP to distinguish itself from the incumbent NDC, in much the same way that free primary education allowed Kibaki to distinguish himself from KANU in Kenya's 2002 election. While the incumbent NDC had explored options for reforming the country's unpopular "cash-and-carry" policy, which required the sick to pay for services before receiving treatment, the NDC had made little substantive progress.[9]

The NPP's victory in the 2000 presidential election reflects the party's "capacity to repackage and market itself as a *national* party" (Ayee 2002, p. 171, emphasis added). Yet, the party came to power with only a slim margin over the NDC. Once in power, the NPP therefore sought out policy initiatives that would deliver concrete benefits across communities and provide a base for its appeal to voters in the subsequent election. Carbone (2011, p. 400) notes that after winning the 2000 election, the NPP "was on the lookout for highly visible measures that it could showcase in seeking a new mandate in 2004." Moreover, the final form of the NHIS reforms bore a clear political imprint. Despite concerns about the cost, the NPP leadership opted for a *universal* plan that would shift a substantial financial burden onto the national budget. The adoption of a universal program was ostensibly motivated by a desire to ensure that the most vulnerable and impoverished would be able to participate in the scheme.[10] Politically, it would allow the NPP to claim credit for delivering benefits to voters in all ethnic communities and help to insulate the party against the inevitable allegations of ethnic chauvinism by the NDC in the coming 2004 campaigns. The NHIS led to substantial increases in access to the healthcare system and a decrease in out-of-pocket expenditures in the years following its adoption—benefits that were widely shared across regions (Witter and Garshong 2009).

The public response to the NHIS was overwhelmingly positive. Figure 7.2 plots performance ratings across Kufuor's two terms using data from four national Afrobarometer surveys conducted between 1999 and 2008. The figure includes data from the 1999 survey, the year prior to Kufuor's victory in 2000, as a baseline. In addition to tracking views about health performance, Figure 7.2 also provides performance assessments on several other sectors probed in the Afrobarometer polls for comparative purposes. The data show that assessments of the NPP's performance on healthcare steadily improved as the NHIS program was implemented. Though it is not possible to isolate the effect of the NHIS program from other factors that might have also influenced popular views, it is likely that the

---

[9] Details are drawn from Carbone (2011).
[10] While participation rates are lower among poorer Ghanaians, overall enrollment expanded rapidly after the program's introduction (Witter and Garshong 2009).

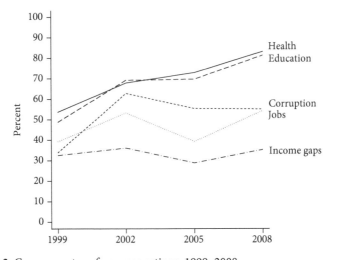

Figure 7.2 Government performance ratings, 1999–2008

Notes: Data from multiple Afrobarometer surveys conducted in Ghana. Figure tracks the percent saying that the government performed "fairly well" or "very well" in selected areas.

NHIS contributed to these positive assessments given that it was the primary health reform implemented during Kufuor's time in office. Performance ratings on healthcare were high both in absolute terms (83% gave the NPP positive marks at the end of Kufuor's second term in 2008) and in relative terms, slightly above education and well above ratings for jobs creation, corruption control, or dealing with inequality.

From a political perspective the NHIS program worked as intended, providing the NPP with a concrete example to which it could point as evidence that the party had delivered widely-shared benefits (see also Mensah, Oppong, and Schmidt 2010). Whether the NHIS helped the NPP at the ballot box remains an open question. Several studies report positive associations between broad performance ratings and vote choice in Ghana (Lindberg and Morrison 2005; Youde 2005; Hoffman and Long 2013), suggesting that the NPP's policies may have bolstered the party's electoral prospects. However, these works do not examine performance in specific sectors such as healthcare. Others suggest that deeply held beliefs about ethnic favoritism limited the political impact of the NPP's social service reforms. Bob-Milliar (2011, p. 469), for example, argues that "even though the NPP regime has a track record of having implemented some of the best social policies in the health and educational sectors, [Upper West] voters have simply ignored such social intervention and stuck with the NDC." Thus, while it is not possible to say with certainty whether the NHIS won the NPP any new supporters at the polls, the politics surrounding its initiation and implementation show that electoral competition in Ghana, as in Kenya, encourages parties to embrace broad, inclusive policies in their efforts to cultivate support across a diverse set of ethnic communities.[11]

Electoral incentives are likely not the only factor that motivates inclusive policymaking in Ghana. Morrison and Hong (2006) note that political culture in Ghana militates against overt forms of ethnic favoritism, pointing to a legacy established by Nkrumah, who sought to cultivate national identities in place of communal attachments, along with legislation—the Avoidance of Discrimination Act, 1957—that criminalized communal mobilization (see also McDonnell (2016) for a complementary argument). Nugent (2001a, p. 427) proposes that fear of inter-group conflict also leads political leaders to steer clear of ethnic politics, noting that "the Ghanaian political class has become acutely aware of the perils of playing the ethnic card, as it witnessed one [nearby] country after another succumb to bitter conflict." Whitfield (2009) claims that Ghana's two ideological traditions provide a ready social cleavage for organizing electoral support that discourages ethnic forms of political mobilization. This chapter does not seek to assess the relative weight of these or other possible influences on policy choices. Rather, it aims to demonstrate that in addition to these forces, *electoral competition*—and particularly the competition for swing voters—encourages the adoption of universal policies.

Finally, it is important to note that ostensibly universal policies may fall prey to political distortions at the implementation stage. Abdulai and Hickey's (2016) examination of education spending in Ghana finds that political factors exert a consistent effect on regional budgetary allocations despite rhetorical commitments to inclusive national principles. These findings provide a useful reminder that party leaders may face competing pressures that undermine broad-based pledges made on the campaign trail.[12] Evidence from Ghana suggests that some types of policy reforms will be more subject to biases at the implementation stage than others. Programs that allow bureaucratic discretion over allocations across districts, like the education policies studied in Abdulai and Hickey (2016), will likely be more prone to influence than programs that create individual-level entitlements, as with the NHIS.[13]

Conclusion

This chapter demonstrates that the swing-targeting approach developed in Kenya helps to explain electoral politics and policymaking in a second case, Ghana, that

---

[11] This discussion complements the account in Harding (2020) which argues that electoral incentives in Ghana and elsewhere in Africa lead politicians to implement nationally-oriented policies that distribute benefits widely, particularly in rural areas where most voters reside.

[12] The potential for political factors to distort universal programs has been documented also in the literature on fertilizer subsidies (e.g., Banful 2010; Brazys, Heaney, and Walsh 2015; Mason, Jayne, and van de Walle 2017).

[13] See also Banful (2010, 2011) and Briggs (2012) for relevant studies of discretionary targeting in Ghana.

differs from Kenya in several important ways. Does the approach have relevance beyond the two cases examined in this book? Limitations in the availability of comparable data and secondary sources from other countries make it difficult to delineate the extent of the argument's applicability across Africa's emerging democracies. Yet, several recent studies indicate that the competition for swing voters defined in ethnic terms is central to electoral dynamics and policymaking in other cases. In Zambia, Scarritt (2006) shows that elections are typically fought by parties with distinct ethnic bases and that the competition for voters outside their respective strongholds compels them to construct broad, multi-ethnic electoral coalitions. Resnick (2014, ch. 6) demonstrates that even as Michael Sata, who came to power in Zambia in 2011, sought to bolster his support among coethnic Bembas, he adopted a broad-based campaign strategy, as did his main rivals. In Sierra Leone, where the electoral landscape shares much in common with Kenya and Ghana, Casey (2015) demonstrates that parties devote greater campaign effort and public resources to swing areas outside of their respective ethnic strongholds. In Malawi, Westberg (2015) and Brazys, Heaney, and Walsh (2015) show that the need to cultivate support from swing communities leads parties to target fertilizer subsidies toward areas outside of the parties' respective core ethnic regions. These scattered results suggest that, as in Ghana and Kenya, the imperative of courting a diverse electorate has important implications for how parties campaign and how incumbents make policy choices in Africa's emerging democracies.

8

Conclusion

The democratic wave that swept across Africa starting in the early 1990s was widely viewed as a new dawn—a second liberation—for a continent where misrule, corruption, and violence had become commonplace (e.g., Nyong'o 1992). Three decades later, opinion remains divided on democracy's prospects and effects in the region (see Ndegwa 2001; Radelet 2010; Cheeseman 2015; Bleck and van de Walle 2019). The benefits for personal freedom and political participation are undeniable. However, progress on social and economic development has been slower. Equally concerning, some observers have noted that multiparty elections, which are now the norm across the continent, have increased incentives for elites to turn to ethnicity as the foundation for their electoral bids, heightening ethnic tensions and contributing to outbreaks of communal violence (Keller 2014). These observations echo longstanding concerns among scholars about the challenges of democratic competition in diverse societies (e.g., Lijphart 1977; Horowitz 1985; Snyder 2000).

This book offers a decidedly positive contribution to the scholarship on multiparty politics in diverse countries. It demonstrates that the path from ethnic diversity to exclusionary politics is not inevitable. Drawing on a wide range of evidence primarily from Kenya, the book shows that electoral competition can encourage broad-based political strategies and universal policies. That these findings emerge from the study of Kenya, a country where elections routinely exacerbate ethnic tensions and spark violence, make them all the more striking. This chapter concludes by exploring the book's implications for Africa's emerging democracies and suggesting avenues for future research.

Electoral Politics and Policymaking

At the most basic level, this book connects to debates about the nature of political representation in multiethnic societies. In Africa, the world's most diverse region, it is often taken as an "axiom of politics" (Posner 2005, p. 97) that public figures act as communal advocates, advancing the interests of their own ethnic groups at the expense of others. Explanations for this distinct style of representation emphasize normative concerns, social pressures, psychological factors and above all, political incentives. The normative approach is developed in works that stress the communal ties that link public figures to their communities and create a moral

Multiethnic Democracy: The Logic of Elections and Policymaking in Kenya. Jeremy Horowitz, Oxford University Press.
© Jeremy Horowitz 2022. DOI: 10.1093/oso/9780198852735.003.0008

imperative to attend to the interests of one's group (e.g., Lonsdale 1994; Berman 1998). Others describe the social pressures that encourage politicians to share resources with their communities or suffer communal sanctions (Bates 1983). In a particularly influential account, Horowitz (1985) outlines a psychological approach—drawing on Tajfel (1970)—in which the desire to overturn group hierarchies leads politicians, particularly those from less "advanced" groups, to target resources and opportunities toward their communities. Political imperatives are generally thought to reinforce these moral, social, and psychological influences, exacerbating patterns of group-centric representation. Thus, a vast literature chronicles what Lonsdale (1994) calls "political tribalism"—the competitive mobilization of political factions along communal lines by political entrepreneurs seeking advantage over rivals. Despite some notable exceptions, this view of representation remains commonplace in descriptions of African politics.[1]

This book offers an alternative view of how political incentives affect representation. It demonstrates that in Africa's emerging democracies electoral competition can encourage politicians to portray themselves as *national* leaders, not communal champions. While African politicians have always portrayed themselves in such terms, their high-minded appeals to shared national interests have often not been reflected in policy choices. Thus, Berman (1998, p. 306) writes that "even as they ritually denounce 'tribalism', African politicians, in the open secret of African politics, sedulously attend to the maintenance of the ethnic networks of patronage that are the basis of their power." The evidence in this book shows that broad-based appeals in Africa's emerging democracies should not be dismissed merely as smoke and mirrors. Multiparty competition in settings like Kenya not only generates an incentive for national leaders to couch their electoral appeals in inclusive language, but also encourages them to make good on such pledges once in office.

As noted throughout earlier chapters, I do not claim that multiparty elections have or will eliminate all form of communal favoritism in Kenya or elsewhere in Africa. Rather, the book shows that at the national level the imperative of appealing to voters across ethnic boundaries attenuates whatever pressures may incline leaders to target rewards toward core ethnic supporters. In advancing these arguments, this book breaks with other works that stress the continuity of patronage dynamics before and after the introduction of multiparty elections in Africa (e.g., Franck and Rainer 2012; Kramon and Posner 2016; van de Walle 2007; Mueller 2020). It joins a smaller literature that shows that democracy can mitigate

---

[1] Several recent works emphasize the limitations of communal representation as a framework for understanding elite mobilization strategies or resource allocation decisions in multiethnic countries. Notable contributions include Resnick's (2014) account of populism as a strategy for appealing to Africa's urban poor; Koter's (2013) work on local intermediaries in West Africa; Huber's emphasis on the interaction between inequality and ethnic diversity (2007); and Burgess et al.'s (2015) study of road construction in Kenya.

ethnic favoritism, though the account offered here traces democracy's salutary effects to electoral incentives rather than constraints on executive power, as in Burgess et al. (2015).

The foundation for these arguments is a view of electoral politics that places the competition for swing voters at the center of national elections. As noted in the introduction, this approach is at odds with much of the traditional literature, which typically assumes that core mobilization is the primary task of electoral competition. Such approaches generally take the view that in the absence of moderation-inducing electoral institutions or cross-cutting cleavages that temper group differences, parties in highly-diverse settings like Kenya will engage in competitive efforts to mobilize rival ethnic constituencies. It is the single-minded focus on whipping up the party faithful—rather than efforts to court voters across ethno-partisan lines—that defines electoral competition.

This book takes aim at the core mobilization model by bringing together multiple data sources to examine what candidates do and say on the campaign trail. My interviews with party strategists, political operatives, and candidates in Kenya's 2007 election revealed that presidential aspirants adopt broad campaign strategies in their efforts to win over potential converts to their cause, a claim verified by data on the location of campaign rallies in multiple elections. To explain this pattern, the account offered in this book emphasizes how uncertainty about the relative return on investment from alternative campaign strategies encourages broad-based campaigning, a dynamic reinforced by the need to blunt rivals' advances in battleground areas and facilitated by the ability to delegate mobilization responsibilities to lower-level actors in party strongholds. In emphasizing the competition for swing voters, this work joins a handful of other recent contributions that examine the distinction between core and swing in Africa and explore how the pursuit of the swing affects electoral politics and policymaking (Weghorst and Lindberg 2013; Fridy 2012; Casey 2015).

Elections and Conflict in Multiethnic Societies

The findings have implications for scholarship that examines the connection between democracy and violence. It is often assumed that when parties seek support across ethnic lines, they moderate their campaign strategies in ways that attenuate ethnic tensions and reduce the potential for violence (e.g., Horowitz 1991; Reilly 2001; Reilly and Reynolds 1999; Sisk 1994). Yet, in Kenya, where parties routinely adopt broad electoral strategies, elections often sharpen inter-communal tensions and contribute to violent outbreaks. In the wake of the 2007 election that triggered a period of intense ethnic violence, observers pointed to the divisive nature of campaigning as a key factor. For example, a report by Human Rights Watch concluded that "the election campaign itself was virulently divisive, with politicians on both sides characterizing their opponents in derogatory terms linked to their ethnicity" (HRW 2008, p. 23). Similarly, Barkan (2008b, p. 147) observed that "the elections polarized the country along ethnic lines, as both parties had mobilized ethno-regional constituencies by appealing to voters' sense of identity." How, then, to reconcile the apparent polarizing effect of campaigns with the extensive data in this book showing that Kenyan parties regularly prioritize efforts to appeal across ethno-partisan divides?

The evidence in this book suggests that the common dichotomy between moderate and divisive electoral strategies found in much of the literature is too simplistic. The examination of campaign speeches in Chapter 5 shows that parties do not adopt a uniform campaign approach, either playing up ethnic divisions or seeking to bridge them. They do not, in other words, choose either to "play the ethnic card" or to bury it in the deck. Rather, parties simultaneously employ messages designed to appeal across ethnic boundaries while also adopting bellicose language aimed at limiting the appeal of rivals by exploiting ethnic fears, antipathies, and resentments.[2] Thus, even as ODM's leaders sought in 2007 to court voters widely by emphasizing Odinga's inclusive intentions, the party's leading luminaries also sought to exploit beliefs that Kibaki had favored the Kikuyu and other groups from the Mt. Kenya region, playing on long-standing grievances about perceived "Kikuyu domination." On the other side, Kibaki's allies in PNU worked assiduously to win over voters around the country by emphasizing the broad reach of his government's reforms, while also demonizing Odinga as a blood-thirsty tyrant whose rise to power would thrust the country into an ethnic war. Broad-based appeals aimed at transcending ethnic divisions and belligerent attacks designed to reinforce them are two sides of the same coin— pieces of a coherent strategy parties adopt in their efforts to advance their cause— not alternative strategies.

Scholars have long hoped that if parties could be made to appeal to voters across ethnic lines, these actors would eschew divisive rhetoric on the campaign trail, opting instead for appeals to common interests that transcend ethnic differences. The Kenyan case shows that these hopes are misplaced. Encouraging parties to pursue voters outside their ethnic strongholds—through institutional fixes or other interventions—is no panacea. This observation should temper enthusiasm for institutional engineering as a strategy for lowering the temperature of competitive elections in diverse societies (e.g., Southall 2009; Horowitz 1991; Reilly 2001).

On a more encouraging note, the book's findings on the link between electoral competition and policymaking have positive implications for peace and prosperity in Africa's multiethnic societies. Chapter 6 shows that education reforms introduced after the transition to multiparty politics in Kenya have gone a long way

---

[2] See also Chege (2008), Kagwanja (2009), and Klopp and Kamungi (2008).

toward rectifying persistent inequalities in access to primary school that have existed since the colonial era. While education quality and the prospects of advancing to higher levels remain unequal, the reforms implemented since the transition to multiparty politics represent a meaningful step toward a more equitable education system. This work joins a small body of scholarship that shows that although democratic transitions in Africa remain incomplete, multiparty competition can alter policy outcomes in socially beneficial ways (e.g., Bates and Block 2013; Burgess et al. 2015; Carbone 2011; Stasavage 2005a; Harding and Stasavage 2013; Harding 2020). To the extent that democracy encourages the adoption of more inclusive policies that help to narrow intergroup inequalities, it has the potential to alter intergroup relations in ways that contribute to political stability (Stewart 2016; Cederman et al. 2011).

Voter Behavior

Finally, this book has implications for scholarship on voter behavior in multiethnic settings. It advances an approach to core and swing that departs both from the American and comparative literatures. Studies of the U.S. electorate, where core and swing have been examined more extensively than perhaps anywhere else, tend to privilege individual attributes, such as political engagement and interest or ideological and partisan orientations, over social identities in theorizing which types of voters will be most responsive to campaign influence (Campbell et al. 1960; Campbell 2001; Greene 2011; Hillygus and Shields 2008; Kaufmann, Petrocik, and Shaw 2008; Mayer 2006; Zaller 2004). For its part, the comparative ethnic politics literature has made considerable progress in unpacking the links between ethnicity and vote choice, but has so far devoted less attention to understanding dynamics in electoral preferences over time. Accounts typically either conclude that swing voters do not exist in ethnically-divided societies (Horowitz 1985) or that non-ethnic factors define core and swing (e.g., Lindberg and Morrison 2005; Weghorst and Lindberg 2013; but see Fridy 2007 and Casey 2015). In contrast, the account offered here shows that in settings where ethnicity is politically salient, social identities play an important role in structuring core and swing. While the book provides a sparse account, it offers a starting point for making sense of how party leaders conceptualize the electoral landscape in diverse settings.

This chapter concludes by asking whether we should expect inclusive policies like the adoption of free primary education in Kenya to reduce the political importance of ethnicity to voters. It is well understood that ethnic voting persists because voters expect that leaders will "favor their own" in office (Bates 1983; Horowitz 1985; Posner 2005; Chandra 2004; Ferree 2011). Thus, one might expect that if favoritism declines, ethnic considerations will become less important determinants of voters' election choices. There are several reasons, however, to believe that ethnicity will remain salient as policymaking becomes more inclusive, at least in the short term.

First, voters hold strong priors that inhibit the adoption of new beliefs. As noted in Chapter 3, survey data show that many Kenyans expect that leaders will favor their supporters at the expense of other groups and continue to see candidates and parties as representatives of narrow ethnic coalitions. Given such beliefs, voters have every incentive to support the candidate or party they believe will best represent their group's interests, and to use ethnic cues to inform such expectations. Parties, despite their efforts to court voters across group lines, find themselves fighting strong headwinds in trying to overcome engrained beliefs.[3]

The second factor that works to keep ethnicity locked in place is an information environment that inhibits voters from updating their beliefs about government favoritism. Many voters in Kenya cannot access the information needed to assess whether incumbents at any level of government are behaving in an inclusive or exclusive manner. While voters can rely on observations of their localities to learn whether the nearby road has been paved, the local primary school has been connected to the electricity grid, or the local clinic is well staffed and provisioned, voters almost certainly cannot make relativistic assessments about how their group is being treated in comparison to others. The difficulty of forming relativistic assessments leaves voters susceptible to elite efforts to shape beliefs. And, as shown in Chapter 6, incumbent and challenger alike have incentives to reinforce negative perceptions about their rivals' ethnic intentions—strategies that fortify existing views about ethnic favoritism. Thus, elite rhetorical strategies keep beliefs about the ethnic logic of patronage politics firmly in place even as incumbents opt for more inclusive policies.

Third, like voters elsewhere, Kenyans more readily internalize messages from trusted political leaders from their own ethnic communities and the party they support. A large body of literature on persuasion shows that voters learn from sources they view as credible and trustworthy (Hovland and Weiss 1951) and that voters rely on source cues—attributes such as race, religion, gender, or partisanship—to form judgments about the trustworthiness of a given speaker (Kuklinski and Hurley 1994; Gilens and Murakawa 2002; Slothuus 2010). In Kenya, ethnic and partisan identities serve as ready cues that signal shared interests and therefore the trustworthiness of political leaders. As a result, voters tend to accept campaign claims made by coethnic and co-partisan politicians and discount those made by non-coethnics and non-co-partisans (Ferree 2011). Given that partisan leaders have incentives to reinforce perceptions of opponents as ethnic chauvinists, these biases likely work to keep prior beliefs in place.

---

[3] See Carlson (2016) and Adida et al. (2017) on how priors may constrain belief formation in similar settings.

Finally, the structure of political information flows may contribute to the persistence of existing beliefs. One-sided exposure to campaign information is common. Data from the 2017 panel study described in Chapter 4 show that voters are considerably more likely to attend rallies held by the party they support than the alternative party.[4] They are also more likely to be contacted during door-to-door canvassing by agents from the party they support than by rivals (see Chapter 4). In addition, because ethnic groups remain relatively geographically concentrated, most voters interact with like-minded individuals who share their own ethnic and partisan orientations. Data on social networks from the 2012–13 panel survey described in Chapter 4 found that only about 1 in 7 respondents (roughly 11%) routinely discuss politics with someone who supports a different party.[5] This means that for many Kenyan voters, campaigns and social interactions likely reinforce—rather than providing opportunities to reassess—existing beliefs about patronage politics.

In sum, prior views, the difficulty of making relativistic assessments of distributive outcomes, voters' own internal biases, and one-sided information flows hinder the formation of new beliefs about ethnic favoritism. Yet, we know from other contexts that changing political dynamics can influence public perceptions even in settings where intensely-held partisan dispositions condition information processing (e.g., Lenz 2012; Hirano, Lenz, Prinkovskiy, and Snyder 2014; though see Nyhan and Reifler 2010). A key task for future research in Kenya and other similar settings will be to investigate the conditions under which voters update their beliefs about ethnic favoritism as political leaders opt for more inclusive policies.

[4] Data from the second wave, conducted shortly before the 2017 election, found that 68 percent of respondents had attended one or more rally held by the party they supported, relative to 45 percent for opposing-party rallies. The first round of the survey (n=2,026) was conducted through face-to-face interviews on May 11–23, 2017; follow-up interviews with 730 respondents were conducted on August 4–7, 2017 by phone.

[5] Data are from the first round of the 2012–13 panel survey (n=1,246). Respondents were first asked to list up to four people they talk to about "politics and elections." 36 percent of respondents listed one or more discussion partners. Respondents were then asked which presidential candidate they thought each of their discussion partners would vote for in the 2013 election.

Appendices

Appendix for Chapter 2

A. The 2015 Survey Experiment

To study how coethnicity affects electoral preferences, I conducted a survey experiment in Nairobi in January 2015 that included 819 respondents from two diverse parliamentary constituencies. The survey was conducted in respondents' households. The sample included respondents from the larger ethnic groups in Nairobi: the Kikuyu, Luo, Luhya, Kisii, and Kamba. Respondents were asked to choose between two candidates in hypothetical by-elections (the elections were portrayed as real in the questions and respondents were informed that they were not actual elections during the debrief). This exercise was repeated twice. Half of all elections featured two non-coethnics and half included a coethnic versus a non-coethnic. The analysis presented in Chapter 2 is based only on trials in which respondents were offered a choice between a coethnic and a non-coethnic. Candidate ethnicity was signaled by the candidates' surnames and the birth location. In elections that featured a coethnic and a non-coethnic, the order of the candidates was randomized. For realism, other features (age, occupation, and campaign appeals) were randomized (attributes are shown below). The text, read by enumerators, is as follows:

> As you may know, there is an upcoming by-election in Kajiado Central constituency on March 12. I will describe two of the people in the race and then ask you how you would vote if the election included only these two candidates.
>
> The first candidate is [NAME]. He was born in [PROVINCE]. Before running for office, he was a [PROFESSION]. He has promised that if elected he will ensure that [CAMPAIGN APPEAL].
>
> The second candidate is [NAME]. He was born in [PROVINCE]. Before running for office, he was a [PROFESSION]. He has promised that if elected he will ensure that [CAMPAIGN APPEAL].
>
> If you were voting in this election, which candidate would you vote for?

After the second trial, respondents were asked: 1) On a scale from 1 to 7, how much would you trust Candidate 1, [NAME], to represent people like you? For this question, 1 means very little and 7 means very much. 2) How much would you trust Candidate 2, [NAME], to represent people like you?

PROFESSIONS: a small business owner; a manager at a civil society organization; a government official in the Ministry of Health; a government official in the Ministry of Education; a government official at the Ministry of Transport and Infrastructure; an IT manager; an accountant at an international export company; an agricultural officer; a manager at a large international bank; an engineer at a construction company; a teacher; a university professor; a lawyer; a jua kali (informal sector).

FIRST NAMES: John; Simon; Thomas; Antony; Joseph; Michael; Wilson; Stanley; Peter; Julius; Kennedy; Bernard; James; Moses; Henry; Vincent; David; Richard; Philip; Jacob; Francis; Robert; Joshua; Alex; Samuel; Bernard; Nicholas; Benjamin; Charles; Fredrick; Samson; Alfred; Daniel; Benson; Edward; Erick; Paul; Jackson; Joel; Elijah; Patrick; Martin; Christopher; Anthony; George; Geoffrey; Andrew.

LAST NAMES:
Kikuyu: Mwangi, Kamau, Kariuki, Maina, Njuguna, Macharia, Kimani, Karanja, Ndungu, Waweru
Luo: Onyango, Otieno, Ochieng, Owino, Okoth, Odongo, Owuor, Omondi, Oloo, Odero
Kamba: Wambua, Mutiso, Mutuku, Muli, Kioko, Munyao, Makau, Mutisya, Mulwa, Musau
Kalenjin: Cheruiyot, Chepkwony, Langat, Korir, Kirui, Kibet, Koech, Ngetich, Rono, Rotich
Luhya: Makokha, Wafula, Barasa, Were, Wanyonyi, Nyongesa, Wekesa, Simiyu, Wanjala, Wanyama
Kisii: Momanyi, Ondieki, Makori, Nyakundi, Mose, Mokaya, Mogaka, Bosire, Nyangau, Mokua

APPEALS: He has promised that if elected he will ensure that:

o people from all tribes in the constituency will receive funds for development projects

o young people from all tribes in the constituency will receive jobs

o people from all tribes in the constituency will receive help with school fees

o people from all tribes in the constituency will receive help when they are sick

o people from all tribes in the constituency will receive piped water in their homes

o people from all tribes in the constituency will receive better lighting in the areas where they live

o people from all tribes in the constituency will receive more police centers to improve security in the areas where they live

o people from all tribes in the constituency will receive more shared toilets and bathrooms in the areas where they live

B. Data and Estimation Methods for Bloc Voting Rates

The analysis of bloc voting rates by ethnic group draws on survey data for 2007, 2013, and 2017, and employs ecological inference (EI) methods to generate estimates for earlier contests for which survey data is not available (1992, 1997, and 2002). Both types of data may contain error. Surveys that ask about electoral preferences are prone to a host of well-known measurement problems: voters may conceal their true preferences (or refuse to provide an answer), especially when being interviewed by non-coethnics (Adida et al. 2016). And even very large surveys provide only rough estimates of preferences when the data is disaggregated to the ethnic-group level, where samples are smaller. The ecological inference approach also suffers from several limitations. The estimates it can generate are only as good as the available data. In Kenya, there is good reason to believe that official election returns may not be fully accurate in most elections. In addition, the election results and census data used to generate group voting rates are only available at the constituency and district level, which limits the precision of the estimates. Finally, because turnout rates by ethnic group are not available, the EI methods assume constant turnout across groups. Despite these issues, the estimates provided here, imperfect as they may be, offer the best available data on group bloc voting trends over time. The analysis presents voting outcomes by ethnic group for Kenya's eight largest communities, which collectively make up about 86 percent of the population (1989 census).

EI Methods

To estimate voter preferences in the 1992, 1997, and 2002 elections I use the multinomial-dirichlet ecological inference (EI) method from Rosen et al. (2001). The method is designed to yield estimates from larger tables (i.e., where there are more than two groups and outcomes). It is available as part of *Zelig* in R; the software package, ei.RxC, was developed by Wittenberg, Alimadhi, Bhaskar, and Lau (2007).

The EI method works by first calculating bounds on possible values for quantities of interest (e.g., the share of Kalenjins who voted for Moi in 1992) and then using statistical methods to estimate where the actual value lies within the range proscribed by the bounds. The method works best when the geographic units for which data is available are relatively homogenous with regard to ethnic groups and electoral outcomes, because this allows for the calculation of narrow bands in the first step. I match electoral outcomes to census information at the district level, using the 1989 census data (the only census from which sub-national data on ethnicity is available). Unfortunately, the census data cannot be disaggregated below the district level, which means that the data for each election includes information from 41 units. Fortunately, districts in Kenya are relatively homogenous with regard to both ethnicity and electoral outcomes. In the 1992 election, for example, the data show that the leading candidate received 70 percent or more of the district-level vote in more than half (22 of 41) of all districts and the largest group makes up 70 percent or more of the population in 65 percent of districts (27 of 41).

One way to validate the EI approach is to compare the results to survey data. Table A2.1 shows a comparison between EI estimates generated using the Rosen et al. (2001) method for the eight largest ethnic groups and a residual "other" category across the three leading presidential candidates in the 2007 race, Kibaki, Odinga, and Musyoka. The estimates are compared to those obtained from a nationwide survey conducted roughly two weeks before the 2007 election (n=6,111). The results show a close correspondence for most ethnic groups, with a difference of less than 10 percentage points between the EI estimates and the survey estimates in nearly all cases. The one notable exception is the Luhya, for which larger discrepancies are noted in support for Kibaki and Odinga, relative to the survey data. The reason is that in the 2007 race, as in previous races, the Luhya community was more evenly divided across the leading candidates than other ethnic groups. As a result, the upper and lower bounds for Luhyas are wider, and the resulting estimates generated by the EI approach are less precise than for other groups.

Tables A2.2 through A2.5 show estimates of electoral preferences for elections held between 1992 and 2017.

Table A2.1 Comparison between EI results and survey data for 2007

	Kibaki		Odinga		Musyoka	
	EI	Survey	EI	Survey	EI	Survey
Kikuyu	.98	.95	.01	.04	.01	.01
Luhya	.40	.26	.54	.73	.05	.01
Luo	.01	.02	.98	.97	.02	.01
Kalenjin	.02	.07	.94	.92	.04	.01
Kamba	.18	.15	.10	.06	.72	.79
Kisii	.32	.40	.56	.57	.13	.03
Meru	.88	.89	.04	.10	.08	.01
Mijikenda	.27	.36	.66	.62	.07	.02

Notes: EI estimates based on ecological inference methods described in Rosen et al. (2001) using official election results and 1989 census data. Survey estimates are based on data from a national survey (n=6,111) conducted by Steadman (now Ipsos) on December 11–16, 2007.

SURVEY DATA

2007: Data is from a national poll (n=6,111) conducted by Steadman (now Ipsos) on December 11–16, 2007. Preferences are measured with a question that asked, "If an election for president were held now, whom would you vote for if the person was a candidate?" Those who refused, said they were undecided, or said they would not vote are excluded.

2012/13: Data is from the first round of a panel study (n=1,246) conducted by Ipsos on December 6, 2012–January 6, 2013. Preferences are measured with a question that asked, "If the election were between only Raila Odinga and Uhuru Kenyatta, which candidate would you vote for?" Those who refused, said they were undecided, or said they would not vote are excluded.

2017: Data come from the first wave of a panel survey (n=2,036) conducted by Ipsos on May 11–23, 2017. Preferences are measured with a question that asked, "If the election was held tomorrow, who would you want to vote for president and deputy president?" Those who refused, said they were undecided, or said they would not vote are excluded.

Table A2.2 1992 vote choice (percentages)

	Moi (Kalenjin)	Matiba (Kikuyu)	Kibaki (Kikuyu)	O. Odinga (Luo)
Kikuyu	1	47	50	1
Luhya	30	41	1	22
Luo	1	1	1	97
Kalenjin	98	0	0	0
Kamba	32	33	26	2
Kisii	31	25	15	19
Meru/Embu	4	9	80	2
Mijikenda	70	9	7	9

Notes: Estimates based on ecological inference (EI) methods described in Rosen et al. (2001) using official election results and 1989 census data.

Table A2.3 1997 vote choice (percentages)

	Moi (Kalenjin)	Kibaki (Kikuyu)	R. Odinga (Luo)	Wamalwa (Luhya)	Ngilu (Kamba)
Kikuyu	2	95	1	1	2
Luhya	35	1	1	59	4
Luo	6	2	88	1	4
Kalenjin	99	0	0	0	1
Kamba	23	28	5	4	41
Kisii	53	27	4	8	8
Meru/Embu	17	74	2	2	5
Mijikenda	77	8	4	3	8

Notes: Estimates based on ecological inference (EI) methods described in Rosen et al. (2001) using official election results and 1989 census data.

Table A2.4 2002 and 2007 vote choice (percentages)

	2002			2007		
	Kibaki (Kikuyu)	Kenyatta (Kikuyu)	Nyachae (Kisii)	Kibaki (Kikuyu)	R. Odinga (Luo)	Musyoka (Kamba)
Kikuyu	70	26	1	95	4	1
Luhya	85	9	1	26	73	1
Luo	94	2	1	2	97	1
Kalenjin	16	79	1	7	92	1
Kamba	82	11	2	15	6	79
Kisii	26	6	62	40	57	3
Meru/Embu	76	16	2	89	10	1
Mijikenda	69	19	5	36	62	2

Notes: For 2002, estimates are based on ecological inference (EI) methods described in Rosen et al. (2001) using official election results and 1989 census data. For 2007, estimates are based on data from a national survey (n=6,111) conducted on December 11–16, 2007.

Table A2.5 2013 and 2017 vote choice (percentages)

	Kenyatta (Kikuyu)	R. Odinga (Luo)	Others	Kenyatta (Kikuyu)	R. Odinga (Luo)
Kikuyu	92	4	3	96	4
Luhya	7	65	27	27	73
Luo	1	98	1	6	94
Kalenjin	83	12	4	84	16
Kamba	15	78	7	28	68
Kisii	16	79	4	28	72
Meru/Embu	84	11	4	88	12
Mijikenda	14	78	8	24	75

Notes: For 2013, estimates are based on data from the first round of a national panel survey (n=1,246) conducted between December 6, 2012 and January 6, 2013. For 2017, estimates are based on data from the first round of a national panel survey (n=2,036) conducted on May 11–23, 2017.

Appendix for Chapter 3

A. Survey Details

2007: The 2007 survey (n=2,020) was conducted on September 21–25, 2007 by Steadman (now Ipsos). The survey was conducted just after the major parties announced their presidential nominees for the election. All interviews were conducted in respondents' homes.

2012–13 panel: The first wave was conducted at the start of the 2012–13 campaign period, just after the main coalitions, Jubilee and CORD, formed in early December 2012. The second wave was conducted shortly before the March 4, 2013 election. All first-round interviews were conducted in person in respondents' homes. To improve re-contact rates in the second round, telephone interviews were used for a small share of respondents (68 out of 829). The survey team succeeded in re-interviewing 829 of the 1,246 (67%) individuals who were included in the first round. Analysis examining changes in voting intentions across waves employs inverse propensity weights to reduce attrition bias on observables following the methods developed by Fitzgerald, Gottschalk, and Moffitt (1998).[1] North Eastern province, which contains less than 1 percent of the Kenyan population (2009 census), was excluded from the survey because of security concerns and the difficulty of reaching the nomadic communities that inhabit some parts of the province.

2017 panel: As with the 2012–13 panel, the survey waves for this study were timed to book-end the campaign period, with the first wave conducted roughly three months before the election (May 11–23) and the second wave conducted just prior to election day (August 3–7). The first wave, which was conducted in respondents' homes as parts of a larger Ipsos omnibus poll reached 2,026 respondents. In the second wave, Ipsos succeeded in reaching 730 of the respondents from wave 1 (36%). The low recontact rate likely stems from having conducted the round 2 interviews by phone and the short period for the second wave (five days). To adjust for attrition on observables, the analysis again employs inverse propensity weights (Fitzgerald, Gottschalk and Moffitt 1998) in all tests that track changes across the two survey waves. The first wave sample was restricted to those who reported being registered to vote.

B. Survey Measures and Variable Definitions

Variables in Models of Preference Change:

Vote choice:

- 2013: If the election were between only Raila Odinga and Uhuru Kenyatta, which candidate would you vote for?
- 2017: If the election was held tomorrow, who would you want to vote for president and deputy president?

Mixed parentage: Constructed from questions that asked about the ethnic identity of each respondent's mother and father.

---

[1] Details are provided in the Online Appendix available on Dataverse (dataverse.org).

Spouse from different ethnic group: Constructed by asking whether respondents were married, and if so, the ethnicity of their spouse.

Non-coethnics in network (2013 only): Constructed by first asking respondents to list up to four individuals with whom they discuss politics ("Is there anyone you talk with about politics and elections?") and then asking about the ethnicity of each individual mentioned. This measure is a count ranging from 0 to 4 of the number of non-coethnics mentioned.

Non-coethnics in EA sample: Constructed as the share of non-coethnic respondents in each respondent's enumeration area (EA).

Political interest: How much interest do you have in politics: a lot, some, a little, or very little?

Education:

- 2013: What is the highest level of education you have completed?
- 2017: What is the highest level of education you achieved so far?

Radio news/newspaper/TV news consumption: During a typical week, how many days do you listen to the radio? How many days do you read a newspaper? How many days do you watch TV?

Vernacular radio source (2013 only): To create this variable, the round 1 survey recorded the name of the radio station from which respondents obtained radio news most frequently. All stations were coded as either primarily English/Swahili or vernacular by a Kenyan research assistant. Among the 73 stations mentioned, we were unable to find information on 11.

Wealth/income:

- 2013: Measured by an asset index constructed using principal components analysis based on a series of seven questions that asked about household ownership of the following items: radio, television, bicycle, motorcycle, car, fridge, computer.
- 2017: About how much do all members of this household earn per month?

Age: How old are you?
Female: Recorded by interviewers.
Days between interviews (2013 only): constructed as the number of days between the round 1 and round 2 interviews.

Additional Variables in Models of Direction of Change:

Beliefs about Kenyatta and Odinga's ethnic intentions: Constructed from questions on both surveys that asked, "How well do you think each of the following candidates would represent the interests of your ethnic group if elected: very well, somewhat well, not well, or not at all?" Changes in beliefs about each candidate are defined as the round 2 response minus the round 1 answer.

Overall evaluation of Kenyatta and Odinga (2013 only): Constructed from questions on both surveys that asked, "For each of the following politicians, please tell me whether you like the candidate very much, like him somewhat, neither like him nor dislike him, dislike him somewhat, or dislike him very much." Changes in beliefs about each candidate are defined as the round 2 response minus the round 1 answer.

C. Voter Preferences at the Start of the 2007, 2013, and 2017 Campaigns

Table A3.1 Voting intentions at the start of the 2007 campaigns (percentages)

	Kibaki	Odinga	Musyoka	Other	Undecided
Kikuyu	90	6	1	1	3
Luo	4	94	0	0	2
Kamba	24	9	59	0	8
Luhya	22	68	3	3	4
Kalenjin	13	76	2	1	8
Kisii	26	68	0	4	2
Meru	89	6	1	0	5
Mijikenda	33	52	5	1	9
Other (each < 5%)	42	50	0	1	7

Notes: Data come from a survey conducted by the Steadman Group on September 8–20, 2007 (n=2,020). RTAs (1.3% of the sample) are excluded.

Table A3.2 Voting intentions at the start of the 2013 campaigns (percentages)

	Kenyatta	Odinga	Undecided
Kikuyu	91	8	1
Luo	3	97	0
Kamba	19	79	2
Luhya	13	78	8
Kalenjin	88	11	1
Kisii	27	70	3
Meru	81	17	2
Mijikenda	11	85	4
Other (each < 5%)	48	50	2

Notes: Data come from the first round of the panel survey (n=1,246) described in the previous chapter, which was conducted in December 2012. Respondents were asked whom they would vote for if the presidential election included only Uhuru Kenyatta and Raila Odinga. RTAs (0.7% of the sample) are excluded.

Table A3.3 Voting intentions at the start of the 2017 campaigns (percentages)

	Kenyatta	Odinga	Other	Undecided
Kikuyu	92	4	1	4
Luo	6	88	0	6
Kamba	25	60	3	12
Luhya	24	65	1	11
Kalenjin	80	15	0	5
Kisii	25	64	0	11
Meru	84	11	0	5
Mijikenda	20	63	1	16
Other (each < 5%)	48	43	2	8

Notes: Data come from a survey conducted by Ipsos in May 2017 (n=2,026). RTAs (2.6% of the sample) are excluded.

Appendix for Chapter 6

A. The Ethnic Composition of Kikuyu- and Kalenjin-Majority Districts over Time

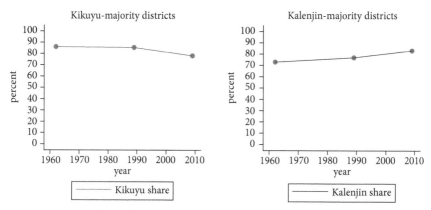

Figure A6.1 Population shares in Kikuyu- and Kalenjin-majority districts over time

Notes: Census data from 1962, 1989, and 2009 is aggregated to the original 41 districts. Data for 1962 is from Burgess et al. (2015) based on the 1962 census data. The 1989 data is from Republic of Kenya (1994). The 2009 data (reported at the County level) is from the Kenya National Bureau of Statistics (2014).

Appendix for Chapter 7

A. Ecological Inference Methods

To estimate vote choice by ethnic group in Ghana, I use the ecological inference methods developed by King (1997) and implemented using *eiCompare* in R (see Collingwood, Oskooii, Garcia-Rios, and Barreto (2016)). For all election years, I generate support for the NPP relative to an "other" category that sums support for all other parties. I use districts as the unit of analysis, the lowest level for which census data is publicly available. Census data for all estimates is taken from the 2000 census. I aggregate the census using the following ethnic categories: Ashanti, Fante, Brong, Akan-other, Ga Dangbe, Ewe, Guan, Mole Dagbani, Grusi, and Other. Aggregating election results to the district level is possible because all constituencies (the lowest level at which election results are made available) nest within districts. For all analyses, there are 110 district-level observations. It is important to note that data on turnout by ethnic group is not available in Ghana, and as a result I assume constant turnout rates for all groups.

To validate the EI estimates, I compare the results for the 2008 election to survey data from an exit poll conducted on the day of the election (see Hoffman and Long 2013). I do not expect a perfect match since the exit poll data differs in at least three ways. First, self-reported information on vote choice is prone to enumerator bias (Adida et al. 2016).

Table A7.1 Comparison between EI estimates and survey data—estimated support for the NPP in the 2008 election (percentages)

Group	EI	Survey	Difference
Akan groups...			
Ashanti	88.3	82.9	+5.4
Brong	55.9	57.6	−1.7
Fante	42.8	51.1	−8.3
Other Akan	61.9	62.4	−0.5
Ga-Adangbe	22.5	32.2	−9.7
Ewe	2.7	17.8	−15.1
Guan	29.5	36.1	−6.6
Gurma	39.8	36.4	+3.4
Mole-Dagbani	31.2	35.0	−3.8
Grusi	37.0	48.6	−11.6
Other	35.9	36.1	−0.2

Notes: Vote choice data is from the 2008 exit poll (see Hoffman and Long 2013). EI estimates are generated using methods described in the text.

Second, surveys provide respondents the option of not providing an answer at all, and in the 2008 exit poll 4.3 percent of respondents chose not to report their vote. Third, because the EI estimates rely on the assumption of constant turnout across ethnic groups, there is imprecision in the estimates. Despite these limitations, Table A7.1 shows a relatively close correspondence between the EI estimates and the exit poll results, with most group-level estimates varying by no more than ±10 percentage points.

Interviews

Cesar Acio, ODM campaign consultant, Nairobi, September 27, 2007

Peter Anyang' Nyong'o, Secretary General of ODM, Nairobi, October 8, 2007

Hamid Hashi, ODM Deputy Communications Officer, Nairobi, October 9, 2007

Janet Ongera, Executive Director, ODM Secretariat, Nairobi, October 11, 2007

Major Matu, PNU Secretariat Executive Director, Nairobi, October 11, 2007

Lee Kanyare, Director of Media and Public Affairs, PNU Secretariat, Nairobi, October 11, 2007

Gabriel Kimani, NARC-Kenya Branch Secretary, Nakuru, December 9, 2007

William Attinga, ODM Branch Secretary for Central Rift Valley, Nakuru, December 9, 2007

Lee Kinyanjui, PNU MP candidate for Nakuru Constituency, Nakuru, December 9, 2007

Mike Brawan, ODM MP candidate for Nakuru Constituency, Nakuru, December 9, 2007

Daudi Mwanzia, LPK MP candidate and incumbent MP for Machakos Town, Machakos, December 11, 2007

Dr. Susan Musyoka, PICK MP candidate for Machakos Town, Machakos, December 12, 2007

Collins Kataka Kaloni, PNU MP candidate for Machakos Town, Machakos, December 13, 2007

Victor Munyaka, ODM-K MP candidate for Machakos Town, Machakos, December 13, 2007

Afiya Rama, ODM-K MP candidate for Mvita, Mombasa, December 20, 2007

Gideon Mung'aro, OMD MP candidate for Malindi, Malindi, December 21, 2007

Lawrence Kamau, PNU Regional Coordinator for Coast Province, Mombasa, December 21, 2007

References

Abdulai, Abdul-Gafaru, and Gordon Crawford. 2010. "Consolidating democracy in Ghana: Progress and prospects?" *Democratization* 17(1): 26–67.

Abdulai, Abdul-Gafaru, and Sam Hickey. 2016. "The politics of development under competitive clientelism: Insights from Ghana's education sector." *African Affairs* 115 (458): 44–72.

Adida, Claire L. 2015. "Do African voters favor coethnics? Evidence from a survey experiment in Benin." *Journal of Experimental Political Science* 2(1): 1–11.

Adida, Claire L., Karen E. Ferree, Daniel N. Posner, and Amanda Lea Robinson. 2016. "Who's asking? Interviewer coethnicity effects in African survey data." *Comparative Political Studies* 49(12): 1630–60.

Adida, Claire L., Jessica Gottlieb, Eric Kramon, and Gwyneth McClendon. 2017. "Reducing or reinforcing in-group preferences? An experiment on information and ethnic voting." *Quarterly Journal of Political Science* 12(4): 437–77.

Ajulu, Rok. 1998. "Kenya's democracy experiment: The 1997 elections." *Review of African Political Economy* 76(275): 275–85.

Ajulu, Rok. 2002. "Politicised ethnicity, competitive politics and conflict in Kenya: A historical perspective." *African Studies* 61(2): 251–68.

Ake, Claude. 1993a. "What is the problem of ethnicity in Africa?" *Transformation* 22: 1–14.

Ake, Claude. 1993b. "The unique case of African democracy." *International Affairs* 69(2): 239–44.

Alesina, Alberto, and Ekaterina Zhuravskaya. 2011. "Segregation and the quality of government in a cross section of countries." *American Economic Review* 101(5): 1872–1911.

Althaus, Scott L., Peter F. Nardulli, and Daron R. Shaw. 2002. "Candidate appearances in presidential elections, 1972–2000." *Political Communication* 19(1): 49–72.

Alwy, Alwiya, and Susanne Schech. 2004. "Ethnic inequalities in education in Kenya." *International Education Journal* 5(2): 266–74.

Ametewee, Victor K. 2007. "Ethnicity and ethnic relations in Ghana," in Steve Tonah, ed., *Ethnicity, Conflicts and Consensus in Ghana*. Accra: Woeli Publishing Services.

Anderson, David M. and Emma Lochery. 2008. "Violence and exodus in Kenya's Rift Valley, 2008: Predictable and preventable?" *Journal of East African Studies* 2(2): 328–43.

Anderson, David M. 2003. "Briefing: Kenya's elections 2002: The dawning of a new era?" *African Affairs* 102(407): 331–42.

Anderson, David M. 2005. "'Yours in struggle for Majimbo'. Nationalism and the party politics of decolonization in Kenya, 1955–64." *Journal of Contemporary History* 40(3): 547–64.

Anebo, Felix K. G. 1997. "Voting pattern and electoral alliances in Ghana's 1996 elections." *African Journal of Political Science/Revue Africaine de Science Politique* 2(2): 38–52.

Anebo, Felix K. G. 2001. "The Ghana 2000 elections: Voter choice and electoral decisions." *African Journal of Political Science/Revue Africaine de Science Politique* 6(1): 69–88.

Ansell, Ben W. 2008. "Traders, teachers, and tyrants: Democracy, globalization, and public investment in education." *International Organization* 62: 289–322.

Arcenaux, Kevin. 2007. "I'm asking for your support: The effects of personally delivered campaign messages on voting decisions and opinion formation." *Quarterly Journal of Political Science* 2(1): 43–65.

Arriola, Leonardo R. 2013. *Multiethnic Coalitions in Africa: Business Financing of Opposition Elections.* Cambridge: Cambridge University Press.

Arriola, Leonardo R., Donghyun Danny Choi, Matthew K. Gichohi. 2021. "Increasing Cross-Ethnic Trust: Political Endorsements as Vicarious Contact." Working paper.

Arthur, Peter. 2009. "Ethnicity and electoral politics in Ghana's Fourth Republic." *Africa Today* 56(2): 44–73.

Asante, Richard, and Emmanuel Gyimah-Boadi. 2004. "Ethnic structure, inequality and governance of the public sector in Ghana." United Nations Research Institute for Social Development.

Austen-Smith, David. 1992. "Strategic models of talk in political decision making." *International Political Science Review* 13(1): 45–58.

Austin, Dennis. 1964. *Politics in Ghana 1946-1960.* London: Oxford University Press.

Austin, Dennis. 1976. *Ghana Observed: Essays on the Politics of a West African Republic.* Manchester: Manchester University Press.

Ayee, Joseph. 2002. "The 2000 general election and presidential run-off in Ghana: An overview." *Democratization* 9(2): 148–74.

Ayee, Joseph. 2017. "Ghana's elections of 7 December 2016: A post-mortem." *South African Journal of International Affairs* 24(3): 311–30.

Bailey, Michael A., Daniel J. Hopkins, and Todd Rogers. 2013. "Unresponsive and unpersuaded: The unintended consequences of voter persuasion efforts." Working Paper RWP13-034. Harvard Kennedy School.

Baker, Andy, Barry Ames, and Lucio Renno. 2006. "Social context and campaign volatility: Networks and neighborhoods in Brazil's 2002 election." *American Journal of Political Science* 50(2): 382–99.

Banda, Kevin K., and Thomas M. Carsey. 2015. "Two-stage elections, strategic candidates, and campaign agendas." *Electoral Studies* 40: 221–30.

Bandyopadhyay, Sanghamitra, and Elliott Green. 2021. "Explaining inter-ethnic marriage in Sub-Saharan Africa." *Journal of International Development* 33(4): 627–43.

Banful, Afua Branoah. 2010. "Old problems in the new solutions? Politically motivated allocation of program benefits and the 'new' fertilizer subsidies." *World Development* 39 (7): 1166–76.

Banful, Afua Branoah. 2011. "Do formula-based intergovernmental transfer mechanisms eliminate politically motivated targeting? Evidence from Ghana." *Journal of Development Economics* 96: 380–90.

Barkan, Joel D. 1979. "Bringing home the pork: Legislative behavior, rural development and political change in East Africa." In Joel Smith and Lloyd Musolf, eds., *Legislatures in Development.* Durham, NC: Duke University Press.

Barkan, Joel D. 1984. "Legislators, Elections, and Political Linkage." In Joel D. Barkan, ed., *Politics and Public Policy in Kenya and Tanzania.* New York: Praeger.

Barkan, Joel D. 1987. "The electoral process and peasant-state relation in Kenya." In Fred M. Hayward, ed., *Elections in Independent Africa.* Boulder, CO: Westview Press.

Barkan, Joel D. 1993. "Kenya: Lessons from a flawed election." *Journal of Democracy* 4(3): 85–99.

Barkan, Joel D. 1995. "Debate: PR and Southern Africa: Elections in agrarian societies." *Journal of Democracy* 6(4): 106–16.

Barkan, Joel D. 2004. "Kenya after Moi." *Foreign Affairs* 83(1): 87–100.

Barkan, Joel D. 2008a. "Progress and retreat in Africa: Legislatures on the rise?" *Journal of Democracy* 19(2): 124–37.

Barkan, Joel D. 2008b. "Will the Kenyan settlement hold?" *Current History* 107(708): 147–53.

Barkan, Joel D. 2013. "Electoral Violence in Kenya." New York: Council on Foreign Relations. Contingency Planning Memorandum No. 17.

Barkan, Joel D., and Michael Chege. 1989. "Decentralizing the state: District focus and the politics of reallocation." *Journal of Modern African Studies* 27(3): 431–53.

Barkan, Joel D., and Frank Holmquist. 1989. "Peasant-state relations and the social base of self-help in Kenya." *World Politics* 41(3): 359–80.

Barkan, Joel D., and Njuguna Ng'ethe. 1998. "African ambiguities: Kenya tries again." *Journal of Democracy* 9(2): 32–48.

Bartels, Brandon, Jeremy Horowitz, and Eric Kramon. 2021. "Can democratic principles protect high courts from partisan backlash? Public reactions to the Kenyan Supreme Court's role in the 2017 election crisis." *American Journal of Political Science*.

Bartels, Larry M. 1985. "Resource allocation in a presidential campaign." *Journal of Politics* 47(3): 928–36.

Bartels, Larry M. 1993. "Message received: The political impact of media exposure." *American Political Science Review* 87(2): 267–85.

Bartels, Larry M. 1998. "Where the ducks are: Voting power in a party system." In John Geer, ed., *Politicians and Party Politics*. Baltimore: Johns Hopkins University Press.

Bartels, Larry M. 2006. "Priming and persuasion in presidential campaigns." In Henry E. Brady and Richard Johnson, eds., *Capturing Campaign Effects*. Ann Arbor, MI: University of Michigan Press.

Basedau, Matthias, and Anika Moroff. 2011. "Parties in chains: Do ethnic party bans in Africa promote peace?" *Party Politics* 17(2): 205–22.

Bates, Robert H. 1983. "Modernization and Ethnic Politics." In D. Rothchild and V. Olorunsola, eds., *State versus Ethnic Claims: African Policy Dilemmas*. Boulder, CO: Westview Press.

Bates, Robert H., and Steven A. Block. 2013. "Revisiting African agriculture: Institutional change and productivity growth." *Journal of Politics* 75(2): 372–84.

Baum, Matthew A., and David A. Lake. 2003. "The political economy of growth: Democracy and human capital." *American Journal of Political Science* 47(2): 333–47.

Beckett, Paul A. 1987. "Elections and democracy in Nigeria." In Fred M. Hayward, ed., *Elections in Independence Africa*. Boulder, CO: Westview Press.

Bennett, George and Carl Rosberg. 1961. *The Kenyatta Election: Kenya 1960–61*. London: Oxford University Press.

Berelson, Bernard R., Paul F. Lazarsfeld, and William N. McPhee. 1954. *Voting: A Study of Opinion Formation in a Presidential Campaign*. Chicago, IL: University of Chicago Press.

Berge, Lars Ivar Oppedal, Kjetil Bjorvatn, Simon Galle, Edward Miguel, Daniel N. Posner, Bertil Tungodden, and Kelly Zhang. 2020. "Ethnically biased? Experimental evidence from Kenya." *Journal of the European Economic Association* 18(1): 134–64.

Berman, Bruce J. 1998. "Ethnicity, patronage and the African state: The politics of uncivil nationalism." *African Affairs* 97(388): 305–41.

Berman, Bruce J., Jill Cottrell, and Yash Ghai. 2009. "Patrons, clients, and constitutions: Ethnic politics and political reform in Kenya." *Canadian Journal of African Studies / La Revue Canadienne des Etudes Africaines* 43(3): 462–506.

Berman, Bruce J., and John Lonsdale. 1992. *Unhappy Valley: Conflict in Kenya and Africa*. Ohio University Press.

Binswanger, Hans P. 1980. "Attitudes toward risk: Experimental measurement in rural India." *American Journal of Agricultural Economics* 62(3): 395–407.

Bleck, Jaimie, and Nicolas van de Walle. 2011. "Parties and issues in Francophone West Africa: Towards a theory of non-mobilization." *Democratization* 18(5): 1125–45.

Bleck, Jaimie, and Nicolas van de Walle. 2013. "Valence issues in African elections: Navigating uncertainty and the weight of the past." *Comparative Political Studies* 46(11): 1394–421.

Bleck, Jaimie, and Nicolas van de Walle. 2019. *Electoral politics in Africa since 1990: Continuity in change.* Cambridge: Cambridge University Press.

Boas, Taylor C. 2010. "Varieties of electioneering: Success contagion and presidential campaigns in Latin America." *World Politics* 62(4): 636–75.

Boas, Taylor C., and F. Daniel Hidalgo. 2011. "Controlling the airwaves: Incumbency advantage and community radio in Brazil." *American Journal of Political Science* 55(4): 869–85.

Bob-Milliar, George M. 2011. "'Te Nyɔgeyɛng Gbengbeng!' ('We are holding the umbrella very tight!'): Explaining the popularity of the NDC in the Upper West Region of Ghana." *Africa* 81(3): 455–73.

Bob-Milliar, George M. 2012. "Party factions and power blocs in Ghana: A case study of power politics in the National Democratic Congress." *Journal of Modern African Studies* 50(4): 573–601.

Bogonko, Sorobea Nyachieo. 1992. *A History of Modern Education in Kenya (1895–1991).* London: Evans Brothers Ltd.

Bold, Tessa, Mwangi Kimenyi, Germano Mwabu, and Justin Sandefur. 2013. "Why Did Abolishing School Fees Not Increase Public School Enrollment in Kenya?" Brookings Institute / Africa Growth Initiative. Working Paper #4.

Boone, Catherine. 2011. "Politically allocated land rights and the geography of electoral violence: The case of Kenya in the 1990s." *Comparative Political Studies* 44(10): 1311–42.

Box-Steffensmeier, Janet M., David Darmofal, and Christian A. Farrell. 2009. "The aggregate dynamics of campaigns." *Journal of Politics* 71(1): 309–23.

Branch, Daniel. 2011. *Kenya: Between Hope and Despair, 1963–2011.* New Haven: Yale University Press.

Branch, Daniel, and Nicholas Cheeseman. 2006. "The politics of control in Kenya: Understanding the bureaucratic-executive state, 1952–78." *Review of African Political Economy* 33(107): 11–31.

Brams, Steven J., and Morton D. Davis. 1974. "The 3/2's rule in presidential campaigning." *American Journal of Political Science* 68(1): 113–34.

Bratton, Michael, and Mwangi S. Kimenyi. 2008. "Voting in Kenya: Putting ethnicity in perspective." *Journal of Eastern African Studies* 2(2): 272–89.

Bratton, Michael, and Nicolas van de Walle. 1997. *Democratic Experiments in Africa: Regime Transitions in Comparative Perspective.* New York: Cambridge University Press.

Brazys, Samuel, Peter Heaney, and Patrick Paul Walsh. 2015. "Fertilizer and votes: Does strategic economic policy explain the 2009 Malawi election?" *Electoral Studies* 39: 39–55.

Briggs, Ryan C. 2012. "Electrifying the base? Aid and incumbent advantage in Ghana." *Journal of Modern African Studies* 50(4): 603–24.

Briggs, Ryan C. 2021. "Power to which people? Explaining how electrification targets voters across party rotations in Ghana." *World Development* 141.

Brown, Stephen. 2007. "From Demiurge to Midwife: Changing Donor Roles in Kenya's Democratizing Process." In Godwin R. Murunga and Shadroack W. Nasong'o, eds., *Kenya: The Struggle for Democracy.* London and Dakar: Zed Books.

Burgess, Robin, Remi Jedwab, Edward Miguel, Ameet Morjaria, and Gerard Padró i Miguel. 2015. "The value of democracy: Evidence from road building in Kenya." *American Economic Review* 105(6): 1817–51.

Bwayo, Philip. 2013. "Raila urges Uhuru to donate 'family' land." *The Nation*, February 21, p. 8.

Campbell, Angus, Philip E. Converse, Warren E. Miller, and Donald E. Stokes. 1960. *The American Voter*. New York: Wiley.

Campbell, James E. 2001. "Presidential Election Campaigns and Partisanship," in Jeffrey E. Cohen, Richard Fleisher, and Paul Kantor, eds., *American Political Parties: Decline or Resurgence?* Washington, DC: CQ Press.

Carbone, Giovanni. 2011. "Democratic demands and social policies: The politics of health reform in Ghana." *Journal of Modern African Studies* 49(3): 391–408.

Carbone, Giovanni. 2012. "Do new democracies deliver social welfare? Political regimes and health policy in Ghana and Cameroon." *Democratization* 19(2): 157–83.

Carbone, Giovanni, and Alessandro Pellegata. 2017. "To elect or not to elect: Leaders, alternation in power and social welfare in sub-Saharan Africa." *The Journal of Development Studies* 53(12): 1965–87.

Card, Emily, and Barbara Callaway. 1970. "Ghanaian politics: The elections and after." *Africa Report* 15(3): 10–15.

Carlson, Elizabeth. 2015. "Ethnic voting and accountability in Africa: A choice experiment in Uganda." *World Politics* 67(2): 353–85.

Carlson, Elizabeth. 2016. "Finding partisanship where we least expect it: Evidence of partisan bias in a new African democracy." *Political Behavior* 38(1): 129–54.

Carsey, Thomas M. 1995. "The contextual effects of race on white voter behavior: The 1989 New York City mayoral election." *Journal of Politics* 57(1): 221–8.

Carsey, Thomas M., Robert A. Jackson, Melissa Stewart, and James P. Nelson. 2011. "Strategic candidates, campaign dynamics, and campaign advertising in gubernatorial races." *State Politics & Policy Quarterly* 11(3): 269–98.

Casey, Katherine. 2015. "Crossing party lines: The effects of information on redistributive politics." *American Economic Review* 105(8): 2410–48.

Cederman, Lars-Erik, Nils B. Weidmann, and Kristian Skrede Gleditsch. 2011. "Horizontal inequalities and ethnonationalist civil war: A global comparison." *American Political Science Review* 105(3): 478–95.

Chabal, Patrick, and J. P. Daloz. 1999. *Africa Works: Disorder as Political Instrument*. Oxford: James Currey.

Chandra, Kanchan. 2001. "Cumulative findings in the study of ethnic politics." *APSA-CP* 12(1): 7–11.

Chandra, Kanchan. 2004. *Why Ethnic Parties Succeed: Patronage and Ethnic Headcounts in India*. Cambridge: Cambridge University Press.

Chauchard, Simon. 2016. "Unpacking ethnic preferences: Theory and micro-level evidence from Northern India." *Comparative Political Studies* 49(2): 253–84.

Chazan, Naomi. 1982. "Ethnicity and politics in Ghana." *Political Science Quarterly* 97(3): 461–85.

Cheeseman, Nic. 2008. "The Kenyan elections of 2007: An introduction." *Journal of Eastern African Studies* 2(2): 166–84.

Cheeseman, Nic. 2015. *Democracy in Africa: Successes, Failures, and the Struggle for Political Reform*. Cambridge: Cambridge University Press.

Cheeseman, Nic, Karuti Kanyinga, Gabrielle Lynch, Mutuma Ruteere, and Justin Willis. 2019. "Kenya's 2017 elections: Winner-takes-all politics as usual?" *Journal of Eastern African Studies* 13(2): 215–34.

Cheeseman, Nic, Gabrielle Lynch, and Justin Willis. 2014. "Democracy and its discontents: Understanding Kenya's 2013 elections." *Journal of Eastern African Studies* 8(1): 2–24.

Chege, Michael. 2008. "Kenya: Back from the brink?" *Journal of Democracy* 19(4): 125–39.

Chege, Michael. 2018. "Kenya's electoral misfire." *Journal of Democracy* 29(2): 158–72.

Chua, Amy. 2003. *World on Fire: How Exporting Free Market Democracy Breeds Ethnic Hatred and Global Instability.* New York: Doubleday.

Colantoni, Claude S., Terrence J. Levesque, and Peter C. Ordeshook. 1975. "Campaign resource allocation under the electoral college." *American Political Science Review* 69(1): 141–54.

Colclough, Christopher, and Andrew Webb. 2012. "A triumph of hope over reason? Aid accords and education policy in Kenya." *Comparative Education* 48(2): 263–80.

Collier, Ruth Berins. 1982. *Regimes in Tropical Africa: Changing Forms of Supremacy, 1945–1975.* University of California Press.

Collingwood, Loren, Kassra Oskooii, Sergio Garcia-Rios, and Matt Barreto. 2016. "eiCompare: Comparing ecological inference estimates across EI and EI:R×c." *The R Journal* 8(2): 92–101.

Commission of Inquiry into Post-Election Violence (CIPEV). 2008. *Final Report.*

Conover, Pamela Johnston. 1981. "Political cues and the perception of candidates." *American Politics Quarterly* 9(4): 427–48.

Conroy-Krutz, Jeffrey K. 2013. "Information and ethnic politics in Africa." *British Journal of Political Science* 43(2): 345–73.

Conroy-Krutz, Jeffrey, Devra C. Moehler, and Rosario Aguilar. 2016. "Partisan cues and vote choice in new multiparty systems." *Comparative Political Studies* 49(1): 3–35.

Converse, Philip. 1964. "The Nature of Belief Systems in Mass Publics," in David Apter, ed., *Ideology and Discontent.* New York: Free Press.

Cowen, Michael and Karuti Kanyinga. 2002. "The 1997 Elections in Kenya: The Politics of Communality and Locality." In Michael Cowen and Liisa Laakso, eds., *Multi-Party Elections in Africa.* Oxford: James Currey.

Cox, Gary W., and Mathew D. McCubbins. 1986. "Electoral politics as a redistributive game." *Journal of Politics* 48(2): 370–89.

Crespin-Boucaud, Juliette. 2020. "Interethnic and interfaith marriages in sub-Saharan Africa." *World Development* 125.

Crook, Richard C. 1997. "Winning coalitions and ethno-regional politics: The failure of the opposition in the 1990 and 1995 elections in Côte d'Ivoire." *African Affairs* 96(383): 215–42.

Cussac, Anne. 2008. "'Kibaki Tena?' The challenges of a campaign." *East African Review* 38: 35–55.

D'arcy, Michelle. 2013. "Non-state actors and universal services in Tanzania and Lesotho: State-building by alliance." *Journal of Modern African Studies* 51(2): 219–47.

Davis, Gavin. 2004. "Proportional representation and racial campaigning in South Africa." *Nationalism and Ethnic Politics* 10(2): 297–324.

Dawson, Michael C. 1995. *Behind the Mule: Race and Class in African-American Politics.* Princeton, NJ: Princeton University Press.

De Sardan, J. P. Olivier. 1999. "A moral economy of corruption in Africa?" *Journal of Modern African Studies* 37(1): 25–52.

Della Vigna, Stefano and Ethan Kaplan. 2007. "The Fox News effect: Media bias and voting." *Quarterly Journal of Economics* 122(3): 1187–234.

Delli Carpini, Michael X., and Scott Keeter. 1996. *What Americans Know about Politics and Why It Matters.* New Haven, CT: Yale University Press.

Dercon, Stefan, and Roxana Gutiérrez-Romero. 2012. "Triggers and characteristics of the 2007 Kenyan electoral violence." *World Development* 40(4): 731–44.

Di Falco, Salvatore, and Charles Perrings. 2005. "Crop biodiversity, risk management and the implications of agricultural assistance." *Ecological Economics* 55(4): 459–66.

Diamond, Larry. 2002. "Elections without democracy: Thinking about hybrid regimes." *Journal of Democracy* 13(2): 21–35.

Diaz-Cayeros, Alberto, Federico Estévez, and Beatriz Magaloni. 2016. *The Political Logic of Poverty Relief: Electoral Strategies and Social Policy in Mexico.* Cambridge: Cambridge University Press.

Dickson, Eric S. and Kenneth Scheve. 2006. "Social identity, political speech, and electoral competition." *Journal of Theoretical Politics* 18(1): 5–39.

Dixit, Avinash and John Londregan. 1996. "The determinants of success of special interests in redistributive politics." *Journal of Politics* 58(4): 1132–55.

Dixon, Robin. 2017. "Kenyans vote in fiercely contested presidential election." *Los Angeles Times* (online edition). August 8, 2017.

Downs, Anthony. 1957. *An Economic Theory of Democracy.* New York: Harper.

Dreher, Axel, Andreas Fuchs, Roland Hodler, Bradley C. Parks, Paul A. Raschky, and Michael J. Tierney. 2019. "African leaders and the geography of China's foreign assistance." *Journal of Development Economics* 140: 44–71.

Dulani, Boniface, Adam S. Harris, Jeremy Horowitz, and Happy Kayuni. 2021. "Electoral preferences among multiethnic voters in Africa." *Comparative Political Studies* 54(2): 280–311.

Dunning, Thad, and Lauren Harrison. 2010. "Cross-cutting cleavages and ethnic voting: An experimental study of cousinage in Mali." *American Political Science Review* 104(1): 21–39.

Easterly, William, and Ross Levine. 1997. "Africa's growth tragedy: Policies and ethnic divisions." *Quarterly Journal of Economics* 112(4): 1203–50.

Ejdemyr, Simon, Eric Kramon, and Amanda Lea Robinson. 2018. "Segregation, ethnic favoritism, and the strategic targeting of local public goods." *Comparative Political Studies* 51(9): 1111–43.

Ekeh, Peter P. 1975. "Colonialism and the two publics in Africa: A theoretical statement." *Comparative Studies in Society and History* 17(1): 91–112.

Elischer, Sebastian. 2013. *Political Parties in Africa: Ethnicity and Party Formation.* Cambridge: Cambridge University Press.

Eshiwani, George S. 1993. *Education in Kenya since Independence.* Nairobi: East African Publishers.

Fearon, James. 1999. "Why ethnic politics and 'pork' tend to go together." Typescript.

Fearon, James. 2003. "Ethnic and cultural diversity by country." *Journal of Economic Growth* 8(2): 195–222.

Fehr-Duda, Helga, Adrian Bruhin, Thomas Epper, and Renate Schubert. 2010. "Rationality on the rise: Why relative risk aversion increases with stake size." *Journal of Risk and Uncertainty* 40(2): 147–180.

Ferree, Karen E. 2006. "Explaining South Africa's racial census." *Journal of Politics* 68(4): 803–15.

Ferree, Karen E. 2010. "The social origins of electoral volatility in Africa." *British Journal of Political Science* 40(4): 759–79.

Ferree, Karen E. 2011. *Framing the Race in South Africa: The Political Origins of Racial Census Elections.* Cambridge: Cambridge University Press.

Ferree, Karen E., and Jeremy Horowitz. 2010. "Ties that bind? The rise and decline of ethno-regional partisanship in Malawi, 1994–2009." *Democratization* 17(3): 534–63.

Ferree, Karen E., Clark C. Gibson, and James D. Long. 2014. "Voting behavior and electoral irregularities in Kenya's 2013 Election." *Journal of Eastern African Studies* 8(1): 153–72.

Figueiredo, Rui de and Barry R. Weingast. 1999. "The rationality of fear: Political opportunism and ethnic conflict." In Barbara Walter and Jack Snyder, eds., *Civil Wars, Insecurity and Intervention*. New York: Columbia University Press.

Finkel, Steven E. 1993. "Reexamining the 'minimal effects' model in recent presidential campaigns." *Journal of Politics* 55(1): 1–21.

Finkel, Steven E., Jeremy Horowitz, and Reynaldo T. Rojo-Mendoza. 2012. "Civic education and democratic backsliding in the wake of Kenya's post-2007 election violence." *Journal of Politics* 74(1): 52–65.

Fitzgerald, John, Peter Gottschalk, and Robert Moffitt. 1998. "An analysis of sample attrition in panel data." *Journal of Human Resources* 33(2): 251–99.

Flores-Macias, Francisco. 2009. "Electoral volatility in 2006." In Jorge I. Domingez, Chappell Lawson, and Alejandro Moreno, eds., *Consolidating Mexico's Democracy*. Baltimore, MA: Johns Hopkins University Press.

Fox, Roddy. 1996. "Bleak future for multi-party elections in Kenya." *Journal of Modern African Studies* 34(4): 597–607.

Franck, Raphael, and Ilia Rainer. 2012. "Does the leader's ethnicity matter? Ethnic favoritism, education, and health in sub-Saharan Africa." *American Political Science Review* 106(2): 294–325.

Fridy, Kevin S. 2007. "The elephant, umbrella, and quarrelling cocks: Disaggregating partisanship in Ghana's Fourth Republic." *African Affairs* 106: 281–305.

Fridy, Kevin S. 2012. "Where are Ghana's swing voters? A look at the voters responsible for alternating power in one of Africa's most successful democracies." *Africa Review* 4(2): 107–21.

Fumey, Abel, and Festus O. Egwaikhide. 2018. "Political economy of intergovernmental fiscal transfers: The rural–urban dynamics in Ghana." *African Development Review* 30 (1): 33–44.

Gadjanova, Elena. 2017. "Ethnic wedge issues in electoral campaigns in Africa's presidential regimes." *African Affairs* 116(464): 484–507.

Gadjanova, Elena. 2021. "Status-quo or grievance coalitions: The logic of cross-ethnic campaign appeals in Africa's highly diverse states." *Comparative Political Studies* 54 (3–4): 652–85.

Gagnon, V. P. 2004. *The Myth of Ethnic War: Serbia and Croatia in the 1990s*. Ithaca: Cornell University Press.

Gans-Morse, Jordan, Sebastian Mazzuca, and Simeon Nichter. 2014. "Varieties of clientelism: Machine politics during elections." *American Journal of Political Science* 58(2): 415–32.

Gelman, Andrew and Gary King. 1993. "Why are American presidential election campaign polls so variable when votes are so predictable?" *British Journal of Political Science* 23(4): 409–51.

Gerber, Alan S., and Donald P. Green. 2000. "The effects of personal canvassing, telephone calls, and direct mail on voter turnout: A field experiment." *American Political Science Review* 94(3): 653–64.

Gerber, Alan S., and Donald P. Green. 2005. "Correction to Gerber and Green (2000), replication of disputed findings, and reply to Imai (2004)." *American Political Science Review* 99(2): 301–13.

Gertzel, Cherry J. 1970. *The Politics of Independent Kenya, 1963–8*. Evanston, IL: Northwestern University Press.

Gibson, Clark C., and James D. Long. 2009. "The presidential and parliamentary elections in Kenya, December 2007." *Electoral Studies* 28(3): 497–502.

Gilens, Martin, and Naomi Murakawa. 2002. "Elite Cues and Political Decision-Making." In M. X. Delli Carpini, L. Huddy, and R. Y. Shapiro, eds., *Research in Micropolitics: Political Decision-Making, Deliberation, and Participation* (volume 6). New York: JAI Press.

Goldstein, Ken, and Paul Freedman. 2002. "Lessons learned: Campaign advertising in the 2000 elections." *Political Communication* 19(1): 5–28.

Goldsworthy, David. 1982. *Tom Mboya: The Man Kenya Wanted to Forget*. London: Heinemann.

Green, Donald P., and Adam Zelizer. 2017. "How much GOTV mail is too much? Results from a large-scale field experiment." *Journal of Experimental Political Science* 4(2): 107–18.

Greene, Kenneth F. 2011. "Campaign persuasion and nascent partisanship in Mexico's new democracy." *American Journal of Political Science* 55(2): 398–416.

Grignon, François. 2001. "Breaking the 'Ngilu Wave': The 1997 elections in Ukambani." In M. Rutten, A. Mazrui, and F. Grignon, eds., *Out for the Count: The 1997 Elections and Prospects for Democracy in Kenya*. Kampala: Fountain Publishers.

Gyimah-Boadi, Emmanuel. 2001. "A peaceful turnover in Ghana." *Journal of Democracy* 12 (2): 103–17.

Gyimah-Boadi, Emmanuel. 2009. "The 2008 Freedom House Survey: Another step forward for Ghana." *Journal of Democracy* 20(2): 138–52.

Gyimah-Boadi, Emmanuel, and Richard Asante. 2006. "Ethnic structure, inequality, and public sector governance in Ghana." In Y. Bangura, ed., *Ethnic Inequalities and Public Sector Governance*. Basingstoke: Palgrave Macmillan.

Harbeson, John. 1973. *Nation-Building in Kenya: The Role of Land Reform*. Evanston, IL: Northwestern University Press.

Harding, Robin. 2015. "Attribution and accountability: Voting for roads in Ghana." *World Politics* 67(4): 656–89.

Harding, Robin. 2020. *Rural Democracy: Elections and Development in Africa*. Oxford: Oxford University Press.

Harding, Robin, and David Stasavage. 2014. "What democracy does (and doesn't do) for basic services: School fees, school inputs, and African elections." *Journal of Politics* 76(1): 229–45.

Harneit-Sievers, Axel, and Ralph-Michael Peters. 2008. "Kenya's 2007 general election and its aftershocks." *Africa Spectrum* 43(1): 133–44.

Harris, J. Andrew, and Daniel N. Posner. 2019. "(Under what conditions) do politicians reward their supporters? Evidence from Kenya's Constituencies Development Fund." *American Political Science Review* 113(1): 123–39.

Hassan, Mai. 2015. "Continuity despite change: Kenya's new constitution and executive power." *Democratization* 22(4): 587–609.

Hassan, Mai and Kathleen Klaus. 2020. "Closing the Gap: The Politics of Property Rights in Kenya." Working paper.

Haugerud, Angelique. 1993. *The Culture of Politics in Modern Kenya*. Cambridge: Cambridge University Press.

Herr, Paul. 2002. "The impact of campaign appearances in the 1996 election." *Journal of Politics* 64(3): 904–13.

Hersh, Eitan D. 2015. *Hacking the Electorate: How Campaigns Perceive Voters*. Cambridge: Cambridge University Press.

Hillygus, D. Sunshine, and Simon Jackman. 2003. "Voter decision making in election 2000: Campaign effects, partisan activation, and the Clinton legacy." *American Journal of Political Science* 47(4): 583–96.

Hillygus, D. Sunshine, and Todd Shields. 2008. *The Persuadable Voter: Wedge Issues in Presidential Campaigns*. Princeton, NJ: Princeton University Press.

Hirano, Shigeo, Gabriel S. Lenz, Maksim Pinkovskiy, and James M. Snyder Jr. 2014. "Voter learning in primary elections." *American Journal of Political Science* 59(1): 91–108.

Hoffman, Barak D., and James D. Long. 2013. "Parties, ethnicity, and voting in African elections." *Comparative Politics* 45(2): 127–46.

Hoffmann, Vivian, Pamela Jakiela, Michael Kremer, and Ryan Sheely. 2015. "Targeting, Discretionary Funding, and the Provision of Local Public Goods: Evidence from Kenya." Typescript.

Holbrook, Thomas M., and Scott D. McClurg. 2005. "The mobilization of core supporters: Campaigns, turnout, and electoral composition in United States presidential elections." *American Journal of Political Science* 49(4): 689–703.

Holt, Charles A., and Susan K. Laury. 2002. "Risk aversion and incentive effects." *American Economic Review* 92(5): 1644–55.

Horowitz, Donald L. 1985. *Ethnic Groups in Conflict*. Berkeley: University of California Press.

Horowitz, Donald L. 1991. *A Democratic South Africa? Constitutional Engineering in a Divided Society*. Berkeley: University of California Press.

Horowitz, Jeremy. 2012. "Campaigns and Ethnic Polarization in Kenya." Ph.D. dissertation, San Diego: University of California.

Horowitz, Jeremy. 2016. "The ethnic logic of campaign strategy in diverse societies: Evidence from Kenya." *Comparative Political Studies* 49(3): 324–56.

Horowitz, Jeremy, and James Long. 2016. "Strategic voting, information, and ethnicity in emerging democracies: Evidence from Kenya." *Electoral Studies* 44: 351–61.

Horsnby, Charles. 2013. *Kenya: A History since Independence*. New York: I. B. Tauris.

Hovland, Carl I., and Walter Weiss. 1951. "The Influence of source credibility on communication effectiveness." *Public Opinion Quarterly* 15(4): 635–50.

Huber, Gregory A., and John S. Lapinski. 2006. "The 'race card' revisited: Assessing racial priming in policy contests." *American Journal of Political Science* 50(2): 421–40.

Huber, John D. 2012. "Measuring ethnic voting: Do proportional electoral laws politicize ethnicity?" *American Journal of Political Science* 56(4): 986–1001.

Huckfeldt, Robert, and John Sprague. 1995. *Citizens, Politics, and Social Communication*. Cambridge: Cambridge University Press.

Human Rights Watch (HRW). 1993. *Divide and Rule: State-Sponsored Ethnic Violence in Kenya*. New York: Human Rights Watch.

Human Rights Watch (HRW). 2008. *Ballots to Bullets: Organized Political Violence and Kenya's Crisis of Governance*. New York: Human Rights Watch.

Human Rights Watch (HRW). 2010. "Kenya: Opposition Officials Helped Plan Rift Valley Violence." Retrieved on August 1, 2010, www.hrw.org/en/news/2008/01/23/kenya-opposition-officials-helped-plan-rift-valley-violence.

Hyde, Susan D., and Nikolay Marinov. 2012. "Which elections can be lost?" *Political Analysis* 20(2): 191–210.

Hydén, Göran. 1980. *Beyond Ujamaa in Tanzania: Underdevelopment and an Uncaptured Peasantry*. University of California Press.

Hydén, Göran. 1983. *No Shortcuts to Progress: African Development Management in Perspective*. University of California Press.

Ichino, Nahomi, and Noah L. Nathan. 2013. "Crossing the line: Local ethnic geography and voting in Ghana." *American Political Science Review* 107(2): 344–61.

Iddi, Ziblim. 2016. "The Regional Balance of Presidential Tickets in Ghanaian Elections: Analysis of the 2008 General Election." In Kwame A. Ninsin, ed., *Issues in Ghana's Electoral Politics*. Dakar: CODESRIA.

Imai, Kosuke. 2005. "Do get-out-the-vote calls reduce turnout? The importance of statistical methods for field experiments." *American Political Science Review* 99(2): 283–300.

International Budget Partnership. 2015. *Parliament and the National Treasure: How Are They Playing Their Roles in Kenya's New Budget Process?* IBP Budget Policy Brief No. 33.

International Crisis Group. 2008. *Kenya in Crisis*. Africa Report #137, February 21, 2008.

IRIN. 2008. "Kenya: Spreading the word of hate." February 11, 2008. http://www.irinnews.org/Report.aspx?ReportId=76346.

Iscan, Talan B., Daniel Rosenblum, and Katie Tinker. 2015. "School fees and access to primary education: Assessing four decades of policy in sub-Saharan Africa." *Journal of African Economies* 24(4): 559–92.

Iyengar, Shanto, and Donald Kinder. 1987. *News That Matters: Television and American Opinion*. Chicago, IL: University of Chicago Press.

Iyengar, Shanto, and Adam F. Simon. 2000. "New perspectives and evidence on political communication and campaign effects." *Annual Review of Psychology* 51: 149–69.

Jablonski, Ryan S. 2014. "Does aid buy votes? How electoral strategies shape the distribution of aid." *World Politics* 66(2): 293–330.

Jackson, Robert H. and Carl G. Rosberg. 1984. "Personal rule: Theory and practice in Africa." *Comparative Politics* 16(4): 421–42.

Jacobson, Gary C. 1990. "The effects of campaign spending in House elections: New evidence for old arguments." *American Journal of Political Science* 34(2): 334–62.

Jeffries, Richard. 1998. "The Ghanaian elections of 1996: Towards the consolidation of democracy?" *African Affairs* 97(387): 189–208.

Jeffries, Richard, and Clare Thomas. 1993. "The Ghanaian elections of 1992." *African Affairs* 92(368): 331–66.

Jockers, Heinz, Dirk Kohnert, and Paul Nugent. 2010. "The successful Ghana election of 2008: A convenient myth?" *Journal of Modern African Studies* 48(1): 95–115.

Jones, Jeffrey M. 1998. "Does bringing out the candidate bring out the votes? The effects of nominee campaigning in Presidential elections." *American Politics Quarterly* 26(4): 395–419.

Joseph, Richard. 1987. *Democracy and Prebendal Politics in Nigeria: The Rise and Fall of the Second Republic*. New York: Cambridge University Press.

Kadima, Denis and Felix Owuor. 2014. "Kenya's decade of experiments with political party alliances and coalitions: Motivations, impacts and prospects." *Journal of African Elections* 13(1): 150–80.

Kagwanja, Mwangi. 1998. *Killing the Vote: State-Sponsored Violence and Flawed Elections in Kenya*. Nairobi: Kenya Human Rights Commission.

Kagwanja, Peter. 2009. "Courting genocide: Populism, ethno-nationalism and the informalisation of violence in Kenya's 2008 post-election crisis." *Journal of Contemporary African Studies* 27(3): 365–87.

Kagwanja, Peter, and Roger Southall. 2009. "Introduction: Kenya–a democracy in retreat?" *Journal of Contemporary African Studies* 27(3): 259–77.

Kamungi, Prisca Mbura. 2009. "The politics of displacement in multiparty Kenya." *Journal of Contemporary African Studies* 27(3): 345–64.

Kanyinga, Karuti. 1998. "Contestation over Political Space: The State and the Demobilisation of Opposition Politics in Kenya." In Olukoshi, Adebayo O., ed., *The Politics of Opposition in Contemporary Africa*. Uppsala: Nordiska Afrikainstitutet.

Kanyinga, Karuti. 2009. "The legacy of the White Highlands: Land rights, ethnicity and the post-2007 election violence in Kenya." *Journal of Contemporary African Studies* 27(3): 325–44.

Kanyinga, Karuti. 2016. "Devolution and the new politics of development in Kenya." *African Studies Review* 59(3): 155–67.

Kanyinga, Karuti, and Sophie Walker. 2013. "Building a political settlement: The international approach to Kenya's 2008 post-election crisis." *Stability: International Journal of Security and Development* 2(2): 1–21.

Kariuki, Joseph. 2005. "Choosing the President: Electoral Campaigns in Northern Central Kenya." In Hervé Maupeu, Musambayi Katumanga, and Winnie Mitullah, eds., *The Moi Succession: Elections 2002*. Nairobi: Transafrica Press.

Kasara, Kimuli. 2007. "Tax me if you can: Ethnic geography, democracy, and the taxation of agriculture in Africa." *American Political Science Review* 101(1): 159–72.

Kaspin, Deborah. 1995. "The politics of ethnicity in Malawi's democratic transition." *Journal of Modern African Studies* 33(4): 595–620.

Kaufmann, Karen M., John R. Petrocik, and Daron R. Shaw. 2008. *Unconventional Wisdom: Facts and Myths about American Voters*. Oxford: Oxford University Press.

Keefer, Philip. 2007. "Clientelism, credibility, and the policy choices of young democracies." *American Journal of Political Science* 51(4): 804–21.

Keller, Edmond. 2014. *Identity, Citizenship, and Political Conflict in Africa*. Indiana University Press.

Kelly, Bob, and R. B. Bening. 2013. "The Ghanaian elections of 2012." *Review of African Political Economy* 40(137): 475–84.

Kenya Human Rights Commission. 1997. *Kayas of Deprivation, Kayas of Blood: Violence, Ethnicity and the State in Coastal Kenya*. Nairobi: KHRC.

Kenya Human Rights Commission. 1998. *Killing the Vote: State Sponsored Violence and Flawed Elections in Kenya*. Nairobi: KHRC.

Kenya National Bureau of Statistics. 2014. *Socio-Economic Atlas of Kenya: Depicting the National Population Census by County and Sub-Location*. Nairobi: Kenya National Bureau of Statistics.

Kenya National Commission on Human Rights (KNCHR). 2008. *On the Brink of the Precipice: A Human Rights Account of Kenya's Post-2007 Election Violence*. Nairobi: KNCHR.

Khadiagala, Gilbert M. 2010. "Political movements and coalition politics in Kenya: Entrenching ethnicity." *South African Journal of International Affairs* 17(1): 65–84.

Kim, Eun Kyung. 2018. "Sector-based vote choice: A new approach to explaining core and swing voters in Africa." *International Area Studies Review* 21(1): 28–50.

Kimathi, Wambui. 1993. "A strategic seclusion – yet again! The 1997 general elections in Luo Nyanza." In Marcel Rutten, Alamin Mazrui, and Francois Grignon, eds., *Out for the Count: The 1997 General Elections and Prospects for Democracy in Kenya*. Kampala: Fountain Publishers.

King, Gary. 1997. *A Solution to the Ecological Inference Problem*. Princeton, N.J.: Princeton University Press.

Kinyungu, Cyrus, and Allan Kisia. "Raila says he would ask corrupt leaders to account for their deeds." *The Standard*, September 23, 2007, pp. 1 and 4.

Kitschelt, Herbert. 2000. "Linkages between citizens and politicians in democratic polities." *Comparative Political Studies* 33(3): 845–79.

Kjær, Anne Mette, and Ole Therkildsen. 2013. "Elections and landmark policies in Tanzania and Uganda." *Democratization* 20(4): 592–614.

Klaus, Kathleen. 2020. *Political Violence in Kenya: Land, Elections, and Claim-Making.* Cambridge: Cambridge University Press.

Klaus, Kathleen, and Matthew I. Mitchell. 2015. "Land grievances and the mobilization of electoral violence: Evidence from Côte d'Ivoire and Kenya." *Journal of Peace Research* 52(5): 622–35.

Klopp, Jacqueline M. 2001. "'Ethnic clashes' and winning elections: The case of Kenya's electoral despotism." *Canadian Journal of African Studies* 35(3): 473–517.

Klopp, Jacqueline M. 2002. "Can moral ethnicity trump political tribalism? The struggle for land and nation in Kenya." *African Studies* 61(2): 269–94.

Klopp, Jacqueline, and Prisca Kamungi. 2008. "Violence and elections: Will Kenya collapse?" *World Policy Journal* 24(4): 11–18.

Koter, Dominika. 2013. "King makers: Local leaders and ethnic politics in Africa." *World Politics* 65(2): 187–232.

Kpsang, Wyclieff. 2013. "Cord calls for tolerance as crowd turns unruly." *The Nation*, February 24.

Kramon, Eric. 2018. *Money for Votes: The Causes and Consequences of Electoral Clientelism in Africa.* Cambridge: Cambridge University Press.

Kramon, Eric, and Daniel N. Posner. 2011. "Kenya's new constitution." *Journal of Democracy* 22(2): 89–103.

Kramon, Eric, and Daniel N. Posner. 2016. "Ethnic favoritism in education in Kenya." *Quarterly Journal of Political Science* 11: 1–58.

Kuenzi, Michelle, and Gina M.S. Lambright. 2005. "Party systems and democratic consolidation in Africa's electoral regimes." *Party Politics* 11(4): 423–46.

Kuenzi, Michelle, and Gina M.S. Lambright. 2007. "Voter turnout in Africa's multiparty regimes." *Comparative Political Studies* 40(6): 665–90.

Kuklinski, James H., and Norman L. Hurley. 1994. "On hearing and interpreting political messages: A cautionary tale of citizen cue-taking." *Journal of Politics* 56(3): 729–51.

Kyle, Keith. 1999. *The Politics of Independence Kenya.* New York: St. Martin's Press.

Ladd, Jonathan McDonald, and Gabriel S. Lenz. 2009. "Exploiting a rare communication shift to document the persuasive power of the news media." *American Journal of Political Science* 53(2): 394–410.

Laitin, David, and Daniel N. Posner. 2001. "The implications of constructivism for constructing ethnic fractionalization indices." *APSA-CP: Newsletter of the Organized Section in Comparative Politics of the American Political Science Association* 12(1): 13–17.

Lake, David A., and Matthew A. Baum. 2001. "The invisible hand of democracy: Political control and the provision of public services." *Comparative Political Studies* 34(6): 587–621.

Langer, Arnim. 2007. "The Peaceful Management of Horizontal Inequalities in Ghana." *CRISE Working Paper* 25.

Langer, Arnim, and Ukoha Ukiwo. 2008. "Ethnicity, religion and the state in Ghana and Nigeria: Perceptions from the street." In Frances Stewart, ed., *Horizontal Inequalities and Conflict*. London: Palgrave Macmillan.

Lawson, Chappell, and James McCann. 2004. "Television news, Mexico's 2000 elections and media effects in emerging democracies." *British Journal of Political Science* 35(1): 1–30.

Lazarsfeld, Paul Felix, Bernard Berelson, and Hazel Gaudet. 1944. *The People's Choice.* New York: Columbia University Press.

Lenz, Gabriel S. 2012. *Follow the Leader? How Voters Respond to Politicians' Performance and Policies.* University of Chicago Press.

Leonard, David K. 1991. *African Successes: Four Public Managers of Kenyan Rural Development.* Berkeley: University of California Press.

Leys, Colin. 1975. *Underdevelopment in Kenya: The Political Economy of Neo-Colonialism.* Berkeley: University of California Press.

Li, Jia. 2018. "Ethnic favoritism in primary education in Kenya: Effects of coethnicity with the president." *Education Economics* 26(2): 194–212.

Lijphart, Arend. 1977. *Democracy in Plural Societies.* New Haven: Yale University Press.

Lindbeck, Assar, and Jörgen W. Weibull. 1987. "Balanced-budget redistribution as the outcome of political competition." *Public Choice* 52(3): 273–97.

Lindberg, Staffan, and Minion Morrison. 2005. "Exploring voter alignments in Africa: Core and swing voters in Ghana." *Journal of Modern African Studies* 43(4): 565–86.

Lindberg, Staffan I. 2003. "'It's Our Time to "Chop"': Do elections in Africa feed neo-patrimonialism rather than counter-act it?" *Democratization* 10(2): 121–40.

Lindberg, Staffan I. 2010. "What accountability pressures do MPs in Africa face and how do they respond? Evidence from Ghana." *Journal of Modern African Studies* 48(1): 117–42.

Little, Peter D., Kevin Smith, Barbara A. Cellarius, D. Layne Coppock, and Christopher Barrett. 2001. "Avoiding disaster: Diversification and risk management among East African herders." *Development and Change* 32(3): 401–33.

Long, J. Scott, and Jeremy Freese. 2006. *Regression Models for Categorical Dependent Variables Using Stata.* College Station, TX: Stata Press.

Lonsdale, John. 1994. "Moral Ethnicity and Politcal Tribalism." In P. Kaarsholm and J. Hultin, eds., *Inventions and Boundaries: Historical and Anthropological Approaches to the Study of Ethnicity and Nationalism.* Roskilde: Roskilde University.

Lynch, Gabrielle. 2006. "The fruits of perception: 'Ethnic politics' and the case of Kenya's constitutional referendum." *African Studies* 65(2): 233–70.

Lynch, Gabrielle. 2008. "Courting the Kalenjin: The failure of dynasticism and the strength of the ODM wave in Kenya's Rift Valley province." *African Affairs* 107(429): 541–68.

Lynch, Gabrielle. 2010. "Histories of Association and Difference: The Construction and Negotiation of Ethnicity." In Daniel Branch, Nicholas Cheeseman, and Leigh Gardner, eds., *Our Turn to Eat: Politics in Kenya since 1950.* Berlin, Germany: LIT Verlag.

Lynch, Gabrielle. 2011. *I Say to You: Ethnic Politics and the Kalenjin in Kenya.* University of Chicago Press.

Lynch, Gabrielle. 2014. "Electing the 'alliance of the accused': The success of the Jubilee Alliance in Kenya's Rift Valley." *Journal of Eastern African Studies* 8(1): 93–114.

MacArthur, Julie. 2008. "How the west was won: Regional politics and prophetic promises in the 2007 Kenya elections." *Journal of Eastern African Studies* 2(2): 227–41.

Makiche, Edwin and Rawlings Otieno. 2013. "CORD ends Rift tour with calls for a united vote." *The Standard*, February 18, p. 4.

Malik, Aditi. 2016. "Mobilizing a defensive Kikuyu–Kalenjin alliance: The politicization of the International Criminal Court in Kenya's 2013 presidential election." *African Conflict and Peacebuilding Review* 6(2): 48–73.

Markowitz, Harry. 1952. "Portfolio selection." *The Journal of Finance* 12: 77–91.

Marris, Peter, and Anthony Somerset. 1971. *African Businessmen. A Study of Entrepreneurship and Development in Kenya*. London: Routledge and Kegan Paul.

Mason, Nicole M., Thomas S. Jayne, and Nicolas van De Walle. 2017. "The political economy of fertilizer subsidy programs in Africa: Evidence from Zambia." *American Journal of Agricultural Economics* 99(3): 705–31.

Maupeu, Hervé. 2008. "Revisiting post-election violence." *Les Cahiers d'Afrique de l'Est/The East African Review* 38: 193–230.

Mayer, William G. 2006. "The swing voter in American presidential elections." *American Politics Research* 35(3): 358–88.

McDonnell, Erin Metz. 2016. "Conciliatory states: Elite ethno-demographics and the puzzle of public goods within diverse African states." *Comparative Political Studies* 49(11): 1513–49.

Meisler, Stanley. 1970. "Tribal politics harass Kenya." *Foreign Affairs* 49(1): 111–21.

Mendelberg, Tali. 2001. *The Race Card: Campaign Strategy, Implicit Messages, and the Norm of Equality*. Princeton, NJ: Princeton University Press.

Mensah, Joseph, Joseph R. Oppong, and Christoph M. Schmidt. 2010. "Ghana's National Health Insurance scheme in the context of the health MDGs: An empirical evaluation using propensity score matching." *Health Economics* 19: 95–106.

Miguel, Edward, and Farhan Zaidi. 2003. "Do politicians reward their supporters? Regression discontinuity evidence from Ghana." Typescript.

Mkawale, Stephen and Nikko Tanui. 2017. "Uhuru braves heavy rains to woo south Rift." *The Standard* (online version), July 30, 2017.

Morrison, Minion K.C., and Jae Woo Hong. 2006. "Ghana's political parties: How ethno/regional variations sustain the national two-party system." *Journal of Modern African Studies* 44(4): 623–47.

Mozaffar, Shaheen, and James R. Scarritt. 2005. "The puzzle of African party systems." *Party Politics* 11(4): 399–421.

Mueller, Susanne D. 1984. "Government and opposition in Kenya, 1966–9." *Journal of Modern African Studies* 22(3): 399–427.

Mueller, Susanne D. 2008. "The political economy of Kenya's crisis." *Journal of Eastern African Studies* 2(2): 185–210.

Mueller, Susanne D. 2020. "High-stakes ethnic politics." In Nic Cheeseman, Karuti Kanyinga, and Gabrielle Lynch, eds., *The Oxford Handbook of Kenyan Politics*. Oxford: Oxford University Press.

Muigai, Githu. 1995. "Ethnicity and the renewal of competitive elections in Kenya." In H. Glickman, ed., *Ethnic Conflict and Democratisation in Africa*. Atlanta: African Studies Association Press.

Mukudi, Edith. 2004. "Education for all: A framework for addressing the persisting illusion for the Kenyan context." *International Journal of Educational Development* 24(3): 231–40.

Murunga, Godwin R., and Shadroack W. Nasong'o. 2006. "Bent on self-destruction: The Kibaki regime in Kenya." *Journal of Contemporary African Studies* 24(1): 1–28.

Muranga, Godwin R., and Shadrack W. Nasong'o, eds. 2007. *Kenya: The Struggle for Democracy*. London: Zed Books.

Mwajefa, Mwakera. 2013. "Uhuru vows to resolve land issues." *The Nation*, February 17, p. 8.

Nasong'o, Shadrack Wanjala. 2007. "Negotiating New Rules of the Game: Social Movements, Civil Society and the Kenyan Transition." In G.R. Muranga and S. W. Nasong'o, eds., *Kenya: The Struggle for Democracy*. Dakar, Senegal: CODESRIA Books.

Nathan, Noah L. 2016. "Local ethnic geography, expectations of favoritism, and voting in urban Ghana." *Comparative Political Studies* 49(14): 1896–929.

Nation Team. 2007. "Kibaki woos western voters." *Daily Nation.* September 18, 2007, p. 4.

Ndegwa, Stephen N. 2001. "A decade of democracy in Africa." *Journal of Asian and African Studies* 36(1): 1–16.

Ndegwa, Stephen N. 2003. "Kenya: Third time lucky?" *Journal of Democracy* 14(3): 145–58.

Ndulu, Benno J., Jean-Paul Azam, Stephen A. O'Connell, Robert H. Bates, Augustin K. Fosu, Jan Willem Gunning, and Dominique Nijinkeu, eds. 2008. *The Political Economy of Economic Growth in Africa, 1960–2000.* Vol. 2. Cambridge: Cambridge University Press.

Nellis, John R. 1974. *The Ethnic Composition of Leading Kenyan Government Positions.* Nordiska Afrikainstitutet.

Ngige, Francis. 2013. "Raila, Kalonzo lead campaign in Meru." *The Standard*, February 15, p. 10.

Ng'Weno, Hilary. 1992. *Weekly Review*, May 8, p. 1.

Nichter, Simeon. 2008. "Vote buying or turnout buying? Machine politics and the secret ballot." *American Political Science Review* 102(1): 19–31.

Nicolai, Susan, Annalisa Prizzon, and Sébastien Hine. 2014. "Beyond Basic: The Growth of Post-Primary Education in Kenya." London: Overseas Development Institute.

Ninsin, Kwame A. 2016. "Elections and Representation in Ghana's Democracy." In Kwame A. Ninsin, ed., *Issues in Ghana's Electoral Politics.* Dakar: CODESRIA.

Nishimura, Mikiko, and Takashi Yamano. 2013. "Emerging private education in Africa: Determinants of school choice in rural Kenya." *World Development* 43: 267–75.

Nugent, Paul. 2001a. "Winners, losers and also rans: Money, moral authority and voting patterns in the Ghana 2000 election." *African Affairs* 100(400): 405–28.

Nugent, Paul. 2001b. "Ethnicity as an explanatory factor in the Ghana 2000 elections." *African Issues* 29(1/2): 2–7.

Nugent, Paul. 2007. "Banknotes and symbolic capital: Ghana's elections under the fourth republic." In Matthias Basedau, Gero Erdmann, and Andreas Mehler, eds., *Votes, Money and Violence.* Sweden: Nordiska Afrikainstitutet.

Nyhan, Brendan, and Jason Reifler. 2010. "When corrections fail: The persistence of political misperceptions." *Political Behavior* 32(2): 303–30.

Nyong'o, Peter Anyang'. 1989. "State and society in Kenya: The disintegration of the nationalist coalitions and the rise of presidential authoritarianism 1963–78." *African Affairs* 88(351): 229–51.

Nyong'o, Peter Anyang'. 1992. "Africa: The failure of one-party rule." *Journal of Democracy* 3(1): 90–6.

Nyong'o, Peter Anyang'. 2017. "The presidential system of government is bad, period!" *The Star* (online edition), August 12.

Obeng-Odoom, Franklin. 2013. "The nature of ideology in Ghana's 2012 elections." *Journal of African Elections* 12(2): 75–95.

Oelbaum, Jay. 2004. "Ethnicity adjusted? Economic reform, elections, and tribalism in Ghana's Fourth Republic." *Commonwealth and Comparative Politics* 42(2): 242–73.

Ogot, Bethwell A. 1995. "Transition from Single-Party to Multiparty Political System, 1989–93." In Bethwell A. Ogot and William R. Ochieng, eds., *Decolonization and Independence in Kenya, 1940–93.* London: James Currey.

Ogot, Bethwell A. 2000. "Boundary Changes and the Invention of 'Tribes'." In B. Ogot and W. Ochieng, eds., *Kenya: The Making of a Nation: A Hundred Years of Kenya's History, 1895–1995.* Maseno: Institute of Research and Postgraduate Studies.

Oketch, Moses, and Caine Rolleston. 2007. "Policies on free primary and secondary education in East Africa: Retrospect and prospect." *Review of Research in Education* 31 (1): 131–58.

Okoth-Ogendo, Hastings W. O. 1972. "The politics of constitutional change in Kenya since independence, 1963–69." *African Affairs* 71(282): 9–34.

Oloo, Adams. 2001. "Patronising the incumbent: Kalenjin unity in the 1997 Kenya general elections." In M. Rutten, A. Mazrui, and F. Grignon, eds., *Out for the Count: The 1997 Elections and Prospects for Democracy in Kenya*. Kampala: Fountain Publishers.

Oloo, Adams. 2016. "Going against the grain of ethnic voting: The scramble for votes in the 2013 presidential election in Western Kenya." *Open Access Library Journal* 3(4):1–13.

Omolo, Ken. 2002. "Political ethnicity in the democratisation process in Kenya." *African Studies* 61(2): 209–21.

Opalo, Kennedy. 2014. "The long road to institutionalization: The Kenyan parliament and the 2013 election." *Journal of Eastern African Studies* 8(1): 63–77.

Oquaye, Mike. 1995. "The Ghanaian elections of 1992 – A dissenting view." *African Affairs* 94(375): 259–75.

Oyugi, Walter O. 1997. "Ethnicity in the electoral process: The 1992 general election in Kenya." *African Journal of Political Science* 2(1): 41–69.

Oyugi, Walter O. 2006. "Coalition politics and coalition governments in Africa." *Journal of Contemporary African Studies* 24(1): 53–79.

Paget, Dan. 2019. "The rally-intensive campaign: A distinct form of electioneering in sub-Saharan Africa and beyond." *The International Journal of Press/Politics* 24(4): 444–64.

Party of National Unity. 2007. *PNU Manifesto*. Nairobi, Kenya.

Pérouse de Montclos, Marc-Antoine. 2001. "Elections among the Kenya Somali: A conservative but marginalized vote." In M. Rutten, A. Mazrui, and F. Grignon, eds., *Out for the Count: The 1997 Elections and Prospects for Democracy in Kenya*. Kampala: Fountain Publishers.

Popkin, Samuel L. 1994. *The Reasoning Voter: Communication and Persuasion in Presidential Campaigns*. University of Chicago Press.

Posner, Daniel N. 2005. *Institutions and Ethnic Politics in Africa*. Cambridge: Cambridge University Press.

Posner, Daniel N. 2007. "Regime change and ethnic cleavages in Africa." *Comparative Political Studies* 40(11): 1302–27.

Prempeh, Kwasi H. 2008. "Presidents untamed." *Journal of Democracy* 19(2): 109–23.

Price, Robert M. 1973. "The pattern of ethnicity in Ghana: A research note." *Journal of Modern African Studies* 11(3): 470–5.

Przeworski, Adam, Michael E. Alvarez, Jose Antonio Cheibub, and Fernando Limongi. 2000. *Democracy and Development: Political Institutions and Well-Being in the World, 1950–1990*. Cambridge: Cambridge University Press.

Rabushka, Alvin and Kenneth Shepsle. 1972. *Politics in Plural Societies: A Theory of Democratic Instability*. Columbus, OH: Charles E. Merrill Publishing.

Radelet, Steven. 2010. *Emerging Africa: How 17 Countries Are Leading the Way*. Brookings Institution Press.

Randall, Vicky, and Lars Svåsand. 2002a. "Political parties and democratic consolidation in Africa." *Democratization* 9: 30–52.

Randall, Vicky, and Lars Svåsand. 2002b. "Party institutionalization in new democracies." *Party Politics* 8(1): 5–29.

Reilly, Benjamin. 2001. *Democracy in Divided Societies: Electoral Engineering for Conflict Management*. New York: Cambridge University Press.

Reilly, Benjamin. 2006. "Political engineering and party politics in conflict-prone societies." *Democratization* 13(5): 811–27.

Reilly, Benjamin, and Andrew Reynolds. 1999. *Electoral Systems and Conflict in Divided Societies*. Washington DC: National Academy Press.

Republic of Kenya. November 2016. *2017 Budget Policy Statement*. National Treasury.

Republic of Kenya Central Bureau of Statistics. *Kenya Population Census. 1989*. Volume 1. March 1994.

Resnick, Danielle. 2014. *Urban Poverty and Party Populism in African Democracies*. Cambridge: Cambridge University Press.

Rosen, Ori, Wenxin Jiang, Gary King, and Martin A. Tanner. 2001. "Bayesian and frequentist inference for ecological inference: The R×C case." *Statistica Neerlandica* 55(2): 134–56.

Rothschild, Joseph. 1981. *Ethnopolitics: A Conceptual Framework*. New York, NY: Columbia University Press.

Rutten, Marcel. 2001. "The Kenya 1997 General Elections in Maasai land: Our 'Sons' and 'Puppets' and How KANU Defeated Itself." In M. Rutten, A. Mazrui, and F. Grignon, eds., *Out for the Count: The 1997 Elections and Prospects for Democracy in Kenya*. Kampala: Fountain Publishers.

Rutten, Marcel, Alamin Mazrui, and François Grignon, eds. 2001. *Out for the Count: The 1997 General Elections and Prospects for Democracy in Kenya*. Kampala: Fountain Publishers.

Sanger, Clyde, and John Nottingham. 1964. "The Kenya general election of 1963." *Journal of Modern African Studies* 2(1): 1–40.

Sayagie, George. 2013. "PM woos Maa with land pledge." *The Nation*, February 23, p. 6.

Scarritt, James R. 2006. "The strategic choice of multiethnic parties in Zambia's dominant and personalist party system." *Commonwealth and Comparative Politics* 44(2): 234–56.

Schedler, Andreas. 2002. "Elections without democracy: The menu of manipulation." *Journal of Democracy* 13(2): 36–50.

Schumpeter, Joseph A. 2013. *Capitalism, Socialism and Democracy*. New York: Routledge.

Sentinel Project. 2011. "The Risk of Genocide in Kenya." Toronto, Canada: The Sentinel Project for Genocide Prevention.

Shaw, Daron R. 2007. *The Race to 270: The Electoral College and the Campaign Strategies of 2000 and 2004*. Chicago, IL: University of Chicago Press.

Shilaho, Western Kwatemba. 2013. "Old wine in new skins: Kenya's 2013 elections and the triumph of the Ancient Régime." *Journal of African Elections* 12(3): 89–119.

Shumway, Rebecca. 2014. *The Fante and the Transatlantic Slave Trade*. Boydell & Brewer.

Sides, John. 2006. "The origins of campaign agendas." *British Journal of Political Science* 36(3): 407–36.

Simson, Rebecca, and Elliott Green. 2020. "Ethnic favouritism in Kenyan education reconsidered: When a picture is worth more than a thousand regression." *Journal of Modern African Studies* 58(3): 425–60.

Sisk, Timothy D. 1994. *Democratization in South Africa: The Elusive Social Contract*. Princeton, NJ: Princeton University Press.

Slothuus, Rune. 2010. "When can political parties lead public opinion? Evidence from a natural experiment." *Political Communication* 27(2): 158–77.

Snyder, Jack. 2000. *From Voting to Violence: Democratization and Nationalist Conflict*. New York, NY: Norton.

Snyder, James M. 1989. "Election goals and the allocation of campaign resources." *Econometrica* 57(3): 637–60.

Southall, Roger. 1998. "Moi's flawed mandate: The crisis continues in Kenya." *Review of African Political Economy* 25(75): 101–11.

Southall, Roger. 1999. "Re-forming the state? Kleptocracy & the political transition in Kenya." *Review of African Political Economy* 26(79): 93–108.

Southall, Roger. 2009. "Alternatives for electoral reform in Kenya: Lessons from southern Africa." *Journal of Contemporary African Studies* 27(3): 445–61.

Stasavage, David. 2005a. "Democracy and education spending in Africa." *American Journal of Political Science* 49(2): 343–58.

Stasavage, David. 2005b. "The role of democracy in Uganda's move to universal primary education." *Journal of Modern African Studies* 43(1): 53–73.

Steeves, Jeffrey. 2006a. "Presidential succession in Kenya: The transition from Moi to Kibaki." *Commonwealth and Comparative Politics* 44(2): 211–33.

Steeves, Jeffrey. 2006b. "Beyond democratic consolidation in Kenya: Ethnicity, leadership and 'unbounded politics'." *African Identities* 4(2): 195–211.

Stewart, Frances, ed. 2016. *Horizontal Inequalities and Conflict: Understanding Group Violence in Multiethnic Societies*. New York: Springer.

Stokes, Susan. 2001. *Mandates and Democracy: Neoliberalism by Surprise in Latin America*. Cambridge: Cambridge University Press.

Stromberg, David. 2008. "How the Electoral College influences campaigns and policy: The probability of being Florida." *American Economic Review* 98(3): 769–807.

Sunday Nation Team. 2013. "Uhuru: We will address the thorny land question." *The Nation*, February 24, p. 8.

Taber, Charles S., and Milton Lodge. 2006. "Motivated skepticism in the evaluation of political beliefs." *American Journal of Political Science* 50(3): 755–69.

Tajfel, Henri. 1970. "Experiments in intergroup discrimination." *Scientific American* 223 (5): 96–103.

Tavits, Margit. 2007. "Principle vs. pragmatism: Policy shifts and political competition." *American Journal of Political Science* 51(1): 151–65.

Taylor, Charles Fernandes. 2017. "Ethnic politics and election campaigns in contemporary Africa: Evidence from Ghana and Kenya." *Democratization* 24(6): 951–69.

Throup, David W. 1987. "The construction and destruction of the Kenyatta state." In Michael G. Schatzberg, ed., *The Political Economy of Kenya*. New York: Praeger Publishers.

Throup, David W. 1993. "Elections and political legitimacy in Kenya." *Africa* 63(3): 371–96.

Throup, David W. 2003. "The Kenya General Election: December 27, 2002." CSIS Africa Notes, no. 14. Washington D.C.: Center for Strategic and International Studies.

Throup, David W. 2008. "The count." *Journal of Eastern African Studies* 2(2): 290–304.

Throup, David W., and Charles Hornsby. 1998. *Multi-Party Politics in Kenya*. Oxford: James Currey.

Tonah, Steve. 2007. "Democratization and the Resurgence of Ethnic Politics in Ghana, 1992-2006." In G. Rosenthal and A. Bogner, eds., *Ethnicity, Belonging and Biography: Ethnographical and Biographical Perspectives*. Hamburg/London: LIT Press.

Travaglianti, Manuela. 2017. "How abolishing school fees increased support for the incumbent in Burundi." *African Affairs* 116(462): 101–24.

Tsebelis, George. 2002. *Veto Players: How Political Institutions Work*. Princeton, NJ: Princeton University Press.

Tufano, Peter. 1996. "Who manages risk? An empirical examination of risk management practices in the gold mining industry." *The Journal of Finance* 51(4): 1097–137.

Twumasi, Yaw. 1975. "The 1969 Election." In Dennis Austin and Robin Luckham, eds., *Politicians and Soldiers in Ghana 1966–1972*. London: Frank Cass.

Valdivia, Corinne, Elizabeth G. Dunn, and Christian Jetté. 1996. "Diversification as a risk management strategy in an Andean agropastoral community." *American Journal of Agricultural Economics* 78(5): 1329–34.

Valentino, Nicholas A., Vincent L. Hutchings, and Ismail K. White. 2002. "Cues that matter: How political ads prime racial attitudes during campaigns." *American Political Science Review* 96(1): 75–90.

Valentino, Nicholas A., Fabian G. Neuner, and L. Matthew Vandenbroek. 2018. "The changing norms of racial political rhetoric and the end of racial priming." *Journal of Politics* 80(3): 757–71.

van de Walle, Nicolas. 2003. "Presidentialism and clientelism in Africa's emerging party systems." *Journal of Modern African Studies* 41(2): 297–321.

van de Walle, Nicolas. 2003. "Presidentialism and clientelism in Africa's emerging party systems." *Journal of Modern African Studies* 41(2): 297–321.

van de Walle, Nicolas. 2007. "Meet the New Boss, Same as the Old Boss? The Evolution of Political Clientelism in Africa." In Herbert Kitschelt and Steven I. Wilkinson, eds., *Patrons, Clients and Policies: Patterns of Democratic Accountability and Political Competition*. Cambridge: Cambridge University Press.

van de Walle, Nicolas, and Kimberly Smiddy Butler. 1999. "Political parties and party systems in Africa's illiberal democracies." *Cambridge Review of International Affairs* 13(1): 14–28.

wa Gĩthĩnji, Mwangi, and Frank Holmquist. 2008. "Kenya's hopes and impediments: The anatomy of a crisis of exclusion." *Journal of Eastern African Studies* 2(2): 344–58.

Wahman, Michael, and Catherine Boone. 2018. "Captured countryside? Stability and change in sub-national support for African incumbent parties." *Comparative Politics* 50(2): 189–216.

Wantchekon, Leonard. 2003. "Clientelism and voting behavior: Evidence from a field experiment in Benin." *World Politics* 55(3): 399–422.

Wantchekon, Leonard, and Thomas Fujiwara. 2013. "Can informed public deliberation overcome clientelism? Experimental evidence from Benin." *American Economic Journal: Applied Economics* 5(4): 241–55.

Weghorst, Keith R., and Michael Bernhard. 2014. "From formlessness to structure? The institutionalization of competitive party systems in Africa." *Comparative Political Studies* 47(12): 1707–37.

Weghorst, Keith R., and Staffan I. Lindberg. 2013. "What drives the swing voter in Africa?" *American Journal of Political Science* 57(3): 717–34.

Weighton, Lisa, and Patrick McCurdy. 2017. "The ghost in the news room: The legacy of Kenya's 2007 post-election violence and the constraints on journalists covering Kenya's 2013 General Election." *Journal of Eastern African Studies* 11(4): 649–69.

West, Darrell. 1983. "Constituencies and travel allocations in the 1980 presidential campaign." *American Journal of Political Science* 27(3): 515–29.

Westberg, Nina Bruvik. 2015. *Exchanging Fertilizer for Votes?* Working Paper No. 12–2015. Norwegian University of Life Sciences, School of Economics and Business.

Whitfield, Lindsay. 2009. "'Change for a better Ghana': Party competition, institutionalization and alternation in Ghana's 2008 Elections." *African Affairs* 108(433): 621–41.

Widner, Jennifer A. 1993. *The Rise of a Party-State in Kenya: From Harambee! to Nyayo!*. Berkeley: University of California Press.

Wilkinson, Steven. 2004. *Votes and Violence: Electoral Competition and Ethnic Riots in India*. Cambridge: Cambridge University Press.

Wilks, Igor. 1975. *Asante in the Nineteenth Century. The Structure and Evolution of a Political Order*. Cambridge: Cambridge University Press.

Willis, Justin. 1993. *Mombasa, the Swahili, and the Making of the Mijikenda*. Oxford: Oxford University Press.

Wimmer, Andreas. 2002. *Nationalist Exclusion and Ethnic Conflict*. Cambridge: Cambridge University Press.

Witter, Sophie, and Bertha Garshong. 2009. "Something old or something new? Social health insurance in Ghana." *BMC International Health and Human Rights* 9(1): 1–13.

Wittenberg, Jason, Ferdinand Alimadhi, Badri Narayan Bhaskar, and Olivia Lau. 2007. "ei. RxC: Hierarchical multinomial-dirichlet ecological inference model." In Kosuke Imai, Gary King, and Olivia Lau, eds., *Zelig: Everyone's Statistical Software*. Available at http://gking.%20harvard.%20edu/zelig.

World Bank. 2009. *Abolishing School Fees in Africa: Lessons from Ethiopia, Ghana, Kenya, Malawi, and Mozambique*. Washington, DC: International Bank for Reconstruction and Development.

Youde, Jeremy. 2005. "Economics and government popularity in Ghana." *Electoral Studies* 24: 1–16.

Zaller, John. 2004. "Floating Voters in the U.S. Presidential Election, 1948–2000." In Willem E. Saris and Paul M. Sniderman, eds., *Studies in Public Opinion: Attitudes, Nonattitudes, Measurement Error, and Change*. Ann Arbor: University of Michigan Press.

Index